THE WAY IT CHANGED

The Way
It Changed

1951-1975

James McMillan

WILLIAM KIMBER · LONDON

First published in 1987 by
WILLIAM KIMBER & CO. LIMITED
100 Jermyn Street, London, SW1Y 6EE

James McMillan, 1987

ISBN 0-7183-0640-6

Typeset by Ann Buchan (Typesetters), Middlesex
Printed and bound in Great Britain by
Billing & Sons Ltd, Worcester

To
my granddaughter

Contents

List of Illustrations

Introduction

When I closed the final volume of my trilogy on the first 50 years of this century it was to yet another desolate scene of war: this time the conflict in Korea. The subsequent 25 years, for Britain and Europe saw a period of peace (if not tranquillity) accompanied by un-exampled prosperity. For instance, in the UK alone the number of cars on the road quintupled; from under 4 million to nearly 20 million.

And yet behind that front of pacific prosperity lay profound changes in social customs and attitudes, changes that marked the end of the Victorian Era more emphatically than mere technological transformation. If a twentieth-century Rip Van Winkle had gone to sleep in the summer of 1914 and awakened 30 years later, his eyes and ears would have been assailed with terrifying sights and sounds: men and women in strange uniforms; flying bombs screaming overhead; many of his contemporaries killed in the First World War, which he'd slept through, and many of their children falling victims to the Second in which he had woken up. The world in flames in 1944 would physically have borne no resemblance to the peaceful one he had known before drifting into his long sleep.

Now had Rip Van Winkle dropped off in 1950 and awakened in 1975 much around him would have been familiar. Cars and planes and radios and television would have been dramatically improved, but there would have been no quantum leap. Even space travel would not have appeared exceptional to one who had witnessed the German V2 rockets over England and their post-war development. The House of Windsor still reigned. A Labour Government was narrowly in office in 1975 as in 1950.

Yet the social mores would be unrecognisable to the Rip Van Winkle of 1950. The films, books, magazines with their explicit sex, the universal acceptance of divorce, the widespread practice of couples living together 'in sin' and the growing practice of young women having babies and living on their own, apart from the father. Indeed the role of women had been revolutionised, with them providing 40 per cent of the labour force, not as a temporary wartime emergency but as a permanent feature of the employment scene. Even more startling would have been the style of dress and hair and pop music which divided the generations more abruptly than anything else.

In Mr Winkle's 1950, boys up to fourteen or so wore short trousers, between fifteen and thirty they took to sports jackets and flannels, graduating to 3-piece suits, or possibly jacket, trousers and pullover. Leisure time was differentiated from work by taking off the tie and opening the shirt at the neck. Girls wore flowered dresses or skirts and blouses, only occasionally slacks. The 'New Look' of the period emphasised the flowing lines of an earlier, more generously ample age.

In contrast, the mid-seventies saw the emergence of the unisex outfit: tight-fitting blue jeans, usually patched, with heavy-duty top – the wholly sexless, wholly classless gear of a generation which said it abhorred conformity and conformed, in dress, to an unexampled degree.

Indeed the de-sexing of the sexes, wearing the same clothes, wearing the same long, unkempt hair, enjoying the same pursuits, gave rise to bawdy stories. Such as the one about the vicar who, faced with an identical pair whom he was supposed to marry, peered timidly at one then the other and finally asked plaintively, 'Which one of you has the menstrual cycle?' To which, in unison, they responded, 'Neither, mate, we've both got Hondas.' (It may be objected that such a pair would never have got married – but then it was only a story.)

Matching dress in its defiance of the old order was taste in music. From the mid-fifties onwards a huge musical gulf opened up between the generations. Bill Haley and his Comets heralded the new age of rock 'n' roll. They were, however, simply the early prophets. The King emerged shortly afterwards in the shape of another American, Elvis Presley. Mr Presley still maintained the conventions of a different era, when young men and women had still to pinch themselves to appreciate their good fortune. Peter Dacre, reporter with the *Sunday Express*, called on Mr Presley at his house in Tupelo,

Mississippi in 1956. Elvis was just 21 but already he was being proclaimed, in one of the favourite phrases of the period, as a 'legend of his own time'. The exchange between this sophisticated London journalist and the ex-truck driver from America's deepest south illustrated the still deferential modesty exhibited by the recipients of good fortune, an attitude which would be blown away in the years to come.

Dacre: 'Mr Presley, do you know the sensation rock'n'roll has caused in Britain?'

Presley: 'No, sir, I don't.'

Dacre: 'Can you explain the success of your singing?'

Presley: 'I wish I knew, sir. I've never been able to explain the reason myself. I just sing the way I do 'cos I like it.'

The Presley way swept the western world and was soon to be transformed by far more outlandish figures, whose gyrations, gestures and gimmicks would set a standard for future performers. The music became more frantic, the lyrics less decipherable. Groups calling themselves 'Scum' and 'Sex Pistols' tried to shock a by now thoroughly bemused older generation.

It was not unknown for youth to breach musical conventions. The tango had been excommunicated by Queen Mary in 1912 (she intimated that she would not visit any house i.e. grand aristocratic mansion, where the dance had been performed). In the twenties scandalised critics wrote about the bright young things:

> Mother's advice and father's fears
> Alike are voted just a bore
> There is Negro music in our ears
> The world is one huge dancing floor

Noel Coward clothed himself in eccentric garb (though not quite as eccentric as Elton John) to command attention. Where the two periods parted company was over the broad appeal of popular music to people of all ages.

Until the mid-fifties, songs were sung or whistled by pretty well everyone who could hum or whistle. Jazz was in a special category, like Wagnerian Operas. Both had their afficionados – jazz having more numerous and younger ones than Wagner – but the mass of listeners enjoyed the popular ballads played daily on the BBC. This changed dramatically with the advent of rock'n'roll. Popular music in the old, melodic, sense almost disappeared from the repertoire of radio and television variety programmes, to be replaced by the heavy pounding beat and raucous arias of rock'n'roll and its successor versions.

Rip Van Winkle brought up in the music of the thirties and forties and returning to the land of the living in 1975 after a span of 25 years would have concluded that the vocalists were in the grip of some terrible disease. Bing Crosby's crooning, Frank Sinatra's velvet phrasing – not even the passion which that evoked in young females – would have prepared him for the sight of a pop group in full cry. He simply would not have understood what was going on. The transformation of music had significance beyond the tonal. The minstrels were being elevated to the place of the prophets: with this proviso; that they would be honoured in their own country and paid a king's ransom into the bargain. With the fifties, and the advent of television, the entertainer was to enjoy a status to which he, or she, had never dared aspire. This too represented a vast change which would have struck Mr Winkle. He was familiar with the Hollywood stars. But in the fifties, sixties and seventies, 'stars' were made overnight. Peter Sellars, the comedian, told the *Daily Express* that he was astounded that the lead position in *Top of the Pops* was not held by an eight-year-old. Peter Sellars was to satirise the cult of youth in a record.

Teenagers (the very term had not existed in Rip Van Winkle's first incarnation) possessed a large disposable income. Their tastes dictated the mass record market and the pop stars they created in that market went on to gain huge audiences at pop concerts. Popular culture was the product of the predominant financial class, as it had been throughout the ages. Except that this was the first age in which the under-21s were dominant.

Maybe that is the key to the dramatic revolution in outlook which gripped western society from the mid-fifties to the mid-seventies. A combination of full employment – itself almost unheard of as a peacetime phenomenon – with the resolve of the older generation to make sure it would not have to endure the privations of the economically depressed thirties, ensured the succession of youth to the consumer throne. The rest followed on and change in music, tastes, fashions, moral attitudes, became constant.

Before examining the many aspects of the Era of Constant Change, look first at the institution which relies for its strength on continuity, the Monarchy of England.

CHAPTER ONE

The Royal Firm

By great good fortune the couple who occupied Buckingham Palace at the opening of the second half of the twentieth century were universally admired. King George VI had a talent for decency and a profound sense of duty. These qualities had helped him overcome his extreme reluctance to shoulder the burden of kingship when his brother Edward VIII abdicated. Now as he celebrated the New Year of 1951 with his beloved wife, their two daughters, son-in-law, grandson and granddaughter, he could look back on fourteen years of devoted service to his people. Thanks to Elizabeth, the Scots girl he had married 27 years before, he had conquered the awful shyness and the stutter which made public speaking a nightmare. Conquered, not in the sense of eliminating them, but of willing them to submit to the demands of kingship. This battle had won him the hearts of millions.

During the war, the picture of the King in his Admiral's uniform and beside him the Queen who was so much more than a Consort, had graced ships at sea, fly-blown messes in the desert, humble homes badly damaged by bombs. The King and Queen (sometimes the picture included the two little princesses) had been used by British propaganda to contrast the domestic virtues for which the Empire was fighting with Germany's fanatical military symbolised by the standard picture of the frowning Fuehrer. The war was five years over but it had taken a severe toll of the slightly-built man who reigned over the British Empire – still far-flung, despite India's recent defection to republicanism.

George VI had only a little over a year to live. Always a heavy smoker he was, at 55, paying the price in his lungs. The pale face – he was obliged to use make-up in public appearances, a fact which shocked those close enough to notice – was gaunt, the prominent cheekbones almost skeletal.

Yet there was no diminution in the relentless royal round. Nor would he have permitted any. The sense of duty, as deeply implanted in his elder daughter as in himself and the Queen, was the dominant feature in Buck House. You did not let the side down.

In this as in so much else, George VI mirrored his countrymen and his time. Strube, the *Daily Express* cartoonist, had developed a character called 'The Little Man'. George VI was The Little Man Writ Large, and his people loved him for it. The succession was secure, Lilibet would become Elizabeth II, at her side the tall strapping figure of Philip her husband, nephew to the legendary Lord Louis Mountbatten, and with two-year old Charles and four-month old Anne, the House of Windsor was in flourishing condition.

It was about the only Royal House that was. King Farouk of Egypt (destined to be overthrown in 1952) had remarked that 'soon there will be only the King of Hearts, the King of Clubs, the King of Diamonds, the King of Spades – and the King of England'. He was too close to the truth for comfort. Crowns had tumbled after the war of 1914-1918. Still more had come down after the 1939-1945 conflict. Why had the British Royal House survived? Partly because the British had not lost a war (abdication or execution was the forfeit paid for defeat by the German, Austrian, Turkish and Russian rulers in 1918 and by the Italian, Rumanian and Bulgarian rulers in 1945). The larger reason seems to be that the Crown and the British are indissolubly linked in a mystical union. The brief experience of the Cromwellian Commonwealth, seems to have inoculated the country against republicanism.

In 1951, of course, there was a third factor: The Empire. The Monarch was the vital link holding together the diverse races and creeds which spanned the globe. George VI, like his father before him, was meticulous in stressing the Empire theme in his Christmas broadcast.

The Christmas broadcast of 1951 was to prove George VI's last. Shortly after his death, six weeks later, the *Express* reported that the King had insisted on making that broadcast. He had been urged to let the Queen or Princess Elizabeth read the message for him. He rejected the suggestion with the words, 'My daughter may have her opportunity next Christmas. I want to speak to my people myself.' It took two days to record the message. His voice betrayed a husky breathlessness.

His people did not suspect then, but George VI had been desperately ill for three months. Bronchial carcinoma had been diagnosed in both lungs. One damaged lung was removed, but his expectation of life was put at between five months and two years. He was already suffering from Buerger's disease, a contracting of the bore of the arteries supplying the legs with blood. Doctors carried out an operation to relieve the pain caused by contractions. The surgery was successful. Even so, he had to sit for hours at a time with his legs in an electrically heated bath and he faced the grim prospect that the disease would recur and he would lose one or both legs.

The *Express* recorded the doctors' decision to allow the King to resume smoking (he had been a heavy smoker since his days in the Navy) to permit him to wave goodbye to his daughter, off on a Commonwealth tour and to spend many hours at his favourite pastime, grouse shooting. He was out shooting (hare actually) the day before he died.

An Empire went into mourning. *The Times* reported, 'On the loneliest outpost – Macquario Islands in the Atlantic Antarctic – the members of the Australian Antarctic expedition stood in the gale with bowed heads'. The *Mail* recorded, 'Seventy-one year old Richard Candle and his wife Euphelia, 70, of Charlotte Street, Barnes, Surrey, dressed up in black and went to teleview the King's funeral at a neighbour's house. There they collapsed and died.'

Following the announcement of the King's death, BBC radio went over to solemn music, cancelling all light entertainment and controversial programmes until the funeral. Theatres closed down for one night. Many cinemas also shut their doors on the day of the funeral. But, as the *Express* pointed out, the period of national mourning – a few hours – stood in marked contrast to the death of Queen Victoria half a century before. Then, restaurants, theatres, museums, music halls, closed for weeks. Edward VII had to curtail official lamentations in order to save the jobs of tens of thousands in the catering and service trades.

What the press termed 'a march of grief' – the funeral procession – exemplified the nation's real sorrow. There was a feeling that this frail man was truly a casualty to duty. Memories of the shared sacrifice of the war stirred. Thus the Merseyside dockers in their wall newspaper in Liverpool wrote, 'Those of us who were working in the port during the war remember with gratitude the informal visits the King paid to give encouragement to all of us whom he knew to be suffering under the heavy strain of enemy attacks.'

A Zulu chieftain recorded his sorrow: 'Our father is dead. He was a great lion.'

Dr Malan, the South African Premier, assured Elizabeth II of his country's, 'Loyal attachment to your Majesty's Throne and person.' A remarkable statement, considering that Malan represented the Nationalist Afrikaaners and that his successor, Dr Verwoerd, was to proclaim a republic only nine years later.

Robert Menzies, in Australia, assured the Queen that Australia's Ministers 'are her sworn counsellors *in this portion of her realm.*'

From the world outside the Empire tributes to the dead King poured in to the new Queen. Belgium suspended the sitting of its Parliament. Broadway dimmed the lights on the Great White Way. France tolled the bells. Russia and China alone ignored the event, which was not altogether surprising for Britain enjoyed the worst possible relations with the Soviet Union and was in a state of undeclared war with China, insofar as Chinese 'volunteers' in Korea numbering half a million were killing – and being killed by – British soldiers. The Royal Artillery marked the passing of the King by firing live rounds into the Communist Chinese lines. Elizabeth II ascended a secure throne in an insecure world.

The strength of the throne was a source of quiet pride to the vast majority of Britons. The fact that the occupant was a lovely young woman of 25 was further cause for satisfaction – and optimism. No sooner had she ascended the throne than her Premier, Winston Churchill, was pointing out that Britain had always flourished under Queens. He was at pains to say 'Britain' for the title, Queen Elizabeth the *Second* was already a contentious issue north of the Border.

Elizabeth I was Queen of England, not Scotland. The union of the Crowns did not come about until 1603 and was accomplished under James VI of Scotland (James I of the United Kingdom) whose mother, Mary Queen of Scots, was executed by Elizabeth. The Scots argued, with considerable logic, that as James had been obliged to alter his number to suit the English, Elizabeth II should do likewise to suit the Scots.

This made no kind of appeal whatsoever to patriotic English folk who revered the memory of the Great Queen. Elizabeth II it must be and most people in the South regarded the Scots as being almost flippantly absurd in quibbling about the matter.

More than a niggling complaint, however, was at stake. Scottish newspapers reported that at the nightly playing of the National Anthem in cinemas ('God Save the Queen' was played at every concert, theatrical performance, major sporting event as well as in the cinema in those days) sections of the audience were shouting 'the first, the first'. Still more serious, Scottish Nationalist extremists planted bombs in new pillar boxes bearing the inscription EII R. This action actually had the opposite effect to that intended. The public reacted against such lunatic violence. The issue died down and disappeared.

Yet it was a reminder of long-lasting folk memories which could flare up and threaten the stability of the kingdom – a distant warning of far worse things to come in Ireland.

The Establishment in London ought to have been much more aware of Scottish sentiment, for a few months earlier the Stone of Destiny on which ancient Scottish Kings had been crowned at Scone was stolen from Westminster Abbey – it having been removed there in the thirteenth century by the all-conquering English Monarch, Edward I, Hammer of the Scots. The thieves were zealous young Scottish students of Glasgow University who, while being in no way anti-Monarchist, wished to spotlight Scottish grievances about the excessive concentration of authority in Whitehall and hit upon this dramatic means of doing so.

The public thought it a bit of a lark, a student stunt. Not so George VI who was grievously upset and who felt that the Stone's disappearance represented a threat to the mystical continuity of Monarchy. He and his ancestors had been crowned on top of the Stone which formed the base of the throne.

The Archbishop of Canterbury expressed the King's deep disquiet. Scotland Yard's Special Branch moved in, and bewildered Glasgow University students, who had never been in London far less hidden in Westminster Abbey, found themselves questioned by hard-faced professional interrogators.

The student conspirators were filled with dread when, in March 1951, the Attorney General let it be known that they could face criminal proceedings. Swiftly they moved to unburden themselves of their guilty secret and to transfer the Stone from its hiding place – a monumental mason's yard – to Arbroath (scene of Scotland's Declaration of Independence) where it was duly collected by the authorities and returned to Westminster. Such an example of the strength of ancient symbols ought to have alerted Church and State to the need for being wary of offending susceptibilities. The dispute over Elizabeth's title demonstrated that this lesson had not been learned.

Disagreement and contention vanished as mist in morning sunshine with the approach of the Coronation. 'Pavilioned in splendour' cried the *Express* on Coronation Day, 2nd June 1953. The front page headline encapsulated the country's surging optimism: 'All This – And Everest Too'. For the news had just been given that a British-led team had, at last, conquered the highest peak in the world. There was life in the Old Lion yet.

Downpours of rain could not douse the people's enthusiasm. For the Queen, for her consort, for her children, for the Empire (the Queen of Tonga disdaining the rain and travelling in an open carriage, received a special cheer), for Prime Minister Winston Churchill, the pilot who weathered the storm, for themselves – the incomparable British. It was the last hurrah of the Victorian age.

The whole splendid scene was televised (much to the consternation and against the advice of the Queen's crustier advisers) and carried into the homes of tens of millions throughout the land, the Commonwealth and friendly foreign nations. It was a triumph for the BBC, the last it would enjoy as a monopoly and the sole broadcasting Voice of Britain.

It was to be Churchill's and Attlee's last major Royal engagement. The Premier and the Leader of the Opposition had both been born in the Victorian era. While Churchill was cast in an earlier mould, Cavalier or Renaissance, Clement Attlee was the very personification of middle class Victorian virtues. Careful, thrifty, sparse with words and sparser still with gestures. Neat and conventional in dress yet with a powerful social conscience which had guided him from privileged childhood to work in the slums and finally to join the Socialist movement. These two politicians, in their way, represented the two strands of the British character; the extrovert and the puritan; the Cavalier and the Roundhead. Both were to retire in two years' time.

Nostalgia was in the air that damp June day. But it was a cheerful nostalgia and it was not for Victoria, but for Elizabeth I.

The *Express* ran a competition to name the New Elizabethans who in the second Elizabeth's reign would dazzle the world as Raleigh, Drake, Frobisher, Bacon, Marlowe, Shakespeare had done in the First. There was no shortage of entries: inventors Robert Watson

Watt (radar) and Frank Whittle (jet engine) jostled with the daring Hillary, along with Tensing, the conqueror of Everest and artists of the calibre of Henry Moore and Benjamin Britten.

The 'New Elizabethans' was the brand identification for the first couple of years of Elizabeth II's reign. It marched with returning prosperity. At long weary last rationing which the British had endured – thirteen years – longer than any other wartime combatant in the West, defeated or victorious, was being wound up. Even in 1952 it had been extremely severe. The *weekly* meat ration, worth 8p, if taken in the form of fillet steak could fit snugly into a Swan Vesta matchbox. The weekly butter ration was 3 ozs, sugar was 10 ozs, chocolate 6 ozs. Motor cars were effectively rationed as all but 60,000 a year were earmarked for export.

Now cars were coming back on to the roads. Houses were being built at a record rate. Prosperity wasn't around the corner, it was here. Young, vibrant, beautiful Elizabeth caught the glittering moment and embraced the country's hopes.

Sympathy for the Royal Family mingled with adoration, when, a few months later, Elizabeth's sister Margaret publicly disavowed the man she loved, Group Captain Peter Townsend, because he was divorced. She had first met and become entranced with the handsome young airman when she was in her mid-teens. Townsend was the innocent party in the divorce, made absolute long before he met Margaret. In every respect – in his devoted service to her father, as a temporary member of the Royal household, as a gallant officer and a steadying influence – he was an ideal partner for the princess. The Church of England, however, was adamantly opposed to the match, as were the Non-conformists – probably more so. With the Queen's permission, Margaret could have married her Group Captain. Instead he went into 'exile' with NATO in Brussels, and she issued a statement ending the affair. *The Times* congratulated her. Most of the Press, at home and abroad – the Scandinavians were especially scathing – soundly condemned the Establishment for thwarting true love.

Whether or not Margaret's decision was her own – publicly she insisted it was – the effect was to stir resentment of what was perceived to be the stuffy, remote, born-to-privilege members of the Court who advised the Queen and controlled the Royal household.

Soon this spilled over to criticism of the Queen herself. Malcolm Muggeridge, a writer and journalist, criticised her mode of speech and dress. His denunciation followed a particularly oleoginous series by a former Royal governess, 'Crawfie', which had set teeth on edge among the rising class of iconoclast commentators and Muggeridge, though unpopular with the Establishment, found himself extremely popular with the radicals of the literary world.

In a wave of antipathy towards the old order, it was inevitable that the throne should be involved. It was associated, said its critics, with outdated practices and classes, was a hindrance to progress and, while not urging its abolition, the critics clearly wanted it ignored. What was to become known as 'radical chic' found eager echoes from a wider circle in the period beginning 1957, as the era of debunking got underway.

The Queen was referred to as 'Brenda'. Her dowdy clothes and upper class manners and mannerisms were subject to giggling jibes. The satirists, who were just coming into their own, had a field day. While the general public did not share this sneer-and-jeer ethic, the ebbing away of respect for the Crown among a significant section of the new communicating class represented a real threat to the Monarchy's standing.

The threat became the more palpable with the election of John Fitzgerald Kennedy as America's President in November 1960. Kennedy himself had the cool, ironic, self-deprecatory speech much admired by aspiring intellectuals. He could also turn a pretty phrase (that these were the works of his speech writer was not then known). Immensely more significant was the fact that Kennedy represented burgeoning power, while the British Sovereign represented unreal pomp in a fading, if not positively decadent, society.

Then there was Jacqueline Bouvier Kennedy. In her book *All the President's Kin* (Robson Books), author Barbara Kellerman remarked: 'When John Kennedy became President, Jacqueline Kennedy's aesthetic, almost ethereal qualities, were finally used to real advantage. . . *occupying the throne* suited her.' She had elegance, taste, culture. She spoke impeccable French. She was well-versed in art. She managed to captivate that Grand Old Sceptic, Charles de Gaulle. Before everything else she represented the feminine side of power 'setting the tone and style of the sixties', according to the Polish Magazine *Swiat*. Charlotte Curtis in *First Lady* referred to the 'Jackie look' sweeping across America and across the world. Almost overnight America discarded the last of its ruffles, tight belts and bows. Millinery shops sold the largest collection of back-of-the-head pillbox hats in their history. Beauty shops reported that women wanted their hair artfully teased into the bouffant Kennedy coiffure. Stores found themselves selling the low-heeled shoes, alligator handbags (!) little white gloves and elbow-length kid gloves, great coats and small furs (!!) that Mrs Kennedy favoured.

It was reported that, 'Her clothes in Paris were sensational . . . her photograph made the front page of every gazette from Madagascar to Outer Mongolia.' It was a pardonable exaggeration. The Kennedy family were plainly outshining the Royal Family. At the very moment when television brought every event immediately into living rooms around the globe, America's first family was walking away with the honours. Historian Arthur Schlesinger recorded that State dinners in the White House were 'elegant and cheerful, beautifully mingling informality and dignity . . . blithe and enchanted evenings'. Could the same be said of dinners in Buckingham Palace? Distinguished figures from the worlds of art, music, literature studded the White House guest lists, while the same dull old courtiers occupied the seats at Buckingham Palace banquets.*

When Mrs Kennedy visited India – still part of the Queen's domain as a member of the Commonwealth – the US magazine *Time* reported that 'She paraded across the sub-Continent in triumph . . . hailed as "Maharani", Queen.' The journal also commented, 'Few women in the world exercise such influence.'

The combination of this cosmopolitan, soignée, sophisticated, youngish woman (Jacqueline was 31 when her husband won the Presidency) and the vibrant, dare-anything, achieve everything Kennedy Clan, had a tremendous impact everywhere. And this was a *huge* family. Depressed opponents of the Kennedy dynasty were ruefully apt to prophesy the fate of the three Kennedy brothers: 'Jack till '68, Robert to '76, then Ted – and it will be 1984.'

It was not to be. John Kennedy was assassinated. So was Robert. Edward, 'Ted', proved himself unworthy even by the low standards of US politics. Jackie Kennedy got married to a very wealthy and extremely ugly Greek shipowner. The Kennedy image dissolved. The American Camelot proved as insubstantial as a dream. In subsequent sceptical writings on the period it often seemed more nearly to resemble a nightmare.

* Lunches at Buckingham Palace, on the Kennedy model, were later instituted.

Would it have been any different if gunmen had not shot down the two Kennedy brothers? Probably not. The Kennedys for all their glamour, talent, money and capacity to manipulate were politicians. Sooner or later the electorate would have tired of them. The Windsors (or their predecessors) had seen off the Bourbons, the Bonapartes and the Hohenzollerns. The Kennedys would have seen themselves off even if they had not been tragically doomed. There is no comparison between the hereditary dynasty and the political one, or the entertainment one, for that matter.

Strangely the turn-around in the Royal family's esteem with the communicating classes (it had never truly been threatened among the populace in general) came with the re-enactment of an ancient ceremony which might well have provoked hilarity: the installation of Prince Charles as Prince of Wales.

In 1969 there were few still living who could recall the last time a Prince of Wales had been installed – Prince Edward, nearly 60 years before. Then, as he recollected, his Tudor-style dress had been a source of acute embarassment to him. No such mistake was committed at the '69 installation.

The ancient ceremony at Carnarvon Castle was brilliantly brought to life on colour television. The presentation by the Sovereign of the heir to the people of Wales as a covenant of the union between Prince and Principality was lovingly evoked. And what struck the audience of many millions most was the display of loving loyalty from the son to his mother. Here was living testimony of the continuity of the British Monarchy, bridging centuries, assuring one generation that what it possessed was in trust for another, as it had 'succeeded to the heritage of generations gone by'.

Had the ceremony been presented as a play it would have won plaudits from the harshest critics. As real life drama it produced a remarkable reaction in favour of Monarchy, pomp and circumstance and the Family as the repository of the nation's best instincts.

As events had wrought terrible injuries to the Kennedy family, events conspired to enhance the reputation of the Royal Family. The number in the family grew to four with the addition of Princes Andrew and Edward. Charles was now able to take part in the round of Royal duties to which he gave himself wholeheartedly. His younger sister, Anne, though still a gawky teenager, and one who would go through a period of intense unpopularity with the photographers and reporters of Fleet Street, would eventually 'come through' as a very considerable person in her own right.

The Family, the Firm, was by the mid-seventies in good heart. The Queen, having celebrated her Silver Wedding Anniversary, prepared to receive a Nation's and a Commonwealth's homage on her Silver Jubilee. She, at least, could take comfort from the passing years. They had brought her closer and closer to her people while in no way diminishing majesty. Rather the years had enhanced it. The communicators who had once jibed now gave her the awe and reverence she had so bravely earned.

The institution of Monarchy stood as proud and sure as the century passed its three-quarter mark as ever it had in British history. It was the only institution that could make such a claim.

CHAPTER TWO

The Guilt on the Gingerbread

To understand the Britain of the third quarter of the twentieth century it is essential to appreciate the passion for security which gripped the mass of people.

When minimal national insurance and old age pensions were introduced in 1909, recipients were astonished at their good fortune (see *The Way We Were* 1900–1914). Self-help and self-reliance reinforced by private charity was the moral absolute of the Victorian age. The Socialist collectivist argument was making headway among sections of the intelligentsia, among some politicians (notably Lloyd George) and a few senior civil servants, but the dominant theme was still that of individual responsibility.

The Great War shook the social framework to its foundations, yet the individualist concept remained paramount. Pensions were increased somewhat; the age limit was reduced to 65; the panel system for doctors attending lower income groups was extended. The ideal, however, of a Welfare State securing everyone against want, poverty and unemployment was regarded as utopian.

The Great Depression and World War II changed all that. The children of the Depression who had fought the war demanded security. Collectivism came into its own. And the Labour Party, which advocated it, came into power.

By 1951, the attraction of almost total economic control by the State was wearing thin. The country was more severely rationed than during the war. Taxation was penal – rising to 98% of income at the top level. (On occasion, a capital levy took it over the 100% mark) Housing was allocated on a points system. Motor cars, except for those who required them for their profession or trade, were virtually unobtainable. The argument that the Nation must endure this austerity for the sake of regaining export markets marched uneasily with the fact that defeated and ruined Germany was enjoying increasing affluence *and* outstanding foreign trade gains.

So in the election of 1951 Churchill's Conservatives narrowly ousted Labour. It was a victory in seats only. In terms of votes Labour still outstripped the Conservatives. The public wanted modification, not transformation, and there was to be no tampering with the Welfare State. The Tories had already conceded that; if they hadn't they would not have won office. The gibe about being 'looked after from the womb to the tomb' was confined to Tory Party zealots. For public consumption, the Conservatives maintained that they would make welfare more effective through freeing enterprise to create more production. The concept of the collective commitment to provide health, public housing, insurance, unemployment benefit, family allowances and social security for everyone regardless of means or needs, remained inviolable. It was a case of, 'This is what we mean to spend, this is what we need to earn.' Mr Micawber had been stood on his head. Happiness was expenditure. Misery had been banished.

Between 1951 and 1975 this was the general will and conventional wisdom, disputed by a mere handful of academic economists and a small parcel of politicians. Nor was there any compelling reason to combat the dominant philosophy. Dismantling absurd and outdated controls did produce the goods. Housing, private as well as public, became freely available. So did cars. In the period the number on the roads rose from under 2 million to more than 16 million. Food and clothes rationing ended. Foreign travel resumed. Customers could actually get telephones without having to wait six or seven years.

With this improvement in living standards, full employment was maintained and the Welfare State remained intact. Why alter a winning combination? The Conservatives triumphantly rode to victory in 1955 and 1959 – both times with doubled majorities in the Commons – on the theme 'Life is Better'. And it was. If it were better still in Germany, so what? The British were content, why work too hard?

However the non-conformist conscience was not dead, merely slumbering. When the Tory Prime Minister Harold Macmillan gave vent to a perfectly accurate, if inelegantly phrased, observation that the people 'had never had it so good', a considerable section of the communicating class suffered a severe twinge of guilt.

Who was having it so good? Well, the mass of the people who could now afford cars, to buy homes, washing machines, refrigerators, TV sets, holidays abroad. The British were getting a taste of the American life-style – and liking it. To those with a non-conformist

conscience there was something thoroughly irksome in that. The
Americans were crassly materialistic. They were also capitalistic.
Under President Eisenhower they were alleged to be complacent
into the bargain. They were atavistically anti-communist. To be like
the Americans was not admirable. To want to be like them was
positively anti-social.

It is necessary here to define two terms, 'non-conformist' and
'communicating class'. The first does not refer to worshippers who
refused to conform to the tenets of the established Church of
England. The twentieth-century non-conformists were not counted
among the worshippers anywhere, but they *were* against establishment attitudes. Their forefathers probably approved of the
revolting American colonists and would certainly have abhorred the
British Empire. From Tom Paine to Percy Bysshe Shelley, poets and
pamphleteers were natural rebels. Their ideological descendants
of the twentieth century regarded the USA not as a gallant rebel
but as a satiated conservative giant. The USSR ought to have
been the object of their respect but it too had fallen far short of the
ideal and while not discarded, was not preferred to other, nobler,
causes.

The British, passing out of the Imperialist phase, could be agents
of change in Africa and Asia where they still had colonies. But they
must change themselves, cleaving to the dictates of a social
conscience and discarding materialism, capitalism and the pride of
ownership.

The non-conformists were not automatically members of the
Labour Party which they often derided for its cloth-cap image. They
tended to favour the Liberals, a few flirted with the progressive wing
of the Conservatives but basically they distrusted political parties.
They used their own leverage, rather as the Fabians had done sixty
years before.

Unlike the Fabians, they were not a group. Their views simply
enjoyed general acceptance among the same sort of people. As with
Shelley and Paine, they were communicators, television reporters
and commentators, newspaper columnists, free-lance writers
figuring in the literary weeklies, the *Manchester Guardian* (later *The
Guardian*), the *News Chronicle* – soon, alas, to disappear – and in radio
and certain of the Scottish and Provincial English Press.

They set the tone. Their opinions were echoed among a number of
leading civil servants who did not wish to be thought 'square' (the

slang has a dreadfully dated ring) and by Members of Parliament who were on the lookout for issues to clothe their ambitions.

From the time that Roy Thomson, a go-getting Canadian millionaire publisher, landed in Scotland – in 1953 – and began acquiring newspapers, the ranks of the dissenting communicating class swelled appreciably. Thomson, an engagingly frank capitalist, made no secret of his all-consuming interest: money. He once offered the author a senior job in his organisation – at half what the said author was already receiving!

'I'm only interested in balance sheets and the bottom line,' he once declared, also offering a hostage to fortune by opining that his ownership of Scottish commercial television was 'a licence to print money'.

This genial soul had no interest in the politics of the papers he owned: so long as they didn't attack the Royal Family (he dearly wanted a peerage and finally got it) they could take pretty well any line they chose. As he became, successively, publisher of the *Scotsman*, many provincial papers in the UK and finally of the *Sunday Times* and *The Times* itself, a glittering prospect was opened to journalists not only to report the news but to shape it.

In his disdain for policy-making, Thomson was totally at odds with that other leading Canadian millionaire publisher, Maxwell Aitken, first Baron Beaverbrook.

Beaverbrook was a political animal first, a newspaperman second and a money-maker by instinct (he was a dollar millionaire at 24). He came to Britain at the height of Imperial splendour when Kipling was hymning the glories of Empire, and the words of Land of Hope and Glory 'wider still and wider shall thy bounds be set' had been set to Elgar's stirring music. The romance of Empire was Beaverbrook's abiding passion. Amid a life of erratic loves and hates, the Empire was a constant theme. Anything which advanced it was splendid; whatever diminished it was evil. Opinions on this and a host of other topics were transmitted to his newspapers – the *Daily Express, Sunday Express*, London *Evening Standard* and Glasgow *Evening Citizen*. As many as 30 instructions a day were received from The Lord, a title well suited to conveying the omnipotence of The Principal Reader.

Beaverbrook gloried in being a propagandist. He trumpeted the fact to a Royal Commission on the Press, set up by the 1945 Labour Government. He was so committed to presenting his convictions that he actually returned money to advertisers when the paper's profits rose above £1 million – or so he told the author. Beaverbrook was Press Lord writ large.

His newspapers had a simple philosophy: The Empire, grudgingly translated to Commonwealth in 1960, first, last and all time. Effectively this meant the old, or white, Commonwealth: the dominions, of which Canada was the most senior. In addition to being strongly patriotic, the *Express* Group extolled the virtues of free enterprise, competition, car ownership, home ownership, share ownership. What could be termed popular capitalism, or rampant materialism, if one held another view.

The other view was held by most of the opinion-forming journalists who moulded the Thomson papers plus those in the Rothermere Group which controlled the *Daily Mail*. Rothermere's father, the first baron, had been a Press Baron in the Beaverbrook tradition, but his son did not have the same combative stripe. The *Daily Mail*, once the bastion of right-wing Toryism, marched to a different note: strident liberalism-with-a-social-conscience.*

The liberalism was not that of the Manchester School of laisser-faire economics, but of social permissiveness. The economic policy was an amalgam of fervent pro-Europeanism with a belief in the central direction of the national economy.

The Europeanism was translated into an insistent demand that Britain join the European Economic Community, or Common Market. This was not so much because the communicating class believed in the rules of competition governing the EEC – which sat oddly with their belief in national economic planning – but rather because Europe was the 'in thing'. It was *new*.

To appreciate the essence of the third quarter of the twentieth century it is necessary to grasp the importance which that word possessed.

The period from the mid-fifties to the mid-seventies was one of constant restlessness and questioning. Whatever was 'new' was obviously untried and that itself was a cardinal virtue. Hence the passionate advocacy of the Common Market by the communicating class. In their way they were but echoing the hucksters on television who urged customers to buy a cleaning liquid simply because it was new.

Nothing aided the communicating class more than the arrival at

* This *Daily Mail* policy applied to the early sixties.

The young Beatles . . . 'more popular than Jesus Christ'.

The heart transplants of Dr Christiaan Barnard and other medical advances
provided the best news of the period.

the BBC as Director-General of Hugh Carleton Greene. Brother of the distinguished author, Graham, Sir Hugh of the round chubby face, spectacles twinkling on the end of his button nose, seemed to sum up the flippancy of the age. His was in the jargon of his day, a 'flip' appointment by that most flip Prime Minister, Harold Macmillan.

Sir Hugh gave the young ones their head at the BBC and so the immensely powerful corporation which, under the great beetle-browed John Reith ('Wuthering Height' in Churchill's immortal phrase) had held back progress by sticking limpet-fashion to old standards, now took the lead in sneering at the Establishment.

So, as the quarter century advanced, the dissenting opinion-formers, the non-conforming communicators, captured redoubt after redoubt in what was coming to be known as 'The Media'.

Almost invariably the brightest and the best communicators in ink or on screen were radical iconoclasts: Bernard Levin, Paul Johnson, Kingsley Amis, John Braine, David Frost, John Osborne, Hugh Thomas, John Vaizey. That they all marched smartly to the Right in later life is another story. At the time when our story was starting they had the ear of the professional classes and their message was 'ring out the old, ring in the new'. They found a receptive audience.

Now this story, like all stories, has to have a beginning. It began in 1956.

CHAPTER THREE

The Year of Change

Certain years ring a bell in most people's mind: 1066, 1776, 1789, 1914. The year 1956 doesn't apparently come in to that category. England wasn't invaded. There was no earth-shattering revolution, no great and terrible war. Yet in turning social attitudes upside down 1956 really marks the end of the Victorian era more accurately than the death of the Old Queen herself.

It was the year which saw rock 'n' roll cross the Atlantic with Bill Haley's 'Rock Around the Clock' and Britain's own Tommy Steele rose to instant fame with his 'Rock with the Caveman'. The 'pop' revolution had arrived.

It was accompanied by what the Press termed 'rock 'n' roll riots', more an indulgence in alliteration than a strictly truthful account. What happened was that teenagers in cinemas and halls started ripping the seats as well as screaming when their heroes gave vent to screeching and writhing. There was a deal of follow-my-leader about it. There was no hate, no malignancy, simply excitement.

Yet such indiscipline would have been unthinkable five years earlier. The rock 'n' roll 'riots' were the first symptoms of the astonishing change that was coming over Western society. The post-war generation was coming into its own, tasting the fruits of affluence, job security and what was later to be called the 'youth culture'.

Unemployment in the UK did not exist in 1956. There were 10 vacancies for every jobless person (300,000). Women provided a much smaller proportion of the total labour force – 2.5 million – than they were to do twenty years later: 8 million. So those between the ages of fifteen – the then school-leaving age – and twenty were in high demand. Their wages, some £4 a week, were theirs to spend. They were the ones record manufacturers pursued. The change in musical tastes first emerging in 1956 marked the decisive switch from an adult-dominated society to a youth-dominated one.

The cinema gave further emphasis to this trend of 1956. There appeared the film *Rebel without a Cause*. The screen adaptation, by Stewart Stern, was from a work written by Nicholas Ray who had spent eight months researching juvenile delinquency in the US. This pictured the kind of social nihilism which gripped the offspring of wealthy self-centred parents who believed every problem could be solved by money. Materially the boy had everything, except the understanding of his elders. So he went to the bad.

James Dean, the actor who played the flawed youth, was himself killed in a bizarre car accident which could have been suicide. He played out the role in real life and swiftly became a legend and a symbol of defiance (albeit pointless) to disaffected youth. Or so the sociologists portrayed his significance.

Matching the surly, inarticulate, rich rebel without a cause on film came 27-year-old John Osborne's stage play *Look Back in Anger* with its surly, articulate, working class rebel, Jim Porter.

Here in dramatic form was the assault on the establishment virtues. Jimmy Porter (even the name had a deliberately common ring to it) spoke in the rough language of the provinces to denounce the middle class upbringing of his attractive young wife. So a class-war twist was given to the growing alienation of the young from their parents. Osborne followed his *Look Back in Anger* with *The Entertainer* which depicted a drunken, broken-down musical hall comedian, Archie Rice, which some critics took to represent post-Imperial Britain, brought low by the Suez episode. Whether Mr Osborne had that in mind when he wrote *The Entertainer* is a matter for speculation. Of a certainty Suez marked the end of the British Empire 'on which the sun never sets' – a phrase that pre-dated even Queen Victoria.

In an article in *Encounter*, 'The Language of Politics', Bryan Magee, the philosopher, summed up the impact of Suez.

I believe there would now be widespread agreement for the proposition that the British invasion of Suez in 1956 was a mistake which was brought about to an important degree by our seeing ourselves in outmoded categories, in this case categories of Empire. Our imperial role, our naval and military strength, our ability to pursue an independent foreign policy, our traditional domination of the Middle East in alliance with France, our prestige in the area, the Backwardness of the Natives – all these only-too-real realities of an earlier time had lost enough of their substance by 1956 to have become delusions, so that our attempts to behave as if they were still reality involved us in humiliating fiasco.*

That is a shrewd, if harsh, assessment; perhaps too harsh. It might be argued – as the *Express* newspaper argued at the time – that if Colonel Nasser, Egypt's mercurial dictator, had been overthrown in 1956, much pain would have been avoided: such as the installation in Iraq of a Nasser-inspired dictatorship of a particularly malevolent character, not to mention the carbon-copy of Nasser himself, Colonel Gadaffi in Libya. The fact was that when Nasser finally *did* vanish he was succeeded by much more reasonable Egyptian leaders who made peace with Israel.

Anthony Eden, the British Prime Minister at the time, may indeed have been suffering from the delusions Magee mentions, but his biggest delusion was that Nasser was another Hitler. Eden was exorcising the memory of appeasement of the Nazi Fuehrer in the thirties by 'standing up' to his Levantine equivalent in the fifties. That was the delusion, and the tragedy, of Suez.

The Anglo-French invasion of Egypt was ostensibly to save the Suez Canal from becoming embroiled in an Israeli-Egyptian war; in truth to wrest the Canal back from Nasser, who had seized it from the Suez Canal company and eliminate him as the major de-stabiliser of the Middle East. The expedition failed miserably: not wholly through military blunders (the Egyptian air force was taken out with surgical proficiency in a matter of hours, paratroopers took much of the Canal) but by the total collapse of the British before American insistence that they bring the venture to an end.

Such surrender exemplified the transfer of world power from London to Washington. At a stroke, the UK demonstrated that it could no longer, as Magee observes, sustain an independent foreign policy. From that conclusion many far-reaching consequences flowed. Anthony Eden, a sick man, resigned. The Cabinet decided on decolonisation at breakneck speed. Within nine years of Suez the entire British Colonial Empire had ceased to exist and Britain no longer had a meaningful presence east of Suez.

The UK turned away from global responsibilities towards involvement in the European Economic Community. Goodbye Commonwealth, Hullo Common Market, as the *Express* quipped.

The United States emerged as the undisputed champion of the

* Reproduced by permission of A.D. Peters & Co Ltd.

non-Communists in a global role. Veljko Micunovic, the influential Yugoslav ambassador to Moscow*, noted that invariably, after Suez, the Russian leadership spoke exclusively of their relations with the USA and not, as in prior times, with the 'Anglo-Saxon powers' or 'The West'. Similarly, Washington saw all world problems in terms of the Cold War against the USSR and China. Thus American involvement in Lebanon and Vietnam was justified by reference to the alleged attempts by Moscow and Peking to promote Marxism and subvert these territories.

Indeed it was the timing of the Anglo-French-Israeli Suez venture as much as its alleged immorality which roused fury in the US for, by chance, the invasion of Egypt synchronised with the entry of a Russian army into Hungary to crush an anti-Soviet revolt there. The American President, Dwight D. Eisenhower and his Secretary of State, John Foster Dulles, were much distressed over the fact that the Anglo-French operations in early November '56 distracted world attention from Nikita Khrushchev's brutal suppression of the workers of Budapest at the same moment.

Here, again, 1956 represents a turning point in world affairs. Until that year Communism could be, was, viewed as a seamless garment. To many in the West it was a substitute religion without sectarian divide. To these people the sight of Russian tanks firing on Hungarian workers who had risen against their local Soviet-controlled rulers, was terribly disillusioning. Almost as disillusioning as Khrushchev's memorable 'secret' speech in February '56 denouncing Stalin.

One of Communism's greatest illusions was that Joseph Stalin, pipe-smoking, avuncular, benign – though shrewd and ruthless when necessary – was the architect of the future, a man of truly heroic proportions. When his successor, Nikita Khrushchev, shattered that fable he touched off a chain of events not dissimiliar to those begun by the protesting monk, Martin Luther. Within four years of that extraordinary speech China had split ideologically with Moscow in much the same way that Northern Europe rejected the Supreme Pontiff in Rome.

When the text of the Secret Address to the 20th Congress of the Soviet Communist Party was leaked (by the US State Department – it was never published nor mentioned in the USSR) the *Express* printed extracts.

Moscow Diary (Chatto and Windus)

'The Moscow atmosphere in the late Stalin era,' (i.e. 1948–1953) said Khrushchev, 'was of a capital ridden by plots, counter plots and intrigues, in which no one knew who might be the next victim.'

When he was asked by someone in the 1600 strong audience of Communist delegates why he didn't do something about it, Khrushchev himself asked: 'Who said that?' No one replied. 'That,' said Khrushchev, 'is why no one did anything about it.'

Even the members of the Politburo (the Soviet's supreme policy-making and executive body) lived in fear when summoned by Stalin. They never knew whether they would return. Nikolai Bulganin (in 1956, Soviet Prime Minister) was once called to Stalin's country house and did not know whether he would end up at a party or in prison.

Stalin dealt with his subordinates by shouting at them. He would intimidate people he called into his office by saying, 'Why are you looking at me that way? Well? Why don't you look me in the eyes? Are you afraid to look me in the eyes?'

'What could we do?' Khrushchev continued. 'You just had to look at him wrongly and you lost your head.'

He then recounted some of those who had:

'Stalin decimated the Communist Party by purges, especially in the years 1936–38.'

'Five thousand of Russia's best officers were murdered during the blood baths which followed the secret trial of Marshal Tukhachevsky on treason charges in 1937 . . . purges resulted in the massacre of innocent people. Even children were butchered.'

'Serge Ordjonikidze, a fellow Georgian and close friend of Stalin who died during the same period, was given the choice of being murdered or committing suicide. He committed suicide and was given a State funeral.'

'Nikolai Voznesensky, the economic planner, was also shot without trial and without even the knowledge of his colleagues of the Politburo. About three-quarters of the 17th Party Congress (in 1934), many of whom spoke against Stalin, were shot soon after the Congress.'

Khrushchev went on to disclose that even in old age Stalin kept the blood lust bubbling.

'Towards the end of his life (he died in 1953) Stalin considered Marshal Voroshilov (wartime commander of the Soviet northern army group, later President of the USSR) a British spy and refused to let him take part in the work of the Politburo, of which he was a member.'

'Stalin humiliated me,' cried Khrushchev, 'at a reception for foreigners. He shouted at me: "Khokhol, dance the gopak".'

(Khokhol is a derogatory name for a Ukranian, the gopak dance involves intricate footwork unsuited to Khrushchev's bulk and undignified for a man of his age.) Khrushchev added: 'So I danced the gopak.'

During the course of his address, which lasted until 4 am, 80 of the 1600 delegates fainted or had seizures.

The fable of the apostolic descent from Lenin to Stalin, the first kindly guiding the latter to lead the world-wide Communist movement, was smashed to smithereens. For Khrushchev disclosed that, in revenge for Lenin warning his colleagues against him, Stalin threatened Lenin's widow, telling her that if she continued to speak out against him in public he would issue a declaration that she had never been Lenin's wife!

So much for the 'old comrades' story.

Truly, after 1956, Communism could never be the same. As a universal system it had been stripped of its fundamentals: its heroes turned into monsters, its 'objective appraisal of history' shown up to be a mixture of real political cynicism and medieval cruelty.*

But if Communism as practised in the USSR lost its appeal as the recipe for the future, its virulent opposition to the employing class still held sway in Britain. And it was this attitude, perhaps prompted, on occasion, by heedless and incompetent management, which produced another phenomenon of 1956: the start of mass coloured immigration into the United Kingdom.

As already mentioned, unemployment did not exist in 1956. What *did* exist was overfull employment: a scarcity of labour, largely caused by woeful misuse, due to incompetence and union-imposed restrictions.

The flavour of unreconstructed union opinion at this period may be tasted in the words of a Mr Hope (surely not Bob) of the Boot and Shoe Operatives, as reported in the *Daily Express*:

---

*Khrushchev himself suffered from denunciation when he was forced out of power in 1964.

There is no such thing as the dignity of labour . . . Away with the idea that there is something dignified about work. Nobody in their senses wants it.

Every employee should get the maximum amount of wages for the least quantity of work his employer will accept.

As a definition of the union aspect of the iron law of wages that is fair enough. Not surprisingly, however, it did not commend itself to employers and, in consequence, municipal and nationalised industries went recruiting in the Empire.

In 1956 the public transport services, notably London's, went a-searching for additional staff in the Caribbean. They sought West Indians for the simple reason that they spoke English and would find even the most menial jobs in England a vast improvement on their way of life at home.

At the time it seemed an innocuous enough policy. The employers were responding to union tactics of demanding more money for less work by increasing the supply of labour: a perfectly normal market action. But the consequences were to be of an utterly unforeseen and wide-ranging nature. The happy news spread throughout the Commonwealth. There was good living to be earned in England.

Until 1956 immigration from the West Indies, Africa and Asia was minimal. Before 1956, it was estimated that there were fewer than 200,000 Africans, Asians and West Indians in Britain. By 1961, 125,000 *a year* were being admitted. The reasons for this huge influx were twofold: the jet engine which made inter-continental travel so much faster and, relatively, cheaper than before and the unchanged rules of once-Imperial Britain.

The principle of unfettered access to the UK was a fundamental tenet of the Old Empire. Everyone within the Crown's dominions was deemed to have equal rights, *including the right of moving to the Motherland*. But, in practice, that applied only to the very wealthy classes. Jawaharlal Nehru, for instance, was educated at Harrow and adopted the fashionable life so comprehensively that he could not be bothered to work, prompting his irate father – a wealthy Brahmin lawyer – to write: 'Have you had any time to devote to the poor cows . . . reduced by nothing short of culpable negligence.' The 'cows' in question were Nehru's mother, wife, sisters and daughters.

There was no question, in the years prior to 1956, of masses of people coming to Britain to settle. Most of the 200,000 in the mid-fifties were seamen (known as 'lascars') awaiting sailings, students, holidaymakers and wealthy offspring enjoying the Western way of life. The idea of millions of immigrants – of any colour – descending on Britain would have appeared ludicrous. For how could one of the most densely-populated states in the world comfortably accommodate millions of immigrants? And where would it end? The Indian sub-continent alone had 600 million people. In theory, every one of them, as members of the Commonwealth, could settle in the UK. To state the prospect was to expose its folly.

Yet the Cabinet, faced with such a prospect, did nothing about framing a British nationality act which would bring the law into line with reality. It was considered 'illiberal' to face the facts, although the *Daily Express* bluntly expressed what many feared when it said that 'if free entry continues . . . the only question will be where to put the British'.

The immigration crisis – for such it became in the early sixties – stemmed from the tremendous sense of guilt which manifested itself in the later fifties. The Conservatives, from a mixture of guilt about their past dealings with the unions (and also from political calculation) did nothing to alter the unions' restrictive practices. As a result a false labour shortage was created, leading to avid recruitment of cheap labour from the Caribbean. In turn, the Labour Party made unrestricted immigration a litmus test of racial equality. Anyone opposing free entry was a 'racist'.

In this way obfuscation and hypocrisy combined to produce a policy which harmed the West Indian newcomers more than anyone else. For it left them to try to make their own way in a hostile environment, falling further and further behind in the competitive race for jobs and social placings, while creating black ghettoes marked by poor housing, violence and self-induced deprivation. The attitude to immigration and the obverse of racial superiority, illuminated the third quarter of the twentieth century.

Guilt lit the sombre scene: guilt at 'oppressing' the coloured peoples: in the Empire, so far as Britain was concerned, and domestically in the case of the US.

Guilt was a predominant feature among Western societies as self-confidence drained away. It took another form in the UK, as the issues of crime and punishment, and again 1956 was the decisive year. For decades before 1956 valiant souls had been campaigning against the death penalty. The burden of their argument was that it degraded the society which inflicted it and that so long as there was always a doubt about the verdict there was a possibility that the wrong man would be hanged. Such reasoning had little impact on public opinion which regularly registered a preference for the death penalty by margins of eight or nine to one.

The communicating class, however, was heavily influenced by three executions in the early fifties. The first was the hanging of Timothy Evans for the murder of his wife and child. Evans, it was claimed at the time, was mentally retarded. But the clamour against his execution increased enormously when it was discovered that he had shared 10 Rillington Place, London, with a landlord, Christie, who turned out to be a necrophiliac who had murdered half a dozen women. It was stretching the bounds of coincidence too far to believe that two murderers shared the same house. The clamour against the death penalty rose several notches at this apparent proof that an innocent man had perished by the rope.

Another execution which roused furious controversy was that of Derek Bentley who paid with his life for the killing of a policeman during a robbery. The fatal shot was actually fired by Bentley's accomplice who, as a 16-year-old, was spared the ultimate penalty. Bentley had shouted, 'Give it to him, Chris' to his companion. The prosecution contended that Bentley meant Christopher should shoot the policeman. The defence maintained that Bentley wanted him to hand over the pistol. The element of doubt concerning intention and the fact that Bentley died in place of the youth who fired the shot, added weight to the case against hanging. Winston Churchill himself, who was Prime Minister at the time, urged the imposition of the death penalty on the grounds that it was needed as a deterrent to violent crime.

Finally came the case of Ruth Ellis who shot and killed her faithless lover outside a pub in Hampstead. No heed was taken of the plea that this was a *crime passionnel*, the prosecution pointing out that Ellis had pumped five bullets into her lover and that killing by gunfire endangered other lives (a passer-by was slightly hurt). The use of firearms was anathema to the law, especially as, in these bygone days, the police were invariably unarmed.

The three cases provoked a furious public outcry from the anti-capital punishment lobby which found a receptive echo in Whitehall and Westminster. Senior civil servants and MPs were becoming increasingly fearful of being regarded as reactionary in the eyes of the communicating class. They therefore welcomed the opportunity to move towards a more humane attitude. They dared not go too far ahead of public opinion, so a half-way house towards abolition was reached. Mr R.A. (later Lord) Butler, the Conservative Home Secretary, introduced a Capital Murder Bill which prescribed the death penalty for killing by shooting, explosion or arson but excluded the ultimate sentence for killing by other means (i.e. poisoning). This differentiation was clearly unsustainable. In 1965 the death penalty was abolished.

Champions of abolition claimed that capital punishment was no deterrent to murder. Advocates of hanging claimed it was.

The figures for murder (England and Wales):-

    1950   123
    1955   123 (last year of mandatory death sentence)
    1975   515

In 1956 the intellectual momentum for change towards a less repressive, more permissive society was unstoppable. That single year marks the true end of the Victorian era and the start of what its critics were to describe as the Soft Option era.

CHAPTER FOUR

The New Morality: 1

From Lady Chatterley to Lord Longford

October 20, 1960 may be said to mark one important aspect of the Permissive Revolution. On that date came the verdict on David Herbert Lawrence's book *Lady Chatterley's Lover*. D.H.Lawrence had been dead for 30 years but his tortured, restless spirit had haunted two generations of communicators. Twice during his lifetime he was charged with writing obscene works. The first time it was *The Rainbow*, the second time, in 1928, it was *Lady Chatterley*. If anyone could be said to represent the victims of Victorian repression it was Mr Lawrence and his Lady.

Now, at last, their vindication was at hand. In days gone by, fearless young folk (or dirty-minded young beggars, according to one's viewpoint) would pore over the pages of *Lady Chatterley*, eagerly absorbing the tale of a rich baronet cuckolded by his gamekeeper – or flicking through the book until they came on the forbidden four-letter word. It was not the motives of the potential readers that were on trial but those who prevented them from getting hold of the book. That was the fact.

In theory, it was the publishers, Penguin Books, who stood in the dock, before Mr Justice Byrne and a jury of nine men and three women at the Central Criminal Court, London: the Old Bailey.

On the one side were mobilised the forces clamouring for change. Their case, expressed through defending counsel, was that the ban on the book was hypocritical, outdated, absurd, and by virtue of the false screen of morality erected round the ban, tending to create the very lewdness it was meant to prevent: for what we are denied, we desire.

Penguin had, of course, invited prosecution by publishing an unexpurgated edition of *Lady Chatterley* thus, technically, breaching the Obscene Publications Act. Under the terms of the Act – a consolidating measure which simplified previous scattered legislative provisions on obscenity – a work deemed liable to corrupt or deprave could be banned.

Naturally there were certain extenuating circumstances. How could there not be, when in Shakespeare's *Lear* eyes were gouged out and in *Titus Andronicus* hands were lopped off. Clearly, the works of literary and artistic merit were excluded from the proscribed list. Moreover, a book, play or poem that might corrupt a 10-year-old might not be held to corrupt a 30-year-old. In its way, the 1959 Act was a liberalising measure. So liberals resolved to test it by provoking prosecution.

Their reasoning was that a definition of obscenity cannot be an absolute. It must reflect the mood of the period – and that meant the mood of the 1960s: not the 1860s or even the 1950s.

The film industry, through the Hays Office in the US and the Board of Film Censors in the UK, had a strict code of behaviour and stern guide lines on sexuality.

Popular literature mirrored the safe attitude to sex. If you wanted a book with dirty words in it, you got it from a back-street bookshop in a plain wrapper.

To put D.H. Lawrence in this class, argued his promoters, was to degrade a fine work of literature. And anyway (this was the nub of their case, though never explicitly stated) who *were* these censors to determine who might read what? The right to read what you wanted was surely as important as the right to free speech. Anything which restricted that right was, by its very nature, hobbling the human spirit. The total abolition of censorship was the pre-requisite for an outpouring of literary merit unequalled since the days of Shakespeare and Marlowe (when, actually, Tudor censorship was extremely severe . . . but let that pass).

The defenders of the old order – though prosecutors in the case – had no real answer to that, nor to the hosts of distinguished witnesses bearing testimony for the freeing of *Lady Chatterley*.

The Press recorded their appearances: 36 being called of the 72 who offered to give evidence in favour of *Lady Chatterley*.

'It is', said Richard Hoggart, author and lecturer in English, 'a highly educative book in the proper sense. Highly virtuous, if not most puritanical.'

Dr Hemming, psychologist, called the book 'an antidote against evil thinkers about sex as a purely physical thrill'.

Norman St John Stevas, Roman Catholic writer and later Conservative MP and Minister, affirmed: 'I would put Lawrence among the great literary moralists of our own English literature who was essentially trying to purge, cleanse and reform.'

The most profound endorsement of Lawrence's pure intentions came from Dr John Robinson, Anglican Bishop of Woolwich, who was later to write *Honest to God*. He described the book as 'Something sacred . . . an act of holy communion. Lawrence's description of sexual relations cannot be taken out of the context of his quite astonishing sensitivity to the beauty and value of all organic relationships. I think the effect of this book is against, rather than for, promiscuity.'

Questioned by counsel for *Lady Chatterley*, Mr Gerald (later Lord) Gardiner, if it were a book Christians ought to read, the Bishop responded: 'Yes, I think it is.'

Again and again – as in these passages quoted from the Court proceedings – witnesses testified to the essential morality of Lawrence's work. There was still respect for the moral feelings of the jury: hence the glittering array of religious, literary and medical figures brought forward as defenders.

Against this formidable battery, what had the prosecution to offer? Mervyn Griffith-Jones, the principal counsel, gave voice to the uncompromising faith of Welsh Nonconformism. He maintained that *Lady Chatterley's Lover* was a dirty book, tending to deprave and corrupt those who might reasonably be expected to read it once it was freely available.

The book had twelve sexual scenes described in great detail (the defence responded that they represented only 30 pages out of 319) . . . 'On the floor of a hut, in the undergrowth, in the forest . . . The jury may think the plot is little more than padding until we can reach the hut again or the forest or the shrubbery.' Then Mr Griffith-Jones made his fatal error. 'Is this the kind of book,' he asked, 'the jury would want factory girls to read?'

The remark was redolent of the Victorian Past, of Nanny-Knows-Best, of Not-Before-the-Children, of caste, privilege, the classes-and-the-masses, all the things that were anathema to the icon-breakers and communicators of the sixties.

In that watershed year of 1956 John Gordon had sounded the tocsin against sexual licence. The *Sunday Express* columnist had thundered:

On Graham Greene's recommendation (in the *Sunday Times*) I bought *Lolita*. Without doubt it is the filthiest book I have ever read, sheer unrestrained pornography. Its central character is a pervert with a passion for debauching what he calls 'nymphets'. These, he explains, are girls from 11 to 14. The entire book is devoted to an exhaustive, uninhibited and utterly disgusting description of his pursuits and successes.

It is published in France. Anyone who published it here would certainly go to prison.

Not by 1960, they wouldn't have. The Presbyterian voice of John Gordon and the Methodist one of Griffith-Jones were as sounding brass against the rants of libertarianism, heavily backed by the Anglican Church.

Gerald Gardiner summed up the case for *Lady Chatterley* by pointing out that Shakespeare, Chaucer and many other revered men of literature had not hesitated to use robust language to describe the body and the impulse of sexual desire. 'The attitude of shame with which large numbers of people have always viewed sex in any form has reduced us to the position where it is not at all easy for fathers and mothers to find words to describe to their children the physical union.'

It was almost impossible for any rational, reasonable person to dissent from that.

Gardiner went on: 'Witnesses have been repeatedly asked, by the prosecution, if it is a book they would like their wives or servants (!) to read. This might be an echo from the Bench of many years ago – it would never do to let members of the working class read it.'

Mr Gardiner was pushing at an open door. The sexual revolution was about to become the new orthodoxy and to go to extremes in the following fifteen years undreamed of by lawyers, literary persons and spectators in the Old Bailey court.

After a two-week hearing the jury found for the defence. *Lady Chatterley's Lover* could now be bought and read by all. One group in the Press hailed the decision as 'the vindication of liberty', another bemoaned that 'licentiousness has been enthroned'. There is no means of weighing such subjective verdicts.

The popular response is, however, measurable. Some 200,000 paperback copies of the book had been printed before the case was heard. Ultimately more than 3,400,000 copies were sold throughout

Britain and the Commonwealth: twice as many people partook in this 'act of holy communion' as partook of Holy Communion on any average Sunday in the Church of England.

In the years that followed a flood of pornographic material filled the bookstalls. In the Metropolitan Police District the number of pornographic materials seized trebled every few years.*

So great did public anxiety become that a committee under the chairmanship of Lord Longford was formed to investigate the fastest-growing industry in the West. It included such distinguished literary figures as the novelist Kingsley Amis, the critic and essayist Malcolm Muggeridge, Lord Shawcross, the former Attorney General and chief prosecutor of the principal Nazi war criminals and the Archbishop of York. It reported in 1972, the year in which the 'hardporn' material – books and magazines – impounded by Customs and Excise passed the 2.5 million: *fifty times* the amount confiscated in 1960.

The Committee found that porno profits for retailers were 45% to 50% of the cost and that, as a sale or return system operated, the retailer was never left with unsold stock. Admittedly there was the risk of prosecution, but the size of the profit took care of the insurance factor.

The extent of the sexual revolution may be gauged from the trial of three young men, Richard Neville, James Anderson, Felix Dennis who were found guilty in August 1971 of publishing an obscene article, to wit a magazine called *Oz*. The issue which provoked prosecution under the law was a 'school kids' one. It showed, among other things, the popular children's character, the *Express's* Rupert Bear, forcing a passage into his grandmother. Teachers and headmasters were presented as sadists and sexual perverts displaying gargantuan private parts. There was a cartoon with the caption 'f . . . your mother'. The work had been largely written by a panel of teenagers and aimed at a teenage market, lavishly produced at a price of 20p and selling – so it was claimed – 40,000 copies.

Lord Longford's committee interviewed Richard Neville. He

outlined for us opinions which we felt fairly represented the alternative society. He saw no problem of pornography since, in his view, sex was one of the revolutionary weapons with which he

*A large number of them portrayed violence against women.

Nikita Khrushchev, the man who toppled Stalin's reputation.

National Servicemen cheering demob prospects.

End of Empire. British troops quit Suez.

hoped to change society; promiscuity, provided the dangers of VD and the need for contraception were pointed out, was one beneficial way of breaking up the family structure that had led to women becoming appendages and children the property of their parents. For him sexual repression and political repression were part of the same tradition and therefore the post-pubertal child should regard any voluntary sexual relationship as freedom, and therapeutic, however . . . he would not feel justified in offering pornography to children against the parents' wishes, although the destruction of all inhibitions was his aim.

On the stage [said the Commission's report] a new watershed was reached in this country when in the summer of 1971 *Oh! Calcutta!* was staged in London with impunity . . . . The late Sir Alan Herbert, doughtiest champion of artistic freedom, who worked hard to promote the 1959 measure liberalising the law on obscenity, wrote to *The Times*, bitterly saddened that 'the worthy struggle for reasonable liberty for honest writers has ended in a right to represent copulation, veraciously, on the public stage.'

On film, *Love Variations* (which characterised the Virgin Mary as a sex-crazed voyeur) was passed for public viewing in rural West Sussex by a casting vote of 6–5. The French film *Belle de Jour* which traced the erotic fantasies, ritual whipping and all kinds of humiliations, of a young frigid upper-class wife went on circuit in the suburbs and was later shown on television.

What was inconceivable to John Gordon in the oh-so-innocent mid-fifties had become, by the mid-seventies, the norm.

Lord Longford's Commission noted that, 'In Britain, neurotic sexual preoccupations have almost reached the point of a national perversion.' Bishop Trevor Huddleston (a Commission member) sadly commented on his return to England after eight years in Africa: 'The moment I came back I felt that things had gone desperately wrong. I think this country is very sick indeed.'

And *Lady Chatterley*? Here is Commission member David Holbrook's conclusion:

Up to the trial of Lady Chatterley, the rejection of the law was a valuable manifestation of the desire for free expression, so that the full range of erotic experience could be the proper object of science and art. But there has since been a mounting exploitation of sexual explicitness, impelled largely by sadistic principles on the one hand and prompted by economic drives on the other . . . The mass media have given everyone a telescopic view of sexual acts and sadistic displays, never available in the past. Scenes of extreme perversion, such as nuns having their vaginas syringed, double rape, women having their breasts cut off with kitchen knives, intercourse and group sex on the stage, are now mass entertainment. Culture looks consciously back towards primitive savagery . . .

Yet the humanity which governs the bawdiness of Chaucer or Shakespeare is markedly absent. Pornography is being thrust upon the whole population.

Or, as Caliban put it:

> You taught me language; and my profit on't
> Is, I know how to curse

CHAPTER FIVE

The New Morality: 2

Sounding Retreat

The alacrity with which the British busied themselves with the sexual revolution of the sixties was matched by other outbursts against authority and convention. This was the era of flower power, of hippies, of the student revolt and what the Press termed the 'fun revolution'.

To take the last first, the fun revolution was, for most people, encapsulated by the Beatles. The Beatles, four young men in their teens, had first come together in 1956 – that seminal year – although the composition was to change when the original drummer was replaced by Ringo Starr. National, then international fame came to the fabulous four – John Lennon, Paul McCartney (the writers), George Harrison and Ringo Starr – when Brian Epstein took over the management of their affairs. At 27 this personable, shrewd, market-wise music-shop owner was six years older than the oldest Beatle, Lennon. Here was youth at the helm with a vengeance. Within two years of the remarkable partnership being formed the Beatles had become the greatest force in show business.

The *Express* reported Sir Alec Douglas Home, the Foreign Secretary, as saying that he could always persuade foreign countries to see the British viewpoint by promising them that he would urge the Beatles to visit them.

Within five years the Beatles had amassed a fortune. Their single disc 'I Want To Hold your Hand' sold 5 million worldwide. Total record sales (counting LPs as five singles) totalled 230 million. Pillowslips on which the Beatles' heads lay in a Kansas hotel were cut into 160,000 one-inch squares, mounted on certificates and sold for 1 dollar each. In New York 100,000 youngsters turned out to greet them. In Adelaide the crowds numbered 300,000. In Manila there was a riot when the Beatles failed to keep an appointment with the Filipino President's wife, Esmeralda.

This was Beatlemania.

The *Express* had this account of the Beatles' performance before

65,000 in the Shea Stadium, New York on 24 August 1965, told by Miss Sandi Stewart, 15, from New Hampshire, USA.

> You really do believe they can see you, just you alone, when they're up on the stage. That's why you scream so as they'll notice you. I always felt John could see me. It was like a dream. Just me and John together and no one else.
>
> Even when you're screaming you can still hear . . . Their sexy movements make you scream even louder . . . as though they were being sexy with you personally.

Miss Sandi Stewart was one of millions, hundreds of millions. When Ringo had his tonsils removed there were hourly bulletins. The *Express* editorial observed: 'How much better it is that people should be concerned with the minor operation of a Beatle than borne down with anxiety about the next move of a Hitler.'

And that was it.

The British were shrugging off responsibility, a world empire, prime defence of the West. The thumping beat drowned the Last Post. One commentator, in the *Daily Mail*, averred that, 'If we don't count for much in the counsels of the globe any more at least we can take consolation in the international success of the Beatles.'

That was hardly enough for the Beatles. John Lennon described them as being 'more famous than Jesus Christ'.

The fun revolution ended in tears. Brian Epstein died in September 1967 from the cumulative effects of bromide in a drug called carbitral. Suicide was suspected, not proved. John Lennon was later murdered in New York. He had unwittingly written the Group's epitaph at the very height of their fame in the mid-sixties when he remarked: 'I'm pleased I made it young . . . it would have been terrible to spend your whole life before you finally make it, just to find out it is meaningless. We knew it was anyway, but we had to find out for ourselves.'

This nihilist philosophy marched with the drug culture which was so much part of the pop scene. Lennon himself observed that 'drugs probably helped the understanding of myself better . . . LSD was the self-knowledge which pointed the way.' Throughout the period from 1950 to 1975, drug abuse rose alarmingly.*

*No reliable statistics exist, for drug registration represents only a proportion of addicts. But by the mid-eighties 100 National Health Service hospitals were providing outpatient treatment for drug abuse and 35 hospitals had special drug treatment units in the UK.

On both sides of the Atlantic affluence and a lack of aim in life seemed to breed a fearful disdain of life. Repeated warnings, newspaper and television campaigns, the despairing pleas of parents, failed to reverse the toll. The numbers involved were not large in proportion to the total population but they involved many of the brightest young people in society. And they were a symbol of a deep malaise. The malaise showed itself in other forms: the 'drop-outs' who renounced conventional labour and took themselves off to communes where they often indulged in drug-taking to defy society (while resolutely accepting society's welfare benefits).

Many of these causeless rebels were ex-students who could not come to terms with the world and the task of making a living after the heady days of university. For in the sixties and early seventies, universities were very heady places indeed. Between 1961 and 1969 the number of students in full-time higher education in the UK almost doubled, from 200,000 to 390,000. The increase in the decade was greater than in the previous 30 years. 'Apart from electronics and natural gas', observed two educationalists, Richard Lager and John King, 'higher education probably grew faster than any other major industry in the sixties.'

Jobs were there in abundance for the newly graduated so the students had no need to fear unemployment. They were assured of work and were doubly assured of society's esteem because they were constantly told so. Their near-contemporaries were already in command of leading posts in the communications business, notably television, where their remarkable satire programmes were rousing tremendous controversy. The students had no need to kow-tow to parents either. Their fees were paid by the State and generous grants for general living costs were provided. Dependence on or implied obligation to their elders did not exist.

In these circumstances of subsidised irresponsibility it was not surprising that a number of students bit the hand that fed them. They launched sit-ins to protest against rulings or personnel they disliked. They were frequently aided and abetted by young members of the university staff. Disrespect of authority was elevated to an academic principle. Dr Roger Freedman, sociologist and graduate of Berkeley, California, was entranced at the manner in which Sussex University embraced the new non-discipline. 'I'm amazed', he said 'at the way the university staff join in militant protests and urge students to do the same.' He thought this revolutionary attitude compared very favourably with the stuffier attitude adopted by lecturers back home in the USA.

Perhaps Mr Freedman found it hard to imagine how American staff could match the ferocity of student protest in America, exemplified by this message from 20-year-old student of Columbia University, Mark Rudd, to the University's President, Grayson Kirk. 'We will take control of your world, your university and attempt to mould a world in which we and other people can live as human beings. Your power is directly threatened since we will have to destroy that power before we can take over.' Mr Rudd didn't take over. But Mr Kirk quit the University.

Such was student power, US style, in the sixties. In the UK it was not so well organised, but made up for administrative shortcomings with an excess of vituperation, as with a young man still, at 27, a philosophy student, who urged his fellow undergraduates 'to go out and start insulting people. Spit up your disgust.' Colin Rogers, son of a banker and student at Essex, put the case more politely: 'Our aim is one man, one vote. That means each student will carry as much weight as each member of the staff. Since we outnumber them, we'll be running things.' As succinct a definition of democracy as one could wish.

At bottom, the students in Britain and America (and in France too where student riots almost brought down President de Gaulle's government in 1968) were reacting against the fact that they had no cause bigger than themselves. They had no cause *other than themselves* – however much they might manufacture one to justify their protests. The self-indulgence of the young élite was a symptom of the West's retreat from responsibility for vast tracts of the world. Affluence and job security merely made the malady worse.

Of course it was not that the students regretted the disappearance of Empire. They rejoiced at that. But they had lost the opportunity to *serve*. They too, had they but known it, were casualties of the retreat of the West.

CHAPTER SIX

Goodbye to Empire

The British Empire was the largest in the history of the world. In 1945 it stretched over one-third of the surface of the globe, including as it did conquered Italian, French and Japanese colonies. Within twenty years it had ceased to exist and been replaced by some 40, later 49, independent states.

Part of this process of de-colonisation was deliberate. From the end of World War I India moved towards self-government, and by 1937 eleven provinces of British India were self-governing. The white dominions – Canada, Australia, New Zealand, South Africa – received total independence with the Statute of Westminster in 1931. In June 1948 a British White Paper decreed: 'The central purpose of British Colonial policy is to guide the colonial territories to responsible self-government within the Commonwealth in conditions that ensure to the people concerned both a fair standard of living and freedom from oppression in any form.'

In that last phrase 'freedom from oppression in any form' lay the rub. There was no way in which the paramount power could sustain that safeguard once it had ceased to be paramount. A very long period of apprenticeship *might* implant Westminster ideas of democracy but such time was not granted to the rulers or the ruled.

A number of factors contributed to this unhappy outcome. First and most important were the consequences of two world wars. These had fatally eroded Britain's economic primacy and her will to govern. They had also fed nationalism in the Empire, notably in India. The politicians of the Congress movement (originally the Anglo-Indian Congress) latched on to the 'fight for democracy' slogans of the Allies to demand democracy for India in the form of self-determination.

Once the Indian sub-continent had gained independence in 1947 – and promptly split into five mutually antagonistic sovereign states – there was no stopping de-colonisation. Indeed once the Jewel in the

Crown had gone, the justification for an east of Suez imperial policy (and for the unhappy Suez campaign of 1956) vanished.

There arose, in the middle fifties, a group of ex-colonial leaders who preached immediate independence for all peoples. They were the members of the Bandung conference, called by Indonesia's President Sukarno, himself a former subject of the Dutch East Indies, Indonesia's previous status. These leaders, they included Nehru of India, U Nu of Burma, Mohammed Ali of Pakistan, Chou en Lai of China, proclaimed it as their mission to 'free' the world from the chains of colonialism.

The Times quoted Sukarno's speech of welcome to the delegates from 27 Afro-Asian states (plus 1700 security guards):

> This is the first inter-continental conference of coloured peoples in the history of mankind. Sisters and brothers. How terrifically dynamic is our time. Nations and states have woken from the sleep of centuries . . . The old age is dying, a better one is dawning . . . We, the people of Asia and Africa, far more than half the population of the world, can mobilise what I have called 'the moral violence of nations' in favour of peace.

Sukarno was overthrown following the defeat – by British and Gurkha troops – of his attempt to colonise Malaya. U Nu of Burma was overthrown by a military coup. So was Mohammed Ali of Pakistan. So too were these prospective candidates for independence who attended Bandung: Archbishop Makarios of Cyprus and Kwame Nkrumah of Ghana. An *Express* editorial was later to comment cynically on 'the emerging Third World of Afro-Asia' that the only question was who was going to emerge next.

The term 'Third World', by the by, appears to have been coined by a Frenchman to distinguish the ex-colonies from the first, industrialised, world and the second, partly industrialised, as represented by states such as Argentina and Brazil.

The Bandung Conference brought tremendous pressure to bear on the remaining colonial powers. If independence was to be given to Ghana, why not to Nigeria, if to Malaya, why not to Kenya? So went the refrain. It was backed by public opinion. The USA with its long tradition of anti-colonialism (though not always by the American administration which feared the advance of communism in the newly-liberated territories) and by Soviet Russia which welcomed the very prospect feared by Washington.

Voices urging caution and reminding the impatient that democracy would not spring fully matured from the womb of Africa were ignored. The momentum for 'freedom now' simply could not be halted. Between 1957 and 1965 the entire colonial structure in Africa, which accounted for all but a handful of territories, was completely dismantled.

At a stroke, the most specific pledges ('Cyprus will *never* be independent' – Mr Hopkins, for the Foreign Office) and elaborate plans were abandoned.

From 1952 to 1955 British troops and white settlers in Kenya fought to keep Kenya free of the Mau-Mau terrorists, a Kikuyu secret society intent on taking over the territory. Mau-Mau, it was alleged, was inspired and directed by Jomo Kenyatta. In the early sixties Kenya was handed over to an African government – headed by Jomo Kenyatta. Within a year of independence British troops were defending him against mutineers and Kenya became the most pro-Western of East African states as well as the only reasonably prosperous one thanks, in large measure, to the European farmers who remained.

From 1955 to 1959 Britain fiercely resisted the demands of Greek terrorists in Cyprus that the island – 78 per cent Greek, 22 per cent Turk, but only 40 miles from Turkey – be handed over to Greece. In the upshot, Cyprus became independent. Within fifteen years, in 1974, the Greeks launched a coup d'état against the Cypriot government of Archbishop Makarios, thereby provoking a Turkish invasion of the island, so that by 1975 Cyprus was partitioned, more than one third of the island being occupied by Turkey and the island *still* not linked, in any way, with Greece.

In 1953 Britain launched the Central African Federation combining white-ruled Southern Rhodesia with Northern Rhodesia and Nyasaland. Ten years later the Federation splintered into independent, black-ruled Zambia, black-ruled Malawi and unilaterally white minority-ruled Rhodesia, which promptly declared independence.

In 1960 Britain established a West Indian Federation. It dissolved itself within five years, when the territories received independence.

Thus without any discernible pattern, without any strategic plan and conforming to no particular moral code, Britain dispensed with her Empire. Certain rearguard actions were fought with exemplary courage and efficiency. The Communists were defeated in a

campaign lasting nine years so that a free Malaya was granted
independence in 1959. Even so, the federation with Singapore
(federations being a favourite method of the soon-to-be-abolished
Colonial Office) swiftly broke up. The Indonesian attempt to
subjugate Sarawak and Borneo – which had become linked to
Malaya – was frustrated leading, as has been mentioned, to the
downfall of the Indonesian dictator, Sukarno.

The British were spared the terrible wars of colonial independence
which the French fought in Indo-China and Algeria. Possibly that
was because the British, having been victorious in World War II,
had no need to prove themselves, while the French, who had lost,
were resolved to show their heroic resolve. But whether by design, by
force, by mischance or pure chance, the European Empires were
wound up in short order.

In their place arose a vast number of small states, some of whom
changed their names two or three times and most of whom changed
their regimes still more frequently. These countries did not welcome
patronising Westerners but they badly needed Western finance. So
money continued to flow to the ex-colonial territories, usually on a
government-to-government basis, while the former employees of the
Colonial Office, district officers and district commissioners, sought
alternative employment.

Idealistic young people enrolled in Voluntary Service overseas,
but as their expertise was often limited and their authority, as guests,
negligible in the developing lands, they gained small satisfaction
from the experience. Opportunity for service-beyond-self in pursuit
of a glorious faith (which, for millions, the British Empire in its
heyday had been) was denied the generation growing up in the
fifties. Not surprisingly they rebelled and sought other ideals.

CHAPTER SEVEN

Into Europe

This search coincided with a relaxation of traditional discipline in the home, school and college, the abolition of national military service and a dramatic decline in established religion.

Before the First World War more than half of the population of England and Wales regularly attended church on Sunday (two-thirds in Scotland, virtually 100 per cent in Ireland). By the middle of the century the figure had declined substantially and it fell precipitately from then on to reach a mere 2 million for Sunday worshippers in the Anglican faith by 1975.

Whereas belief was probably not nearly as strong as the early century figures would imply (children were simply told to 'come along' to church and there was an end of it), the moral precepts taught at church must have had a considerable effect on a young population that was still basically deferential to authority. By the sixties moral precepts were a subject for titters, if anyone even bothered to mention them. Peter Evans, writing in the *Daily Express*, remarked that most people thought 'ethics' was the mispronunciation of a county in south-east England.

Given the encouragement to indulgence, security of employment, the pressures of advertising to 'buy, buy, buy' what was 'new, new, new' it is understandable that the younger generation indulged itself. And then found it wasn't truly satisfied and searched for fresh experiences which in some cases (fortunately relatively few) took the form of drugs or open, usually rather pointless, defiance of authority. Rebels without a Cause defined, pretty accurately, those energetic, altruistic and articulate young men and women who in earlier times would have found an outlet for their enthusiasm and sense of service in the outlying parts of the Empire.

When Harold Macmillan, the Conservative Prime Minister, flippantly told the electors in 1959 that they 'had never had it so good' he was saying no more than the truth. But he was later to be excoriated for it as betraying a gross materialism which sat ill with youthful idealism.

Politicians agreed that Britain needed a new focus. The Commonwealth, the loose connection of all the former colonies plus the white dominions and the nations of the former Indian Empire, had not enough identity to satisfy such aspirations. It gave some international lustre to the Crown and some opportunities for voluntary services but it was a diminishing economic asset to Britain as Imperial Preference and the Sterling Area (the system of tariff arrangments which gave UK manufacturers a preferential place in Commonwealth markets and Commonwealth foods and raw materials a similarly favoured place in British markets) gave way to homogenised global trade.

So, principally for economic purposes but also to provide a new fulcrum for the expression of British influence and a new arena for idealism, the British Government of the day turned towards the European Economic Community, or Common Market.

Its founders and main champions – the Frenchmen Monnet and Schumann, the German Adenauer and the Italian Gasperi – were motivated by the common resolve to resuscitate a prostrate Europe and bound together by a common Catholic conservatism. They succeeded in bringing a degree of political unity to Western Europe that it had not enjoyed for many centuries. In this they were decisively assisted by the threat from the Soviet Union and the nuclear balance of terror between the West and the USSR.

You hang together if the alternative is to hang separately. That is exactly what Western Europe did, starting with NATO in 1949 and developing into the EEC in 1957. The purpose of creating a Common Market was to provide the economic foundation for a political union. This was how the German states had first come together in the Zollverein, or customs union in the nineteenth century. The same pattern was to be applied to the original six of the EEC: France, Germany, Italy, Holland, Belgium and Luxembourg. Britain did not partake of the Messina negotiations which resulted in the Treaty of Rome, establishing the European Economic Community.

For one thing, the UK's trade was global – in the late fifties only 14 per cent of British exports went to the Six. Secondly, the agricultural policy of the Six ran directly counter to the British cheap food policy which combined low-cost imports from the Commonwealth with subsidies for domestic production. Finally, the Labour Opposition disliked the Common Market which it regarded as a rich man's club founded by reactionary Catholics (the Treaty of Rome!) and governed by rules of competition expressly designed to frustrate socialism. So, initially, the British official view of the EEC was distant and frigid.

However, the explosive growth of the European economies, multiplying exports five-fold in as many years (which actually was due to industrial reorganisation and re-equipment) gave the Common Market a whole new dimension in British eyes. The UK was lagging behind badly. The Commonwealth was not advanced enough – not unified enough – to stimulate trade in the rising technical manufacturers and sophisticated consumer products. So, swallowing prejudices about Continental Catholics and cheap food, the British Government in 1961 applied to join the European Economic Community.

This pragmatic decision, redolent of Harold Macmillan's off-the-cuff style of government, prompted furious political debate. Hugh Gaitskell, the Labour Leader, talked of 'reversing 1000 years of British history'. Lord Beaverbrook, the Empire trade crusader, launched all-out war against the policy (though not against Harold Macmillan who remained high in Beaverbrook's affections).

What Macmillan and his chosen representative for the negotiations, Edward Heath, were proposing was to change Britain from an island power with global responsibility to be a part of Europe. In terms of trade this was swiftly accomplished. Even before membership of the Market was consummated in 1973, British trade was undergoing a transformation with the share going to the Commonwealth and USA diminishing while that with Western Europe rose to half of all British exports. Membership of the Market merely confirmed a trend.

Unforeseen by the politicians were some of the internal consequences. Glasgow and Liverpool, which had enjoyed boom times as the principal ports for trade with North America, suffered from the switch to the east and trade with Europe. This aggravated the decline of Clydeside and Merseyside and produced political and union militancy – which gave another twist to their downward spiral.

Unforeseen too was the fading of the vision of United Europe. This Grand Design, it was believed, could provide a fresh impulse for the British people, most especially British youth.

Harold Macmillan cleverly placed it in historical perspective. 'The British', he told the *Express*, 'are coming Home. After 400 years of venturing across the oceans they are returning to base and the young people here on this island and on the Continent, so often enemies in the past, can together build a better tomorrow.'

But 'building Europe', a favourite phrase of the administrators in Brussels, proved a frustrating task, more often flawed by farce (such as stopping the clock in the Council chamber so that deadlines could be met) than marked with nobility.

First of all the British application, which demanded special terms for the Commonwealth – particularly the right of access for New Zealand lamb – was turned down. General de Gaulle suspected, with good reason, that the British were as intent on preventing a Franco-German axis from dominating the Community as on helping to 'build Europe'. He could not veto British entry on a straight, unconditional application, for the Rome Treaty specifically opened entry to any European nation which accepted the rules. But de Gaulle could, and did, block a British application which required that the rules be bent in her favour.

The huge towering Frenchman with the giraffe-like neck and a voice made for enunciating history, declared that Britain was essentially an Atlantic nation and her entry 'would create a colossal Atlantic community under American dependence and leadership which would soon completely swallow up the EEC'. This last reflected de Gaulle's visceral anti-Americanism. He judged them a vulgar, shallow people, lacking true nationhood, a nation of borrowed cultures, borrowed law, borrowed language: a place to live, not truly a lived-in place. American nationalism was crass commercialism writ large. In that, along with language, law and custom, America was also England writ large. The Anglo-Saxons were de Gaulle's *bête noire*. He had tolerated Churchill during the war – as his host he could do little else – but he had gagged at Franklin D. Roosevelt, the US President, who wanted to run Europe and France (without de Gaulle) after the war.

Now, on 14 January 1963, Charles de Gaulle firmly established as French President and presiding over his country's renaissance was, at last, able to take revenge for the humiliations, real or imagined, that he had suffered at the hands of the Anglo-Saxons. *'Non.'* There would be no diluted European Community, accommodating the interests of a huge amorphous Commonwealth and opening the way for American domination. There would remain the Europe of the Nations, reflecting the values of Catholicism, the heritage of

Charlemagne, the traditions of a Latin inheritance.

The British were stunned – or, more accurately, Mr Harold Macmillan was stunned. The public had shown downright opposition to the European experiment by defeating a pro-Market candidate in a Dorset by-election at the end of 1962. Among the British anti-Marketeers de Gaulle was a hero.

The Americans were nonplussed. They had not realised they were so unpopular with the French President. Later they would be still more upset when de Gaulle removed France from the NATO infrastructure and ordered American army, navy and air force units to leave France. For France, reconciliation with West Germany (the absorption of East Germany in Russia's Communist empire meant that France and West Germany were roughly comparable in population and could more easily be partners) and naturally good relations with other Latin states such as Italy and Spain was at all times to be preferred to alliance with the Anglo-Saxons. Nationalism with a European flavour found favour with the French. It even gave them a sense of pride and vigour while their economy took off in a manner almost as striking as the German Wirtschaftswunder, the economic miracle which turned the shambles of Germany 1945 into the country with the highest gold reserve per head in 1965.

De Gaulle was fine for France – for a while. But neither his historic vision of the Europe of tomorrow nor the remarkable resurgence of the French economy (industrial output trebled between 1957 and 1972) could prevent the extraordinary student revolt in 1968 which almost brought down the Fifth Republic. France too had her rebels without a cause. De Gaulle dismissed them as 'a dog's mess'. Yet the fact that they almost toppled him (he had to get the reassurance of the French Army) demonstrated the still-fragile state of the Gaullist framework.

It survived. De Gaulle didn't. In 1973 the British got into the European Community, three years after de Gaulle's death. But the idealism which might have fired the English ten years earlier had gone, the vision had perished. The bureaucrats had taken over. The one real achievement of the European Community was the Common Agricultural Policy which protected Europe's farmers against outside competition by a complex and ultimately ludicrous system of State intervention to sustain food prices at a much higher level than they would otherwise have been. Another effect of the CAP was to deny underdeveloped countries access to European markets for temperate-type foodstuffs. This, in turn, angered idealistic young people so that the Common Market which had been intended to fire youthful imagination had by 1975, when it was grudgingly endorsed by the British electorate, produced the opposite effect.

More hopeful appeared something which had, on the surface, nothing to do with politics and little to do with Europe, but which was calculated to lift spirits, open dazzling new horizons and unite the peoples of the world in a crusade for knowledge. The exploration of space.

CHAPTER EIGHT

To the Stars – and Beyond

The third quarter of the twentieth century saw intense interest in space travel. To millions the space race seemed to be the answer to the arms race. Uniting mankind instead of dividing it, providing a common objective – the conquest of space – in a competitive environment.

The reality was very different from this altruistic dream. Having captured German rocket scientists at the end of World War II, both Russia and America set about giving further thought to the application of missile technology, the process having been set in motion by the Nazis with their V2 rocket attacks on England.

Russia was the first in the field, launching an artificial satellite into outer space, just before the fortieth anniversary of the Bolshevik revolution. Nikita Khrushchev crowed about the triumph of Communist technology. Bob Hope quipped that 'their Germans are better than our Germans'. An American general sourly observed that he didn't see any point in hurling a bit of metal into the wide blue yonder.

The reaction of most of the world was of thrilled wonderment: Jules Verne, H.G.Wells, Arthur C. Clarke come to life. In Washington the reaction was somewhat different. The US had been beaten in the very sphere, technical competence, in which she believed herself supreme. President Eisenhower's White House was besieged by patriotic demonstrators demanding that he should 'shoot the moon'.

Eisenhower was unimpressed. He saw rocketry as just one more military option. He did not want to involve America in a space version of the Olympic Games. When the US did launch a satellite it weighed a mere 30 lbs against the Russian Sputnik's 184. The miniaturisation was part of a military programme.

A sea change in US attitudes occurred, however, when the USSR launched the first man in space – Yuri Gagarin – in April 1961. John F. Kennedy had just become US President pledged to 'meet every challenge'. He is reported to have stormed at his aides: 'What can we do? Can we put a man on the moon before them? If somebody can just tell me how to catch up!'

Eight days later a memorandum arrived on the desk of Vice-President Lyndon B. Johnson from the President. It read:

> In accordance with our conversation [of the previous day] I would like for you as Chairman of The Space Council to be in charge of making an overall survey of where we stand in space.
>
> Do we have a chance of beating the Soviets by putting a laboratory in space, or by a trip around the moon, or by a rocket to land on the moon, or by a rocket to go to the moon and back with a man? Is there any other space program which *promises dramatic results in which we could win?* [Author's italics.]
>
> How much additional would it cost?
>
> Are we working 24 hours a day on existing programs? If not, why not? If not, will you make recommendations to me as to how work can be speeded up?
>
> In building large boosters should we put emphasis on nuclear, chemical or liquid fuel, or a combination of these three?
>
> Are we making maximum effort? Are we achieving necessary results?

This was the charter of the moon mission. Right from the start, Kennedy latched on to public relations as part of the space race. So, to a still greater extent, did his VP, Lyndon Johnson.

Johnson did not like the Kennedys, most specially he disliked Jack's brother Robert, the Attorney General, who treated Johnson as a hick Texas politician (which he was) who was ignorant and naive (which he wasn't). In the space programme Johnson saw a wonderful chance to carve out a niche for himself and to strengthen his political base in Texas.

His home state got the bulk of the orders and Houston, the oil capital of Texas, became its space capital as well. He appointed a publicity-conscious buddy of his, Jim Webb, to pull the whole project together under the auspices of the National Aviation and Space Agency with the overriding objective of putting a man on the moon. For this target had been publicly proclaimed by Kennedy in a speech to college graduates on 16 May 1961. What is more, the President had pledged that this would be done 'before the end of the decade'.

Nothing could have been better calculated to fuse America's business interests, technical expertise and patriotic fervour into an unbeatable combination than this clarion call which combined a headline and a deadline.

Public relations on a national-political scale was invented by President Franklin D. Roosevelt. He gathered round him men well-versed in selling ideas to the public and inspired them to write and talk glowingly of his huge schemes for re-employment and regeneration in the era of the Depression. Since then it has been difficult to separate US policy imperatives from PR objectives. Thus, during World War II, American troops were as liable to be launched on public relations ventures as on purely military ones. General Mark Clark won the glory of capturing Rome – but the German Army it was his business to trap escaped. US forces stormed the beaches of southern France in August 1944 providing excellent footage for the cameramen, but to no discernible military purpose, as the enemy had long since withdrawn. General George S. Patton raced Bernard Montgomery to enter more towns in Sicily than the British and corner the hallelujah market.

Dwight Eisenhower, with his infectious grin, lent himself as a natural to public relations during the war but, as President, he kept himself more and more aloof from the PR men, earning himself and the White House the dismissive epithet of the 'Tomb of the Well-Known Warrior'.

Kennedy had no such inhibitions. He had been elected to 'get America moving'. Moving upwards and outwards and on to the moon was the perfect answer to the increasing complexity of problems on earth.

In the spring of 1961 – four days before Kennedy's frantic memorandum to Johnson – the US had suffered a humiliating rebuff at the hands of Fidel Castro, the Communist ruler of Cuba. Cuban exiles armed and backed by the CIA, stormed ashore at the Bay of Pigs to settle accounts with Castro. They were routed and the US, having encouraged them to invade, did nothing to help them. Castro consolidated his position, killing or imprisoning the dissenters who had been misled by American promises. For Kennedy, the embodiment of virile, tough-minded young America, it was a bitter blow. It was failure in the very honeymoon of his administration. He had inherited the plan and allowed it to go ahead. And at the first test of nerve he had fumbled and lost. In the long run, the consequences were to be fatal for Kennedy himself. The burden of evidence suggests that his murderer, the ex-Marine Lee Harvey Oswald, was acting as Castro's agent when he gunned down the President in November 1963.

In the short run, the disaster at the Bay of Pigs had to be answered. As had the Soviet challenge of putting Yuri Gagarin into orbit and making a propaganda spectacular of the affair. The Moon mission was America's public relations response to two severe setbacks. And there was a third reason: the need to impress the developing world with America's matchless technology. Talk of mankind's 'urge to explore' came afterwards, to justify the expenditure of 24 billion dollars and to persuade critics that it was better to spend the money this way than any other.

In space, politics were in charge of the space programme from the start. There were no distractions. 'Get there fastest with the mostest' was the simple command in the true American tradition.

There were setbacks. Yet even the rocket that crumpled on the launching pad – prompting the jeer, 'Four . . . Three . . . Two . . . One . . . Hell!' – served a purpose. For it emphasised the scale of the challenge and drew forth the necessary response. The tragic death of the astronauts on the grounded Apollo spacecraft in 1967 did not halt the majestic Moon Mission. This was gloriously accomplished on 20 July 1969 when Neil Armstrong and Edwin Aldrin landed on the moon. With five months to spare the Kennedy promise was redeemed. In public relations terms it was triumph, triumph all the way.

Drama was sustained throughout the entire programme of manned flights from John Glenn's orbit, through the first walk in space to the landing itself.

Treatment of the space race provided a fascinating contrast between the USA and the USSR. The Russians shrouded their space experiments in complete secrecy, only acclaiming success after it was accomplished; they could not bear to have their image tarnished with failure. But once success was achieved, how the Soviets gloated! Veljko Micunovic, the Yugoslav ambassador in Moscow from 1956–58 has recounted (in *Moscow Diary*, Chatto and Windus) the Soviet glee at the successful launching of the world's first Sputnik in October 1957.

It will soon be a month [he recorded] during which this epoch-making achievement has not left the front pages of the

Soviet Press. Films have been made about it and popular scientific meetings are being held throughout the country to glorify the Soviet state and society. They reveal a tendency to suggest that the Sputnik itself is sufficient to make up for all the weaknesses of the Soviet Union, as though it could provide the answer to everybody who has criticised the Soviet Union ... Leading articles describe what the Russians have invented in modern times: the Cherepanovs invented the steam engine; Mozhaisky invented the airplane; Sopov invented radio. Khrushchev says the development of the Sputnik means that bombers could be put on the scrap heap ... The Russians have demonstrated that they possess powerful rockets with which tomorrow they may launch an atomic bomb to any place on the world's surface.*

Propaganda euphoria only ceased when it appeared that the continual drum-beating was provoking the Americans into expanding *their* space/military efforts. 'We hear', Micunovic observed to his diary, 'that the Presidium (the Soviet "Cabinet" of the Party) has decided that nothing further is to be published about Soviet superiority in the field of rockets and that the propaganda machine is to revert to the question of peaceful co-existence.'

When the Americans launched their satellite, Micunovic

found Khrushchev in a bad mood. . . . The Russians had boasted too much – but Khrushchev spoke scornfully of the size of the American satellite ... 'about as big as an orange', he said. 'Tomorrow we will show them,' clenching his fist, 'we'll launch a sputnik weighing over 1,000 kilograms'.

So much for the unifying implications of space.

The *diplomatic* implications were of more substance. The uniqueness of the Soviet-American space race led directly to the conception of the Super Powers, and to the view, in Moscow, that it was only relations between the Super Powers that really mattered. This was made clear to Micunovic by Soviet deputy foreign minister Nikolai Patolichev.

So: the Russians made a meal of initial space landings *after the event* (and this applied, in double measure, to Yuri Gagarin's flight in 1961) but gave no details before the event and merely propagandistic

* Reproduced by permission of Chatto & Windus.

ones after. They retreated whenever they thought that their propaganda was being counter-productive and would provoke the US or damage their relations with the world's other Super Power. In short, the space race was, for them, diplomatic war by another name.

In contrast, the Americans gloried in the great game for the game's sake. Their triumphs and disasters were televised for all to see; as they happened. Not that they neglected propaganda. It was said that no rocket left Cape Canaveral until the weight of published material equalled the weight of the launcher. From details of the grapefruit segments which the astronauts had for breakfast to descriptions of every single piece of equipment on the capsules, the Americans told everything, several times over.

Peak viewing times were carefully synchronised, whenever possible, with major manoeuvres of the spacecraft. It was surely no mere chance that Apollo VIII went round the moon at Christmas 1968. This allowed astronaut Frank Borman to read out a Christmas message to an awed world. The Book of Genesis from outer space, courtesy of US technology. It was the perfect ideological riposte to God-less Communism.

Moreover the astronauts were men of genuine Christian belief and uncomplicated patriotism. Their whole attitude bespoke the best of America. They were crew-cut, clean-climbed cheerful challengers of the unknown who chatted to earth control about familiar, happy things: Snoopy, golf, baseball.

Whether by chance or design, the world was given an insight into the American way of life which was pure gold. It did for America's image what Hollywood musically had done twenty years previously. The whole space programme was used to buttress patriotism. It was something in which every red-blooded American could rejoice. Each launcher and capsule bore the national emblem and each major launching was attended by major American figures. The astronauts wore the Stars and Stripes on their shoulders. The command ship for the moon landing was named Columbia, symbol of America. The module which put Armstrong and Aldrin on the moon was called Eagle, another American symbol. Almost the first thing the astronauts did on landing was to hoist the US flag, salute it and exchange telephone salutations with 'the Chief' – President Richard Nixon.

Whether the moon will prove any more use to the earth than

Mount Everest or Antarctica is for the future to decide. It was the breathtaking technical achievement which took the world by storm. The London *Evening News* wanted Monday re-named Moon-day in awed recognition of the American triumph. At a moment when the US was assailed by troubles at home and abroad, the victory in space was balm to the soul. The moon landing of 20 July 1969 was the most truly emotional moment of the whole 25-year span covered by this book. The astronauts were likened to the heroes of Greek mythology, to whom the elements bowed. 'Man has broken his earthly shackles,' trumpeted the *Express*. On a slightly more mundane note, Dr Thomas Paine, acting director of NASA, remarked: 'I call this [he was referring to the circumnavigation of the moon accomplished by Apollo VIII] a triumph for the "squares" of this world; the men who are not hippies, who work with slide rules and are not ashamed to say a prayer.'

No doubt true, but the deepest meaning of the space race was not the enhancing of the individual but his diminishing importance under the lengthening shadow of the machine. The astronauts were mature men who had undergone long periods of training, lasting several years. It was almost as if they had been programmed along with the computers. They had, after all, to respond to ground control instructions accurately and phlegmatically. There was no call for individual flair and individual initiative might have invited disaster.

How little impact the astronauts/cosmonauts (the latter being the Soviet title) actually had on the public, despite huge publicity campaigns, was revealed in a poll taken in 1965 which showed that only 3 in 100 could name the first man in space. Ten times as many could name the first man to fly the Atlantic solo (Lindbergh). Lindbergh was one man pitting himself against the elements, in total control of his frail craft and out of contact with anyone else. Yuri Gagarin, the first man in space, was a human mechanism who might have been just as effectively replaced by an inanimate one.

Man was diminished not by the immensity of space, but by the very machines he had created. Television again and again recorded the reaction of men returning from hazardous space missions saying, in effect: 'We are just the tip of the pyramid.' A pyramid of mathematical calculation, computer readings and robot-like responses.

A correspondent wrote to the *Evening News* that the space race had more in common with the pyramids than its supporters would care to admit. It had much to do with self-glorification and nothing whatsoever to do with value for money. He added that it was not surprising that the Soviets had been the first to launch space-craft. That was traditional for dictatorships. Witness the Pharaohs.

For a brief, a very brief, moment America, Russia and the rest of the world were united in watching man in space on TV. But when the spectacular was ended the real, harsh world closed in again. By 1975 space shots were relegated to the end of the news bulletins, if they were mentioned at all.

By a sad irony the US performed its greatest feat of space exploration, in the late sixties, when on earth it was suffering its greatest humiliation – in the swamps and jungles of Vietnam.

CHAPTER NINE

The War America Lost

The British 'won' the first Vietnam War in 1945-46. In that year General Gracey's British-Indian troops, fresh from triumph over the Japanese, fought and defeated the Vietminh rebels in what was then known as French Indo-China. The role of captured Japanese troops in containing the rebels was decisive. The readiness of Japanese soldiers to obey whoever was their temporary commander – Japan having just surrendered unconditionally to the Allies – was remarked upon and indeed it is possible that if Japan had been left in uncontested control of Indo-China that country would never have occupied centre stage for almost the whole of the period 1950-1975.

In its world-wide ripple effect, the Vietnam wars had a more profound influence than any other event. They helped to bring down the fourth French Republic, to spread anti-Americanism throughout the West and to unleash a bloody terror (in Cambodia) the like of which the world had not seen since Hitler's massacre of the Jews.

France had become the paramount power in the three principal areas of Vietnam – Tonkin, Annam and Cochin – in the late nineteenth century with the collapse of the old Vietnam Empire. To these territories the French added Cambodia and Laos to make Indo-China. It was a classical European take-over of an area that lacked political cohesion and was ripe for colonisation. There were occasional spasms of protest against French rule, the most notable in 1930, but generally the natives accepted the dominance of outsiders and French language, manners and culture permeated the upper levels of Vietnamese society and its intellectuals.

All this changed in 1941 when the Japanese entered the territory in agreement with Vichy France. The Japanese used it as a base from which to advance against the British colonies of Malaya and Burma. The peoples of Indo-China were now involved in a global struggle and the revolutionary elements in the State were armed and urged to fight the Japanese. The most revolutionary were the Vietminh, a combination of Nationalists and Communists led by Ho Chi Minh, a

French-educated Communist operating mainly among the Ton-kinese. Ho accepted arms from the Americans and greatly impressed those US agents sent to liaise with the guerrillas.

When, on the defeat of Japan, the French tried to re-assert their authority, the Americans on the ground appear to have sided with the Vietminh. On one occasion at least an American agent stood aside when the guerrillas killed a French official.* It was at this point that General Douglas Gracey's forces entered and put down a Vietminh rising, restoring Hanoi, in the north, and Saigon, in the south, to the French.

The British, being then the major colonial power in the Far East, were naturally anxious to restore all the European properties to their former owners – they applied the same system in the Dutch East Indies (later, Indonesia). What the British, French and Dutch colonists did not realise was that that era of *European* colonialism was dead. It had been killed by Europe's two 'civil wars' of 1914 and 1939 and by the Japanese conquest of South-East Asia which had destroyed the mystique of the white man's supremacy. If the Japanese had been left in possession they would have succeeded to the Europeans' patrimony. However, they were defeated and the nation principally responsible for their defeat and now Super Power No 1, the USA, was steeped in anti-colonialism. There was therefore no successor colonialist to the exhausted and discredited Europeans.

The retreating British moved skilfully to frustrate the Communists in Malaya between 1948 and 1957 and so hand over a territory to independence that could genuinely reflect the wishes of the inhabitants. But the French, smarting from their defeat by Germany in 1940 and their passive submission to the Japanese in the East, were resolved to impose their will on a once-prosperous, still Frenchified territory. So the second Vietnam war began.

Initially the Americans were cool towards the French whom they regarded as played-out colonialists. But when it became obvious that the Vietminh were Communist-controlled, US views hardened. When the French accorded Vietnam, Cambodia and Laos nominal independence within the French Union, Washington became yet more friendly towards Paris. In addition, it was felt essential to the security of Western Europe that France regain her confidence by

See Peter M. Dunn's *The First Vietnam War* (Hurst).

successfully re-establishing her military prestige in the East. She might even have done that had her brilliant commander in Indo-China, General de Lattre de Tassigny not died in 1951. From then on the French position deteriorated rapidly.

The crisis was reached at the battle of Dien Bien Phu in April 1954. The French command envisaged it as a Verdun-in-reverse. In 1916 the Germans had enticed the French to fling themselves into the defence of the fortress of Verdun. 'That will be the anvil,' declared the German commander, von Falkenhayn, 'on which the life of France will be hammered out.' The French reckoned that Dien Bien Phu, strategically placed in a valley astride communications, would be the anvil on which General Giap's Vietminh jungle fighters would meet their match in a conventional battle.

Unfortunately for the French, Giap's men were superbly equipped. Russia and China (still Red allies) had so comprehensively and fulsomely supplied Giap's men with powerful weapons that the French found themselves hopelessly out-gunned. The fortress fell. And with it fell the determination of France to continue the struggle. In July of the same year a new French government, under the premiership of Pierre Mendès-France, agreed to a cease-fire. France quit Indo-China. The north, the area of the Tonkinese with its capital at Hanoi, was handed over to Ho: the southern section of Vietnam below the 17th Parallel and the two states of Cambodia and Laos remained within the Western orbit. Elections were due to take place within two years concerning the re-unification of the country.

But by this time a fresh complication had arisen. The US had been financing France's military effort to the extent of 80 per cent. John Foster Dulles, the American Secretary of State, was implacably opposed to Communism. His country had just fought Communism in Korea where the Reds had breached the agreed frontier on the 38th Parallel. The North Korean Communists had been forced back. Dulles was in no mood to concede to North Vietnamese Communists what, at the cost of so much blood, had been denied the North Koreans. He was contemptuous of the Europeans and particularly dismissive of the efforts of Britain's Foreign Secretary, Anthony Eden, in negotiating the Indo-China settlement (this may well have prompted his anti-Eden stance at the Suez crisis two years later).

Dulles and his President, Dwight Eisenhower, refused to sign the accords. They simply transferred the military aid they had been giving the French to the new independent South Vietnamese government of Ngo Dinh Diem and they supported Diem in his refusal to submit to a referendum on the re-unification of North and South. Thus did America begin to get involved in South Vietnam. And so began the third Vietnam War.

Why did the Americans step in to South-East Asia when their European allies were moving out? Basically because they believed the time had come for the Pax Americana to replace the Pax Britannica and its junior French equivalent. It was a natural, logical, even inevitable progression. The British were exhausted and probably effete. Ditto the French. The Americans were virile, successful, brimful of energy and money and, quite obviously, the wave of the future.

Impeccably anti-colonialist, they were the big guys to forge a new partnership with the little guys striving to build their own futures under the shadow of the Communist Russian Bear and the Communist Chinese Dragon (still, in these days, closely united).

Of course it wasn't expressed in these terms in State Department missives. George Kennan in his memoirs records a memo he submitted in 1950 arguing that it was preferable to allow 'the turbulent political currents of that country (Vietnam) to find their own level' – at the probable cost of a Communist take-over. But that view had become much less acceptable in Washington after Korea and Dien Bien Phu. As the Vietcong – the Communist underground army in the South – launched outright war on the Diem regime, President Eisenhower declared at a press conference: 'The loss of South Vietnam would set in motion a crumbling process that could, as it progressed, have grave consequences for us and for freedom.'

There was reason number two for US intervention. Ever since the Berlin airlift in 1949 the Americans had become convinced – with good cause – that the Communists had to be stopped by the threat, or the application, of force. The threat had been sufficient in Berlin; force had been required in Korea when the Communist North had crossed the 38th Parallel and invaded the non-Communist South.

This was regarded by Washington as part of the world-wide Communist conspiracy, a view reinforced when Communist China sent in troops to support the North Koreans. It was both logical and understandable that the US should consider a breach of the 17th Parallel separating non-Communist South Vietnam from Communist North Vietnam, as comparable in every respect to their experience in Korea when the Reds had breached the 38th Parallel.

If the North Vietnamese had been mere satraps of Moscow and Peking they might well have recoiled at the appearance, or even the threat, of US involvement. In truth, the Tonkinese of the North were ready to wage war for a century to bring the whole of Indo-China under their domain. Communism merely added a revolutionary ideology to fervent nationalism and unsparing sacrifice.

In his book *A History of the Modern World**Paul Johnson, a strong admirer of President Eisenhower, admitted 'it was Eisenhower who committed America's original sin in Vietnam'. The 'sin', if it was such, was putting the US in a position where it could be drawn in, step by step, to an Asian swamp.

With young Mr Kennedy the possibility of such a fate became reality. He had assured the world, in his inauguration address, that the US would 'pay any price, bear any burden, meet any hardship, support any friend, oppose any foe to ensure the survival and the success of liberty.' He was now expected to deliver. Like Eisenhower he had his doubts ('it is like taking to drink, you don't know when to stop', he confided to an aide) but he was convinced that the US must support its ally. So the first 7,000 'advisers' were sent to South Vietnam.

Thus was launched the first post-colonial war.

Unlike the British in Malaya the Americans did not control the country they were fighting to defend. They were dependent on the South Vietnamese government, which Kennedy soon decided was not pure or democratic enough to satisfy the criteria of a 'free world'.

Ngo Dien Diem, the South Vietnamese leader, his family and followers, were fervent Roman Catholics. They clashed with the pacifist-minded Buddhists. Diem practised nepotism on a considerable scale and he – or at least his relatives – appeared corrupt. So Kennedy condoned his 'liquidation'. From then on the Administration in Washington felt more and more committed to a country whose ruler they had removed.

Lyndon Johnson, the tough-talking Texan who succeeded the murdered Kennedy, saw himself as the symbol of American masculinity. Large, raw-boned, brash, vulgar (almost deliberately so) Johnson breathed the Alamo spirit: Texans didn't give up. The Americans would 'go it alone' to win decisive victory.

* Weidenfeld and Nicolson.

It had long been argued that allies had somehow held the US back from intervening decisively against the Communists in China and had cribbed, cabined and confined the US effort in Korea, robbing the GIs of victory. No-win wars had plagued other administrations; they were not to plague Johnson's.

Using an attack by North Vietnamese torpedo boats on a US warship in the Tonkin Gulf, Johnson persuaded Congress to grant him authority to wage all-out hostilities on the North, including air attacks. The number of troops on the ground rose from 70,000 in 1963 to 100,000 in 1965, to 560,000 in 1968, Johnson's last year of office. To no avail. The Americans may have been fighting in the wrong place; they were certainly fighting the wrong sort of war.

Their conscript troops were too frequently rotated, so that they never got to know the jungle, far less how to cope with the Vietcong guerrillas. The Americans were weighed down by the impedimenta of war: too many gadgets; too many weapons; too much Coca-Cola. And dominating everything, distorting everything, and finally paralysing everything: the television camera.

As always, American generals were intent on making favourable public relations their first objective. So when US marines landed in divisional force in March 1965 they were portrayed storming up the beach, as though flinging themselves at the enemy. In truth, there was no enemy for 100 miles or more. It was a television spectacular.

As it began, so it continued. With this exception: the television reporters turned sour as the war went badly. Boasting that it would cost them 'lighter fuel money' the American Defence Department entered the war believing that fire power alone could, and would, overwhelm the Vietcong and their North Vietnamese allies. The Americans disposed of more fire power than Allies and Axis powers together in World War II (and that *excluded* the American nuclear arsenal) so their expectations were understandable. They were not, however, realistic.

B52 bombers and off-shore battleships could not destroy the Vietcong underground lairs, nor the jungle trails, nor the camouflaged peasants. If the Americans had been prepared to fight total war, destroying the Northern capital of Hanoi and its port of Haiphong and thereby disrupting the Communists' supply lines to China and Russia, they might well have won the war. But they might also have found themselves in a nuclear exchange with the Communist super powers. And they were not prepared to risk that.

As the fireworks war manifestly failed to produce results so the US reporters, Press, radio and TV, concentrated on American search-and-destroy operations which, inevitably, showed the brutal aspects of soldiers searching villages for guerrillas. American boys were also shown crumpling to the ground, victims of enemy fire.

Night after night these scenes of slaughter were brought into American living rooms. The distorting lens of the camera gave the impression that the US was suffering terrifying losses. This was not true, at least in comparison with other forms of violent death to which Americans had become accustomed.

Thus, twice as many Americans died from gunshot wounds in the USA as died from gunshots in Vietnam. And *five times* as many Americans were killed on the roads of America as were killed in Vietnam.

If the Americans had been winning the war these casualties – tragic though they were – would have been borne. But America was patently not winning the war and someone had to be blamed. Occasionally it was an individual soldier as with Lieutenant Callan who was accused of massacring the villagers of My Lai and tried as a war criminal (based upon the legal code established for the Nuremberg trials). More often it was the Pentagon and the military in general. And always it was the Administration.

Lyndon Johnson, who had enjoyed an extremely good press, was hounded out of office. Crowds outside the White House – televised as a matter of course – chanted, 'Hey, hey, LBJ, how many kids have you killed today?' The 'kids' could have been American soldiers or Vietnamese civilians. They were all grist to the anti-war propagandists.

Richard Nixon, Johnson's successor, was brought down by the Watergate scandal but that, in turn, was a product of the anti-war fury where everyone in politics saw conspiracy on one side or the other.

The rebellion in the colleges was fuelled by the same issue. Students were deferred from selective call-up until they had completed their studies. Many prolonged their studies, or fled to Canada or went into hiding to avoid the draft. This further exacerbated the divisions in society between the 'hard hats' (what used to be called the working class) and the intellectuals.

Gerald Ford, the stand-in President who took over from Richard Nixon in 1974, had the unenviable task of bringing down the curtain on the Vietnam affair in April 1975.

The *Express* headlined the flight of the last Americans to quit Saigon as 'The Flight of the Eagle'. The bird was not mortally wounded but it was sadly reduced in plumage. Countries abroad – notably in the Middle East – drew their own conclusions and made their own dispositions. In Indo-China a fearful tragedy supervened.

Cambodia, which had been drawn into the war as US forces tried to prevent it being used as a conduit for war supplies from the North to the Vietcong, fell to its own brand of Communist fanatics, the Khmer Rouge.

Led by Pol Pot, the Khmer Rouge entered the Cambodian capital, Pnom Penh about the same time as Saigon fell. Straightway they fell upon the city dwellers and drove them into the countryside 'to work or starve'. As many as one quarter of Cambodia's population succumbed in what was, proportionately, the biggest massacre of modern times. Pol Pot was not however charged as a war criminal but, instead continued to enjoy recognition by the United Nations, the body specifically charged with implementing the legal structure defining war crimes and crimes against humanity established at Nuremberg.

In this Pol Pot was following the lead of his guide and mentor Mao Tse-tung. In 1966 the Communist Chinese leader had launched the so-called 'Cultural Revolution' whereby the most violent and illiterate sections of Chinese society were encouraged to beset and harass the 'spectacle wearers'. Teachers and other academics with soft hands were sent into the fields for 're-education'. Many were simply butchered for the crime of not being 'toilers'. It is reckoned that the Cultural Revolution claimed 400,000 victims. The dying Mao left this as a legacy to China and an inspiration to Pol Pot in 1975.

Both of course, were following the example of the Bolshevik Revolution of 1917 when Red Guards would go through trains examining people's hands. Those who had pale soft ones were ordered to leave the train while it was still moving.

The death of perhaps 1,000,000 people in Cambodia and half that number in Laos and Vietnam, marked the bloody close of the era of the West in the East. If the Americans had ever hankered after an empire it had had the shortest life on record: 'From infancy to senility with no intervening period of maturity'.

The Americans had tried to spare the countries of Indo-China the

The New Look of the early fifties . . . a return to elegance.

Lord Longford launched a crusade against pornography.
(Reproduced from a marked news photograph)

horrors that befell them, and, for their pains, were accused of brutal repression. They were also accused of bullying their allies, yet if the Alliance was really dominated by the US it was a singularly ineffective domination. For not one of the NATO powers gave the slightest help to the Americans in Vietnam. Just the reverse. They constantly and loudly condemned the American presence, provoking the then US Secretary of State, Dean Rusk, to lament 'one would have been grateful for the Black Watch band'.

Defied by a modestly-sized Asian state, betrayed by its allies, flayed by articulate critics at home and abroad, the US Administration retreated in upon itself. Both major parties, Democrats and Republicans alike, bore responsibility for the Vietnamese disaster, so neither could reap political benefit from it.

The American public, other than the rancorous opponents of the war, was hurt and baffled. The loss of confidence was palpable, and the US was but the latest white nation to suffer the stinging reminder that the Caucasians were no longer the 'master race'.

Britain's headlong retreat from Empire – liquidating London control of one-quarter of the globe's surface in eighteen years – France's mortal defeat in Indo-China and Algeria (1954–1962) had now been followed by the disastrous expulsion of the most powerful nation on earth from one corner of a foreign field that it had expected to make its own.

As the second half of the twentieth century advanced the issues of race and guilt came to dominate the public debate in Western societies. From unquestioning belief in superiority at the start of the century, through Europe's civil wars, the West had, by the sixties, reached a position of self-questioning doubt and self-loathing. The wars of Vietnam played a significant part in this transformation. But the issue of race and guilt was most dramatically seen in the relations not between Asians and Westerners but between White and Black.

CHAPTER TEN

A Question of Race

When shortly after World War II Winston Churchill referred in admiration to 'The British race around the globe' he could never have imagined that such a phrase could have branded him as 'racist', a term of abuse in the second half of the 20th century to rival that of 'papist' during the rule of Oliver Cromwell in the 17th.

Why this was so requires explanation and that starts with Churchill's great foe, Adolf Hitler.

Hitler advocated the most extreme form of racial discrimination imaginable. The Nordic race – embracing most of Northern Europe – was born to dominate, naturally with the Germans in the van. Hitler's respect for and envy of England rested largely on the British achievement of ruling hundreds of millions of Africans and Asians by the force of will. The sight of the elite ruling few governing India, for example, entranced him. Part of their story was told in the film *Lives of a Bengal Lancer*. It was one of the Fuehrer's favourite movies.

The British held no such illusions about themselves but, equally, there was no perception that racism was a bad thing. People of all classes talked of 'the natives', meaning blacks or Asians. There were terms of abuse – 'wogs, wops, dagoes', but as they also included 'huns' – for Germans – they cannot be classed as advocating racial, as against national, superiority.

Race before World War II simply was not a matter for controversy. All that changed when the monstrous ovens of Auschwitz were opened for inspection and the world gazed with anguish at the results of a racial 'final solution'.

The Jewish holocaust was the first indication that racial theories, carried to the ultimate, led to mass murder. As more and more became known of the Nazi handiwork, especially in Eastern Europe where Russian and Polish *Untermenschen*, or sub-humans, had suffered uncountable miseries, the conviction grew that racial divisions of any kind were intrinsically evil. Hitler, the chief protagonist of racial discrimination, was the principal cause of making racism a crime.

Revulsion against Nazi atrocities was reinforced by the withdrawal from Empire. What were we, the Europeans, doing in these countries anyway? Weren't we just exploiters, grabbing as much loot from the colonies as we could and providing nothing in return?

Such were the routine charges from the Socialist and anti-colonialist lobbies, often indistinguishable, epitomised by the Movement for Colonial Freedom. They were not echoed by the mass of people in Britain (nor France, for that matter). But they had much appeal for the communicating classes, the articulate and politically active journalists, TV commentators, writers, lecturers and so on.

Arguments on these lines meshed neatly with the conviction that colonialism had had its day and that racialism was a vital element in supporting colonialism. From there it was a short step to the simplistic notion that all 'oppressed people' should be lumped together. Jews and Negroes, Asians and Arabs, Cypriots and Malay Chinese.

After a while it was recognised that the Jews did not quite fit into this category (for one thing, they were white) and amendment was made. Similarly with the Cypriots. But the remaining distinctions held firm. 'Black' (embracing brown, yellow, red) was persecuted by White. Any deviation from this grand and simple design was treated as an aberration, unfortunate but untypical. Arab enslavement of Africans; African enslavement of Africans; Zulu annihilation of the Sothos, Ndebele of the Shonas, Hindus of Moslems, Moslems of Hindus, Chinese exploitation of Malays and Malay retribution on Chinese, and scores more of black cruelty to black, brown to brown, black to brown, brown to black, and so on, were conveniently ignored or swiftly brushed aside. There was but one crime: racism. One defiler: the white. One victim: the coloured.

As a distortion of history and fact, the exclusive guilt of the whites is probably without parallel. Hitler would have approved, believing, as he did, that the bigger the lie, the more it was repeated, the more people would believe it. It was, after all, the foundation of his racial policies.

A study of colonialism is out of place here but it does no harm to recall Churchill's wry observation on a visit to the USA that the quintupling of the Indian population during the 200 years of the Raj compared favourably with the virtual elimination of the Red Indians during 200 years of anti-colonialism.

One day there will be dispassionate accounts. Between 1950 and

1975 the thrust of contemporary, informed opinion, was in favour of national liberation *from the whites*. If persecution of minorities followed the installation of a black government that was something that couldn't be helped, as the Biafrans of Nigeria and the Bagandas of Uganda among many others were to find out to their cost.

'One man, one vote – once' was the pattern across Africa as single-party or military dictatorships replaced colonial administrations and corruption – and worse – replaced impartial rule. None of this mattered compared with the emotive cry *Uhuru* – freedom.

As has been related, Ghana, formerly the Gold Coast, was first to the tapes in 1957. The treasury was full, the rule of law well-established, there were no tribal problems. Within six years Ghana was bankrupt. The rule of law had been overthrown (with the leader of the opposition in jail) and tremendous divisions had opened up in Ghanaian society. Two years later Nkrumah was ousted by the army. Six years on and he died in exile. It was a pattern that was to be repeated again and again. In Nigeria. In the Congo (later Zaire). In Uganda. In Sudan. In Chad.

Yet still the propaganda drums beat out that if only the whites would quit all would be well.

The fallacy could not be explained in a rational fashion, but some understanding could be had by reference to the West's growing lack of faith in itself, in its standards, beliefs, perceptions of progress; that the West had nothing to offer and had been responsible for most of the sufferings of the coloured peoples for centuries.

From the mid-fifties these ideas had conquered the citadels of power in the ruling Tory Party and the Civil Service. For their arguments, backed by black and Asian politicians, Nehru and Nkrumah to the fore, who naturally saw themselves as successors to the colonial administrators, were persuasive. Why should the West, which had torn itself to pieces in two world wars, regard itself as superior? Compared with the crimes committed during these conflicts, African tribal disputes were mere storms in a teacup.

Land-grabbing, money-grabbing traders had gone out in the seventeenth and eighteenth centuries from Europe to seize tribal lands and enslave the populations of 'lesser breeds'. Sometimes trade had followed the flag, more often the flag had followed the traders to impose law and order and so protect the profits of the traders. In the nineteenth century a gloss was added to this ruthless bondage in the shape of canting missionaries who converted the heathen to a totally alien God and his Son, Jesus Christ. The heathens were then required to worship not as their forefathers had done but as their colonial masters told them. Thus were their souls bonded as effectively as their bodies. And these oppressed subjects had been obliged to fight in two terrible wars for their white masters. Great was the guilt of the West. Great must be its payment for redemption. Starting with immediate independence for the territories in Africa which the Europeans had carved out for themselves, accompanied by generous financial subventions to compensate the Africans for the exploitation of centuries.

To such sweeping condemnation, the apologists for Empire had no effective answer. They were uneasily aware that they were 'on the wrong side of history'. Ever since the fall of Singapore in 1942 (when the 'gin-swilling planters' had been held up to ridicule and scorn) they had been on the defensive. At most they could plead that colonialism had given the locals peace, impartial justice, a welcome absence of corruption, full treasuries and at least enough health and education to have produced the claimants to the colonial throne. They also hesitatingly suggested that perhaps the colonial peoples were not yet ready for Westminster-style government. To which their critics replied that if they weren't that was itself a terrible indictment of colonial rule and, anyway, why should the Africans necessarily adopt Parliamentary government?

On that note the argument ended and the dissolution of the British Colonial Empire began. So too, at precisely the same moment, 1956–57, began the inward movement of peoples from the Old Empire (New Commonwealth) to the Home Country. This wave of immigration created heightening tensions in England, while the withdrawal from Empire left dangerous legacies, above all in South Africa.

Everything to do with Empire was bundled up in the Commonwealth, so that coloured immigration to the UK and UK policies towards Rhodesia and South Africa were subject to scrutiny, by other Commonwealth countries and to the risk of the charge of 'racial discrimination' being flung at the UK.

As with so much in history, the Commonwealth was created to massage away racial tensions through the application of goodwill. Strictly speaking, the British Commonwealth of Nations was that group of countries – Canada, Australia, New Zealand, South Africa – self-governing dominions recognised as such by the 1931 Statute of

Westminster. The Commonwealth, without the precedent British, came into existence in 1949 to accommodate India and Pakistan. When, in January 1950, India became a republic the British Sovereign was acknowledged as Head of the Commonwealth. In the subsequent flood of independence celebrations the newly-created sovereign states announced their adhesion to the Commonwealth, almost always as republics though occasionally recognising the British monarch as their own head of state.

From the British point of view, the Commonwealth soothed the wound to pride suffered by loss of Empire. In its early days it had positive trading advantages as most of the Commonwealth also formed the Sterling Area, with preferential tariff and currency arrangements. Later these were dismantled as Britain moved towards the European Common Market (see Ch.VII) leaving the Commonwealth as a disparate collection of nations with little in common except the English language, quadrennial Games and cultural exchanges. The Sovereign however still presided over regular Commonwealth gatherings of heads of state or governments and so was given a global character, personally pleasing to the Monarch and nationally comforting to the British people.

However, in the period 1950–75 the perception of the Commonwealth underwent a dramatic transformation in Britain. The Tories had long been regarded as the party of Empire, wrapping itself in the Union Jack, concluding its conferences with 'Land of Hope and Glory', surely the brashest of all hymns to national supremacy. Labour had a wholly unsympathetic attitude to Empire and even viewed the Commonwealth with suspicion as a selective grouping which conflicted with the party's internationalism. Labour concluded its proceedings with 'The Red Flag' in which there was no mention of Britain.

By 1975 the Tories could cheerfully have strangled the Commonwealth for having allegedly exacerbated the problems of immigration and Southern Africa, whereas Labour was hymning its praises as a fine example of non-racial co-operation and a worthy alternative to the capitalistic Common Market.

Again we have a seminal date for this change: 1960. Harold Macmillan went off to South Africa to tell the all-white Parliament at the Cape that the 'wind of change is blowing throughout Africa'. The Afrikaaner-ruled country then announced it meant to become a republic and requested continuing membership of the Commonwealth analagous to India's. The rest of the Commonwealth refused this application on the grounds that the minority whites were oppressing the majority blacks by practising apartheid, or separate development. South Africa, having narrowly voted to become a republic, promptly quit the Commonwealth.

In that same year coloured immigration, under the special aegis of 'Commonwealth citizenship' reached its height: 160,000 landing in the UK for settlement.

Britain's policy towards Southern Africa and her policy towards immigration were now influenced decisively by Commonwealth sentiment. When the Central African Federation, a union of Nyasaland (later Malawi), Northern Rhodesia (later Zambia) and Southern Rhodesia broke up following the independence of Malawi and Zambia, the Commonwealth strenuously objected to independence being granted white-ruled Rhodesia. That country then unilaterally declared its own independence in 1965. Spurred by the Commonwealth the UK imposed economic sanctions designed, according to Mr Harold Wilson, the British Premier, to bring the rebellious white Rhodesians to heel 'in weeks, not months'. Nearly fifteen years were to pass before the whites surrendered power to a black government: during that time much of Britain's market in Central-South Africa was taken by the Germans, French and Japanese. Still more dramatic was the change effected in Britain's relations with South Africa: again largely due to the promptings of the Commonwealth.

In the 25 years that mark the third-quarter of the twentieth century it is safe to say that no nation aroused such passionate antipathy as South Africa. It was truly the pariah state, hated, derided, denounced. South Africa represented all that was monstrous: white supremacy, black humiliation, brutality, insensitivity and prosperity for a European minority built on the exploitation of the black majority. That, in short, was the case for the critics who demanded sanctions and, if necessary, war on the white-ruled republic.

During that period it was undeniable fact that the European minority (about 18 per cent of the total South African population) alone had the vote. The judiciary was a European preserve. So was the senior Civil Service, as were the commanding positions in the Armed Forces. African workers were wholly without political rights in cities such as Johannesburg where they supplied 60 per cent of the labour force. They lived in their own townships outside and had to return there at the end of the day or be in the possession of a pass, signed by a magistrate, permitting them to be elsewhere. They travelled by separate buses and trains into separate stations. They played in segregated sports fields and sunbathed on segregated beaches. They could not drink what they pleased, where they pleased, but had to submit to white-made licensing laws. In the goldfields, source of so much of South Africa's wealth, they were obliged to learn a 'new' language, were kept in compounds and their earnings remitted to their homelands. They were subjected to group area acts which reserved the choicest parcels of land to whites and marriage, or cohabitation, between members of different races was specifically banned on pain of severe punishment.

South Africa was ruled by the National Party, which came to power in 1948 and which was almost entirely Afrikaaner – a mix of Dutch, French Huguenot, German Moravian settlers. They had their own language, a stern Calvinist-like church and a conviction that they had a covenant with God to farm the good earth, sustain white rule and keep the Kaffir in his place – paternally, of course.

A number of the Afrikaans politicians had, in their youth, supported Hitler and the Nazis on the grounds that any enemy of Britain was a friend of theirs. The Afrikaaners were, on all counts, the foe of Western liberals. And as, increasingly during the fifties, the English element of the 4.5 million whites drew nearer to the Afrikaaners (following the demise of Colonial Africa) so they too came under the lash of disapprobation. So when, in 1960, a labour dispute led to a riot in Sharpesville on the Rand, and 67 Africans were tragically and brutally shot, the world waited for the explosion. Nothing happened. Civil wars raged between blacks in Nigeria, Ethiopia, Angola, Mozambique and elsewhere, but the long-foretold uprising of South Africa's blacks against the whites did not happen.

In fact almost all the deaths in South Africa – a violent country in a violent continent – arose from inter-tribal or inter-factional fighting among blacks. The reason for the invented language of the goldfields was that the Africans themselves were of different stock. They had to have a common language because they could not understand one another.

The enormous complexities of a land with a white minority, a Zulu minority, a Xhosa minority, a Sotho minority, a coloured (mix of black, white, Malay and Chinese) minority, an Indian minority, was never dispassionately considered. The indisputable fact that a white minority was ruling the rest was enough to damn South Africa.

Those countries most dependent on South Africa's burgeoning economy – Zambia and Zimbabwe – were foremost in the counsels of the Commonwealth in demanding economic war on that country until political power was transferred from the whites to the blacks. Dictatorship, economic collapse, unlimited corruption, even tribal warfare were preferable to the ultimate evil of white domination.

Thus, in Africa, in much less than one generation, the assumed superiority of the whites had been turned into outright detestation of them, at least in the role of rulers. And, among the whites in the West, self-adulation had turned to self-distrust. Among activists this led to race being placed in the very centre of political life.

The first intimation the British had that they had a 'race problem' on their hands was when in March 1958 Mr Justice Salmon sent four young white men to jail for four years for attacking coloured people in London's East End. His judgement 'men must be able to walk the Queen's highway in peace and without fear' was commended by all sections of the media: the *Daily Express* commenting that 'justice must be colour-blind . . . Mr Justice Salmon has spoken for us all.'

As the months rolled on and the immigrants reached out towards a million . . . a million and a half . . . two millions, a whole new decisive element entered British life. It was not a matter of 'black versus white', but of a fundamental conflict over human nature among whites themselves. On the one hand were the integrationists and, initially at any rate, advocates of unrestricted immigration. Generally they were on the left of the political spectrum, though their ranks also included paternal Tories who believed the British had an after-Empire duty to those whom they had once ruled.

Their argument was that West Indians and Asians should be welcomed and that they should be spread about the country as widely as possible. How this was to be achieved, other than by forcible residence based on something similar to the South African pass laws was not made clear. Although it was admitted, on all sides, that the 'ghettoes' of America were not healthy.

The American experience, however, was repeated in the UK. West Indians and Asians naturally congregated in the same areas occupied by earlier arrivals. To counter this, to ensure equal schooling and job opportunities for the coloured population, the integrationists demanded a system of bussing on American lines whereby white children were taken by bus from predominantly white schools to predominantly black ones and the reverse process to take black children to white schools. In addition a race relations body should monitor discrimination in housing and work which disadvantaged the coloured applicants.

The bussing proposal did not find favour, largely because it was believed comprehensive education would deliver equality and also because America had discovered that bussing was a two-edged sword. Thus the whites in Boston* simply took their children away from municipal schools subject to the bussing programme and enrolled them in private schools. In three years the number of white pupils enrolled in Boston's municipal schools fell from 90,000 to 70,000.

Anti-discrimination measures, however, were legislated by Harold Wilson's Labour Government. In 1965 and 1968 a Race Relations Board and a Community Relations Commission were established to impose equal treatment. Social engineering designed to alter human nature (or eliminate bigotry) was well and truly launched; racial harmony was to be created by law.

The *Express* reported that the Race Relations Board had censured a Scottish doctor in Eastbourne for advertising for a Scottish cook.

Inevitably in attempting to mould human nature to fit certain pre-conditions those engaged in what came to be known as the 'race industry' were obliged to practise 'positive discrimination', i.e. urging that coloured people be given preference in housing, jobs, services. The black people needed no special help in sport. They advanced disproportionately on their own merit, as did many Indians.

In the realms of culture and popular entertainment a considerable effort went into advancing the rights of the coloured population. Sometimes the effort took a bizarre turn. As when the nursery rhyme (and Agatha Christie thriller) was changed from 'Ten Little Niggers' to 'Ten Little Indians'. As when Bob Hope's *Call me Bwana* disappeared from the film libraries.

'Racist' became a term of exceptional emotional content. Was it racist to talk about 'nigger in the woodpile' but acceptable to refer to 'Taffy was a Welshman, Taffy was a thief'? Could a West Indian

---

* See *Common Ground* by J. Anthony Lukas (Knopf): a study of race relations in Boston.

prospective house purchaser claim he had been victim of racial discrimination if the vendor refused his offer? Would employers be obliged to hire the 'statutory black', regardless of performance, to satisfy the Race Relations Board? Such fear and doubt did little for race relations but much to promote ill-feeling.

Inevitably it also produced a reaction, articulated by John Enoch Powell, Tory MP for Wolverhampton, a prime area for immigrants to settle. On 20 April 1968, (Hitler's birthday, as critics were swift to point out) Powell addressed a meeting in Birmingham, another site of large-scale immigration.

This is how the *Express* recorded his speech:

In 15 to 20 years, on present trends, there will be in this country 3,500,000 Commonwealth immigrants and their descendants. That is not my figure. That is the official figure given to Parliament by the spokesman of the Registrar General's office. There is no comparable figure for the year 2000, but it must be in the region of 5–7 million, approximately one-tenth of the whole population and approaching that of Greater London.

Of course it will not be evenly distributed from Margate to Aberystwyth, from Penzance to Aberdeen. Whole areas, towns and parts of towns across England will be occupied by different sections of the immigrant and immigrant-descended population.

So insane are we that we actually permit unmarried persons to immigrate for the purpose of founding a family with spouses and fiancés whom they have never seen . . .

The immigrant and his descendants should not be elevated into a privileged and special class. The citizen should not be denied his right to discriminate in the management of his own affairs between one fellow-citizen and another or be subjected to inquisition as to his reasons and motives for behaving in one lawful manner rather than another.

The effect of this immigration has been to make Britons feel strangers in their own country. They find their homes and neighbourhood changed beyond recognition.

At work they find that employers hesitate to apply to the immigrant worker the standards of discipline and competence required of the native-born worker. They begin to hear, as time goes by, more and more voices telling them they are the unwanted.

As I look ahead I am filled with foreboding. Like the Roman, I seem to see 'The River Tiber, foaming with much blood'.

The last, classical phrase aroused furious denunciation. Its allusion was ignored, the assumption made that Powell was talking about the Thames, not the Tiber. Edward Heath, the then Tory leader, immediately dismissed Powell from the Shadow Cabinet, the Opposition's inner council. One bishop referred to Powell as 'an evil smell'. There were demands from the Labour benches that he be impeached.

The polarity of thinking in the country between the horn-rimmed and the horny-handed was evidenced by the march of London dockers in favour of Powell. It must have been the first time that particular body of men had displayed sympathy for a Tory. Newspaper polls showed a surprising uniformity: by 7–3 the public appeared to back Powell, especially his proposal for voluntary repatriation, providing public funds and free passage for Africans, West Indians and Asians wishing to return to their countries of origin – a proposal evoking no little support among the immigrants themselves who, very properly, wanted to diminish the prospect of violent racial conflict.

Three years later, in 1971, a Conservative Government enacted an Immigration Act which provided for voluntary repatriation and restricted immigration for non-patrials (i.e. those whose parents or grandparents were not British) to those holding work permits. These permits did not carry with them right to permanent residence but only the right to work for a year in a specific place at a specific job. Dependants of such work-permit-holders would not have the right to enter the UK. Special powers were taken to deal with illegal immigrants.

So the flood was stemmed. The measure was not seriously contested even by those who had once advocated unlimited Commonwealth entry. Yet the problems created by the period of unrestricted or barely restricted immigration from 1956–1971 remained to haunt politicians.

Allegiance to the Commonwealth (for foreign immigration into the UK had been severely limited since 1905) had caused British policy towards Southern Africa and towards immigrants to depart radically from what it might otherwise have been. Following his dismissal from Front Bench service, Powell devoted himself to denouncing the Commonwealth and generally to attacking what he regarded as the 'dangerous myths' to which many in Britain clung.

First among them, ahead of the Commonwealth, was the paternalistic way in which British industry was run, leading to the very inefficiency and overmanning that had produced a 'labour shortage' and encouraged Commonwealth immigration.

Collectivist dogma, married to social engineering, was the dominant theme of the 1950–75 generation, with the twin thrusts of security and equality.

CHAPTER ELEVEN

'When Everybody is Somebody . . .'

The drive towards equality has been a basic urge among political activists for aeons. In modern times Robespierre in France, Lenin in Russia, Mao Tse-tung in China, have pursued compulsory equality with the same single-minded ruthless devotion as that exhibited by those who sought the Holy Grail. Total equality has always eluded its pursuers. Wherever it has been tried with the full force of the State the search has ended in terror and dictatorship.

Even local, voluntary and benign endeavours, such as the kibbutz scheme in Israel, have falsified the hopes of their founders. Yet the impulse remains and in the space of the 1950–75 generation it took different forms as first one aspect of equality, then another, failed to live up to expectations.

In 1951 a remarkable experiment in equality-by-State-control in Britain was ending. Coming to power in the immediate aftermath of World War II, Clement Attlee's Labour Government had found all the levers in place for the continuation of a State-regulated war economy to a State-regulated peacetime one. Much of the public, especially the younger ones, were eager to try socialism, wished Labour well and wanted to see co-operation replace competition: the latter being blamed for the disastrous slump of the thirties.

Labour sought to achieve equality by transferring ownership of the major industries from private to public hands and by a tax system which reached confiscatory levels – 103 per cent of income when the capital levy operated – on the 'wealthy'.

It was widely believed that the workers would toil far more eagerly and effectively for British Rail, or the National Coal Board, or British Gas than they would for private employers: for would they not be working for themselves in the form of the State rather than for greedy capitalists?

Income differentiation there had to be to induce certain individuals to accept additional responsibility, but that would be equalised to vanishing point through the operation of transfer payments, taking a disproportionately high tax from the bigger incomes and providing those on the lower level with social benefits.

Capital transfer – of industries and cash – was the major instrument of transformation. It was not the only one. New housing was to be almost entirely municipal with allocations going to families on a points basis: so many for ill-health, so many for the number of children, so many for length of time on the waiting list. 'Priority is the language of socialism,' declared the Minister of Housing, Aneurin Bevan. Private home-ownership (then about 30 per cent in the UK) would gradually wither away as the advantages of municipal provision became clear. Rents of these municipal houses were kept extremely low (in one Scottish town, Dumbarton, local authority rents were 2s 11d – 15p – per week) while the local rates paid by owners dramatically increased. There was, therefore, good reason to believe that home ownership would eventually disappear as the privately-let market was disappearing, thanks to rent control which denied landlords sufficient income to keep their property in reasonable repair.

In addition, food and clothes were rationed, so that no one could eat better or wear finer apparel than his or her neighbour. 'Utility' furniture – price and quality-controlled – meant that everyone, eventually, would have the same furnishings.

So, in all the essentials, food, clothes, shelter, work, life-style, the levers were pulled to ensure equality. Only they didn't – ensure equality, that is.

Private enterprise, in every kind of guise, secured for people what they most wanted. Despite an army of inspectors, the black market in foodstuffs flourished. Those who were prepared to pay received food 'off the coupon'. Motor cars slipped through the strict allotment procedure. The same happened with petrol, also rationed. The more officialdom tried to block the loopholes – colouring commercial petrol so that it could be spotted by police as ration-breaking when they carried out spot surveys – the greater was the ingenuity of those dedicated to frustrating officialdom.

During the war it was considered unpatriotic to support the black market, or the so-called 'spivs' who operated it. By 1951 it had become a popular pastime to outwit restrictions. The contrast between the defeated Germans enjoying unrationed food and an unrestricted housing market with the victorious British enduring tighter rations than they had experienced during the war, was too much to bear.

Equality by rationing broke down in the face of human nature and native craftiness. It was spiritually dead three years before it was finally buried by Winston Churchill's Conservative government.

Equality through housing broke down because the supply of housing never came close to meeting demand. Rigid controls on house-builders, obliging them to seek permission for this, that and the other so restricted output that fierce public resentment set in. The Conservatives, on regaining power in 1951, reintroduced free market methods and from then on private ownership rapidly overhauled municipal rented property, reversing the proportions by 1975.

But, for egalitarians, the greatest disappointment was reserved for the workers in the nationalised industries. Not only did they not respond joyfully to the prospect of working for the State, but production sagged below pre-war levels. In coalmining it sank far below pre-World War I levels (230 million tons then; less than half in 1951). Yet the miners had been the most doughty champions of State ownership and the mine owners among the most despised of capitalist bosses who had starved the pits of investment.

Why then had the pitmen not worked with a will when the banner of the National Coal Board was raised above the pitheads? Because the miners wanted the mines for themselves. They had no more interest in working for the sake of engineers and shopworkers than engineers and shopworkers had in toiling for the miners.

The fallacy of nationalisation was to believe that men and women are motivated by certain ideals which, at one time or other, happen to appeal to intellectuals. Faith in State control as the instrument of obligatory equality broke against the rock of human nature. The irony of the miners, who had been in the van of the nationalisation brigade, 'betraying the cause' was not lost on those who planned a Socialist resurgence.

The 'solidarity' of the working class, once the bedrock conviction of Socialists, clearly did not extend beyond the self-interest of each section of the working class. The workers were no less selfish than the capitalists or the bourgeoisie. Nationalisation and the planned economy had failed not because the theory was unsound but because those who had been trusted to carry the programme forward had proved weak and unreliable crusaders.

General William Westmoreland, commander of American troops in Vietnam.

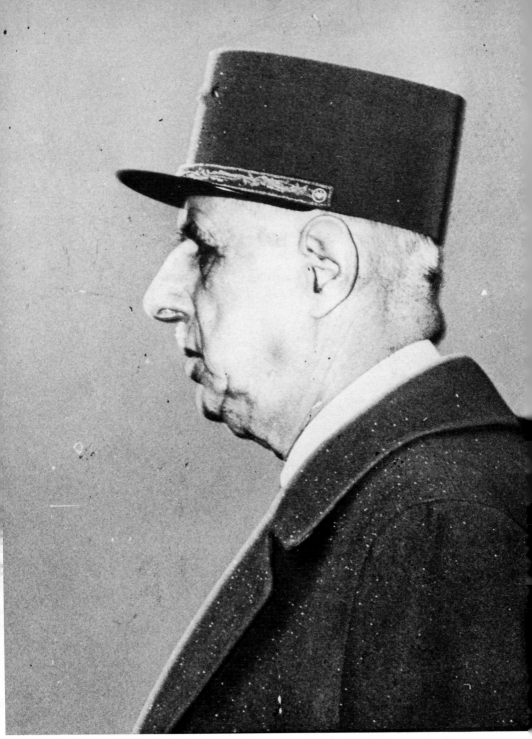
Charles de Gaulle, the President who rebuilt France.

After six years of war and six of deliberate Socialist austerity, the voters were ready for a change, but they gave power to Churchill and Conservatives in October 1951 by the grudging margin of a mere 16 seats. Indeed Labour actually polled more votes than the Tories.

Fear of Churchill's warmongering and anxiety that full employment – which the country had enjoyed since 1940 – would be jeopardised probably accounted for much of the degree of Labour support. But it must be acknowledged that the appeal of the Welfare State, of security from the womb to the tomb, held considerable attraction for the bulk of the people. Certainly the Tories had to agree to sustain the National Health Service and to make no substantial changes in the industrial organisation of the economy (steel was the only industry de-nationalised).

The British settled down to a judicious mixture of job scarcity and a fair dispensation of free enterprise, known as the 'mixed economy'. Mandatory egalitarianism was postponed; not abandoned.

Education was the key to Act II of the Evolution of Equality. Of all the grand illusions of the rational age, none was more appealing than that of 'education'. It was a matter of unequivocal conviction that most of the world's woes, not least crime and other unsociable behaviour, could be put down to lack of education.

Teach the children of the poor, the wrongdoer, the thriftless, the right way to do things and self-inflicted injury would disappear. This comforting belief had sustained many a reformer disillusioned by the working classes' lack of social awareness. Education, and its limitless capacity to change the human condition, came to the rescue of Britain's eager reformers in the 1950s.

More specifically, attention was focused on education's capacity to create equality. For decades, critics of Britain's performance had fastened on the class bias of the classroom as the bedrock reason for the country's failings. Educational snobbishness – the division of the nation into first-class fee-paying pupils at independent schools, second-class at merit-only grammar schools, third-class (75 per cent) at secondary moderns – was the major and scandalous cause of national decline. The 'old school tie' strangled natural talent and reserved the jobs for those who attended 'public' (i.e. private) schools.

Confirmation of this belief came with the publication, in 1960, of Anthony Sampson's book *Anatomy of Britain*. It detailed the nation's leaders in industry, commerce, finance, politics, the civil and armed services, in law, medicine, the Church; and, almost without exception, they turned out to be the products of the public schools and Oxbridge (Oxford and Cambridge) universities.

A few years earlier, journalist and author Henry Fairlie had instituted the word 'Establishment' to describe the interlocking figures whose attitudes and personalities had a common root in schooling and who, by virtue of their positions, virtually decided the country's politics.

As the UK's economic growth declined relatively – though *not* absolutely – to other countries, criticism of the injustice of the educational system grew. It was unfair. It perpetuated inequality and privileges. It made children feel inadequate.

This latter point became a bull one for Labour Party researchers who were searching for a new cause to replace the outworn and discredited one of State-ownership. They came up with the answer: comprehensive education. The method to attain the Socialist objective, equality.

Comprehensive schooling was a most attractive electoral proposition. At a stroke it would remove the stigma attaching to 11+ pupils who failed entry to the grammar schools. The 11+ examination would simply be abolished. In its place would be automatic transference from primary schools to the neighbourhood comprehensive. Those with academic ability would mix with those whose talents lay with manual dexterity, or sport, or art. As co-educational establishments they would teach males a proper appreciation of the female sex and as very large establishments they would be able to offer superb facilities for science, craft, design and technology: the very spheres in which England was falling behind.

True, the comprehensive school, while eliminating discrimination between grammar and modern in the state sector, did nothing about the private sector. However, it was confidently expected that when the benefits of comprehensivisation were seen, the private sector would wither away. For who would spend money on inferior, old-fashioned education in sub-standard buildings with outdated equipment when brand new, custom-built, buildings were available free?

So was born a new crusade for equality. It was accompanied by an unprecedented increase in educational expenditure. Between 1950 and 1975 spending on schools increased fifteen-fold from £370 million a year to £4,864 million, absorbing seven per cent of the gross national product.

While the Labour Party made by far the most effective use of comprehensive education as a vote-gatherer, the Conservatives, afraid of appearing fuddy-duddy and class-conscious, swiftly boarded the bandwagon. In a press interview their spokesman on education, Sir Edward Boyle (Eton and Oxford) explained that comprehensives were good for everyone. 'After all,' he smiled, patting his fine round belly, 'Eton is a comprehensive too.'

With such bi-partisanship and naivety the number of comprehensive schools grew from an experimental two in 1952 to 2,596 in 1975, accounting for the vast majority of pupils in the State sector. Yet the magical equality they were to bring about never transpired. Britain's economic growth slowed still further. Far from withering away, the number of pupils attending schools in the private sector increased. Indeed the comprehensives actually enhanced *inequality*. Parents who could afford to move, set up house in areas where neighbourhood schools had a good reputation. So, if anything, class divisions were more marked than heretofore.

Once again the search for equality through legislation had proved sadly futile.

As educational attainments dropped, the Conservatives nimbly abandoned the bandwagon, explaining that, 'It is now apparent, to say the least, that their (comprehensives) introduction has not been accompanied by the conspicuous advance in educational attainment which the more uncritical proponents of reorganisation promised.' And their spokesman, Mr St John Stevas, added: 'The Socialists are much more concerned with the use of comprehensive schools as a means of social engineering to further the egalitarian society which they favour, than they are with the educational merits, or otherwise, of comprehensive schools.'

The reason why comprehensive education failed to produce the promised transformation was simply human nature. The idea that bright pupils would raise the less bright (and probably tougher) flew in the face of experience. The opposite occurred and because custom-built comprehensives were exceedingly large, accommodating 2,000 or more pupils, headmaster and staff were so out of touch that they could not prevent the less academic from pulling down the more academic to the level of the lowest common denominator.

The more extreme form of egalitarianism – classes of mixed

abilities which deliberately mixed the dumb with the smart – were swiftly abandoned as totally unworkable. 'Streaming' was reintroduced though, to avoid the stigma of being in 1F rather than 1A, the streams were given names such as Avon and Somerset. It is doubtful if the pupils were fooled.

In the end, many headmasters introduced the house system to give pupils an identity that they could not feel for a huge impersonal school. Ironically the house system was the classical product of the very public schools which the comprehensives were designed to supplant.

So the crusades for equality achieved the opposite of their intentions. Yet the more schemes for obligatory egalitarianism foundered, the more were thought up, each more bizarre than its predecessor. Rationing, confiscatory taxation, nationalisation, racial mixing, educational mixing having been tried and either abandoned or tacitly dismissed, it was the turn of sex equality to be the magic key that would unlock a wonderful world. The right of women to total equality; the right of homosexuals to total equality; the right of lesbians to total equality.

Campaigning for women's rights, long pre-dated the post-1950 period of course. In my first volume *The Way We Were 1900–1914*, I quoted Mrs George Corbett, an authoress, complaining to the *Daily Express* in 1900 that while she was infinitely more literate than most men – many of whom could not even spell c-a-t – she was denied the vote while they were granted it. And in 1912 Miss Ann Dugdale shocked public opinion by refusing to utter the promise to obey her husband in the marriage vow.

The Suffragette movement, led by the Pankhurst family, gave voice and organisation to the demand for female franchise, from which reforms in matrimonial law would flow to ensure equality between the sexes. The violence of the suffragette movement, including arson, bombing and physical assault, proclaimed the depth of anger among a section of intelligent women at being denied the vote and treated, at law, as inferior creatures.

But by 1950 these grievances lay far in the past. If the number of women MPs remained disappointingly low – fewer than in 1929 when all women over 21 finally received the vote – the fault lay with women who, while being in the majority in every one of the Parliamentary constituencies, resolutely refused to select, or elect, women members.

Injustices still existed in the courts, but with America setting the pace in divorce legislation heavily favouring women (indeed almost discrimination-in-reverse, against men) there was every reason to suppose that the legal injustices in the British system would be removed. And it was just at this time, the early sixties, that events led to a change in the economic status of women which, in turn, gave impetus to the feminist cause.

The contraceptive pill freed women from the fear of inadvertently giving birth to children and placed in their hands the power to prevent pregnancy, which had hitherto been a male preserve in the form of the sheath. Women could now determine the course of sexual relations and adjust child-bearing to income-earning. This happened at a period of full employment when labour scarcity led to an unprecedented demand for female labour. So women found themselves with a greater degree of sexual freedom than they had ever before enjoyed and a labour market moving increasingly their way (a development which continued even with increasing unemployment).

Yet still women tended to be dominated by men. Only a handful of the top posts in industry, commerce, finance, the civil service were held by women. Clearly the same hidden hand was at work denying women their place in the sun. That could only be a malevolent male conspiracy which must be countered with legislation. Once again the compulsion to achieve egalitarianism through legislation operated.

The Tory Government of bachelor Edward Heath published a consultative document on the topic in September 1973 entitled: 'Equal Opportunities for Men and Women'. It stated: 'The Government has decided to introduce legislation to make unlawful discrimination in employment on the grounds of sex and to encourage the changes in attitudes which are required if women are to obtain opportunities equal with men.'

By one of the delicious ironies with which politics abound, Mr Heath was displaced as Tory leader by Mrs Margaret Thatcher, an example of equal opportunities which he showed no sign of appreciating.

Under the Sex Discrimination Act it was deemed unlawful to discriminate on grounds of sex in the field of employment and in the provision of educational facilities, housing, goods, services and facilities. Those who believed themselves discriminated against were given access to the courts and tribunals. An Equal Opportunities Commission was empowered, on its own initiative, to investigate practices and issue non-discriminatory notices enforceable at law.

'Equality' proved a two-edged sword. If men and women were to be treated equally should, the *Express* newspaper asked, women enjoy a handicap advantage at golf or their own championship at Wimbledon, as distinct from an all-comers competition which did not discriminate on the grounds of sex?

Such objections were less frivolous or risible than the lengths to which the extreme feminists took their case for the abolition of male domination. It was suggested that the English language should be re-written to eliminate such terms as 'mankind'. 'God the Father' should be referred to as 'God the Person' and, indeed, the term 'chair-person' replaced that of 'chairman' at Labour Party gatherings. Sexual harassment at work was solemnly debated at tribunals with women employees complaining that they had been unfairly dismissed for objecting to patronising endearments from their boss.

While this charade in a minor key continued, in the real world violence against women in the form of rape took such an ugly turn for the worse that Germaine Greer, an Australian feminist writer, and others formed rape centres. Once more the brutal facts of human nature made a nonsense of good intentions written into a legal framework.

Yet still the belief persisted that individuals could be made pure by decree.

Homosexuality, 'the love that dare not speak its name', had been regarded as a crime in Britain since the late nineteenth century and as a sin from far, far, earlier. Oddly enough, lesbianism was not embraced in the criminal code; allegedly because Ministers in the Victorian era had no wish to explain to the Great Queen how lesbians operated.

Homosexuals argued, with considerable justification, that if it was not a crime for women to indulge in single sex relations why should it be so for men? Had the Equal Opportunities Commission pre-dated the Wolfenden Report they would have had an unanswerable case. As it happened, however, Parliament pre-empted this argument by accepting the recommendations of the committee chaired by Professor Wolfenden and freeing homosexual relations between consenting adults in private from criminal prosecution.

Few people opposed this in principle. So long as boys were not corrupted, it was surely better to remove the threat of blackmail from men whose only 'crime' was to love other men.

Unfortunately the uncontrollable itch for 'equality' affected homosexuals, or at any rate the articulate ones, so that a campaign was mounted in the early seventies to ensure that homosexuals 'came out'; that is, proudly proclaimed their proclivities, and demanded that they be accorded equal rights with heterosexuals. In the case of teaching and child care this raised delicate issues. But 'Gay Rights' (the term, as with so much else in the twentieth century, was of American origin) would brook no discrimination. Lesbians naturally took up the same policy, and both sections were encouraged by political activists to press their case against the 'dictatorship of the heterosexual majority'.

The world was truly turned upside down in the search for that elusive quality, equality.

The search often produced paradoxes. In Ireland it produced tragedy.

CHAPTER TWELVE

Island Of Bloody Memories

Few people in 1950 would have selected Ireland as the site of a terror campaign, bloody street fighting and murder and mayhem encompassing the death of thousands.

The island, North and South, was at peace. Political controversy in Dublin was concentrated on the establishment of a health service and Ulster seemed so much part of the British scene – its ten Unionist MPs voted automatically with the Conservatives – that its political and economic issues were seen simply as extensions of those in the rest of the UK.

True, a Mr O'Callaghan had contested an election in Coatbridge and Airdrie as an 'anti-partition' candidate. To the vast majority in this Scottish industrial seat the partition of Ireland meant nothing at all. Predictably, Mr O'Callaghan forfeited his deposit, receiving less than 3 per cent of the vote from the considerable Catholic population of the burghs. Yet it was a reminder that the division of Ireland still rankled; that the Protestant ascendancy in Ulster was not to remain uncontested.

Still, the dispute seemed to be safely set in a peaceable mould. Even the bombing of custom-houses on the Northern Ireland-Republican border in 1956–58 did not excite much indignation. It had long been recognised that a handful of IRA extremists, the residue of the irreconcilables who had never accepted Ireland's partition, would resort to violence. They had done so in 1939 in a bombing campaign on mainland Britain. They were simply reverting to type in 1950. As no one was killed – in contrast to the '39 campaign – and as damage was minimal, few gave much thought to the matter.

It should, however, have sparked some anxious questioning. The bombers of '56 were clearly new recruits to the cause. How was it that bitter memories of battles long ago should find an echo in the affluent fifties?

If anyone did ask that question it would have been put down to the recrudescence of nationalism on a world-wide scale. British troops were being killed in Malaya, Egypt, Cyprus, Kenya. Damage to customs houses in Ireland was of small moment compared with loss of life elsewhere.

So little attention was paid to the Irish overture. Ten years later, Ireland appeared to be moving steadily towards resolution of her decades-old split between the Protestant North and the Catholic South. The Premier of Ulster, Terence O'Neill, paid an official visit to Dublin. The Southern Irish Premier, Sean Lemass, reciprocated by journeying to Belfast. British politicians congratulated themselves on this 'natural' progression. They rejoiced too soon and with a total ignorance of Irish realities.

Ulster (or strictly speaking, six of the nine counties of Ulster constituting the political entity of Northern Ireland) was, in the words of one of its founders, Sir James Craig, the place where 'a Protestant Parliament would look after a Protestant people'.

Many of the people themselves were of Scottish stock, having settled there in large numbers in the 17th century. The linen and shipbuilding industries were their creation. So was the Province's flourishing agriculture. There was, however, no real mixing of the races. The Scottish and English plantations kept apart from the native Irish and looked down on them.

The religious strife of the seventeenth century lent sectarian aggravation to racial discord. The Scots tended to a staunch, nay bigoted, Protestantism and shared the fear of the English that Charles I would use his Roman Catholic Irish subjects to subdue Protestant Britain and destroy the hard-won liberties. Fifty years later when William, Prince of Orange, defeated the Catholic Irish supporters of James II, Charles's son and a zealous Papist, at the Battle of the River Boyne, Protestant relief knew no bounds.

'Boyne Water' entered into popular legend. Bloodthirsty songs – 'We were up to our knees in Papist blood' – were sung to rousing melodies. The Orange Order was founded to perpetuate the 'glorious memory' of King Billy. Pictures of him astride a white horse adorned many an Ulster home. And the celebrations of the Victory of 1690 were held with increasing passion as the years passed. To such a degree that even the great Whig champion of the Orange King, Thomas Babington Macaulay, felt obliged to caution the fervent Orangemen of Ulster against overdoing the jubilation – 150 years after the event!

Needless to say, the Roman Catholics bitterly resented the taunts of their Protestant neighbours as they, the Protestants, marched in triumph on 12th July, the anniversary of the Boyne (a Bank Holiday in Northern Ireland) and again the following month when they exulted over the successful defence of Londonderry against James's besiegers.

Protestant children drank this heritage with their mother's milk. When, in the 1870s Gladstone started his campaign to give Home Rule to the whole of Ireland (which would secure perpetual domination by the Roman Catholic majority) Randolph Churchill, for the Tories, 'played the Orange card'.

Absolute, implacable opposition to Home Rule ('Home Rule means Rome Rule') was Ulster's answer or to be precise, the answer of the two-thirds Protestants of the six most populated counties of Ulster. The remaining one-third, the Catholics, were not consulted. By playing the Orange Card, Randolph Churchill secured the Ulster Protestant vote for the Tories for nigh on a century. Solidly working class constituencies regularly returned blue-blooded landowners because they stood for No Surrender to the Papists.

In 1914 Ulstermen under Edward Carson vowed to fight rather than be included in Mr Asquith's bill for all-Ireland Home Rule. Carson played on ancestral themes by asking men to sign a solemn Covenant – echoes of the anti-Papist Solemn League and Covenant that Scottish Presbyterians had signed 300 years before. Many Lowland Scots actually pledged themselves to fight with Ulster. Arms were smuggled in. The country stood on the brink of civil war – when the guns of August on the Continent put a temporary end to civil war in Ireland.

Yet although both communities gave generously of blood to the British cause, the Great War produced terrible symbols of divisiveness. In April 1916 the extremists seized the Dublin Post Office and proclaimed an Irish Republic. They were swiftly crushed, but the Easter Rebellion had entered Irish folklore. The Irish Republican Army was born. And when the British hanged the ringleaders, indifference among the bulk of the Southern Irish population turned into sullen hatred of England. 'The grass grows over the battlefield, never over the scaffold.'

Three months later the 36th Ulster Division, composed of Pals Battalions and all-Protestant, was decimated at the Battle of the Somme. So the legend grew that while Protestant Ulster shed the blood of her best for the Union flag and the cause of freedom on Flanders field, the treacherous Southern Irish took German gold and betrayed the Kingdom. The scores of thousands of Catholic boys who fought in the trenches had no part in this story. Symbolism thrives on simplicity.

When in 1918 the South returned a solid phalanx of extreme nationalists, Sinn Fein, to the Westminster Parliament, the Protestants of Ulster responded by sending a solid phalanx of Unionist members to Westminster. The battle lines were drawn and Ulster actually got her own Parliament a year before the South, the Irish Free State, got hers.

The more the Free State drifted away from Britain, which it did with increasing speed under Mr De Valera whose Fianne Fail party came to power in Dublin in 1932, the more firmly did Ulster cleave to the Union. Until in 1939, another climax was reached when Eire opted for neutrality in the war against Hitler.

In fact many Southern Irishmen fought with Britain (and the North was spared conscription). But, as always in Ireland, the prosaic facts were drowned in a welter of emotionalism. So furious was Ulster's resentment at De Valera's attitude that they nearly precipitated an invasion of the South in 1940 when German invasion, via Eire, seemed a real possibility. The terrible Orange drums beat out their message across the border, but Churchill held his hand and the danger passed.

Such were the memories the Northeners carried with them into the years of peace. These folk memories were Ulster's reason for existence. It was, argued the spokesman for the Province's million Protestants, the totality of differences with the Catholic South – historic, religious, racial – that meant there could never be a United Ireland.

The ruling caste in Northern Ireland did not, however, fully realise the depth of feeling among their voters. Men such as Terence O'Neill and Major Chichester-Clark, leaders of the Unionist Party and Prime Ministers of Northern Ireland in the sixties had far more in common with society in London and the rural pursuits of Southern landowners than with the gritty, hard-faced Orangemen of the North. O'Neill and Clark honestly believed that the ancient war cries and tribal loyalties had no place in the latter part of the twentieth century and could safely be ignored. As one Unionist chief told the *Express*: 'The Sash' (a Protestant song to a stirring melody,

eulogising the sash worn by The Orange Order) 'is as much part of
Ulster history as "Speed Bonnie Boat" (the Scottish Jacobite lament
for departing Bonnie Prince Charlie) is part of Scottish history. But
that is what it is: history. It should have no relevance today.'

He meant it had no part in modern life. And his view was wholly
shared by the politicians of Westminster and their senior civil
servants in Whitehall. It was inconceivable that in the swinging
sixties anyone could be motivated by events in 1690 or that anyone
would particularly care whether they were Catholic or Protestant,
Irish or British. Weren't the two more or less one at any rate?

The Dublin Government laid claim to the six counties. Their
Republican constitution embraced the North. They offered Irish
passports to Ulster and many Catholics there accepted them in
preference to the British. The UK government admitted Irish
citizens on the same basis as those from the Channel Islands and the
Isle of Man. The Irish had the right of domicile and the right to vote,
but were freed from obligations such as national service. Southern
Irish agriculture was actually supported by grants from the British
Treasury. The Irish labour force in England was not far short of that
in Ireland – half a million by 1963. In short, the Irish Republic was
granted a status unprecedented between sovereign states.

A feeling of guilt – allied to pragmatism – probably explained this
indulgent British attitude. It was a kind of 'making up' for the years
of exploitation, absentee landlordism and the Great Famine.
Anyway, as the Irish had been intermingled with Britain for eight
hundred years there was no point in creating artifical barriers just
because politicians in Dublin deemed themselves 'independent'.

A provision in the Government of Ireland Act, 1920, allowed for a
Council of Ireland to oversee and co-ordinate legislation passed by
the Parliament in Dublin and the Parliament (known as Stormont)
in Belfast. That provision had lain dormant. Now, in the 1960s, it
seemed possible that in the new climate of toleration it might
gradually, imperceptibly, come into use. It was just this possibility
which sparked off the Ulster revolt.

The booming voice of the Rev Ian Paisley was the authentic voice
of bedrock Ulster. Looking not unlike the great Edward Carson, the
founder of the State, Paisley articulated the fears of Ulster folk in the
apocalyptic language which captured attention and inflamed the
imagination. The priest-ridden South, condoned by effete aristoc-
rats in the North and flippant fools in London, was preparing the

take-over of Ulster. All that their forefathers had fought for was in jeopardy. The call to the colours – the Union Jack and the Orange heritage – produced a resolute response. Once again the battle cries of old rang out: 'No Surrender'. 'Ulster will fight and Ulster will be right.'

Reaction in London was to pillory Paisley as a latterday Titus Oates, a self-publicist doomed to an early return to obscurity, the sooner the better. Little did those commentators, steeped in the sophisticated frivolity of swinging London, realise that they were about to witness the rebirth of terrorism which would prove, for the umpteenth time, how thin was the crust of civilisation.

The IRA had lain dormant since the customs house war. It was split between one wing which advocated political advancement towards an all-Ireland Socialist Republic and those who urged a violent overthrow of the British presence in the North and ultimately of the tepid English appeasers in Dublin. The latter became known as the Provos, or Provisionals. They awaited their opportunity. It came in 1968.

Sectarian warfare in the back streets of Belfast had been growing since 1966 when the illegal Ulster Volunteer Force had started to pick off selected Republicans in the North. This provoked counter-measures, but it was the world-wide protest movement of the sixties which prompted the crisis.

Northern Ireland's half million Catholics had genuine grievances. In a Protestant province with a perpetual Unionist majority Catholic republicans were not likely to get preferential treatment. Nor did they. They alleged that they were passed over for employment in Protestant-owned concerns – notably Harland and Wolff shipbuilders – and did not get their fair allocation of council housing. They complained also about segregated schooling, although it was their own church which demanded that.

The Protestants replied that the Catholic minority had a higher unemployment because many of them didn't want to work. They enjoyed the British social service payments which explained why they didn't take themselves off to the Republic. These views may have been true, or partly true. But they were the equivalent of blasphemy in the England of the sixties, when all must be paid for existing and none must pay for their sins. The Unionist cause was, from a public relations stance, lost before it was launched.

So when the big protest rallies began in Ulster, demanding

'justice' for the Catholic minority, the weight of sympathy in mainland Britain was overwhelmingly on the side of the protestors and against the Unionists. The latter, fearful that the British Parliament would legislate to withdraw their privileges* and even abolish Stormont (which did eventually happen) over-reacted against the demonstrators. Scuffles turned into riots. Rampaging loyalists burst into Catholic Republican areas of Belfast and Londonderry and were themselves subject to counter-attack. To the media, concentrating on small segments of Belfast or Londonderry it seemed that civil strife was about to become civil war. Units of the British Army were despatched to restore order. The IRA's moment had come.

Terror, which Europe had not known, and that in restricted form, since the anarchist outbreaks of the 1880s and nineties was now about to be unleashed and was soon to have its imitation in Spain, Germany, Italy and France.

Yet as the first bombs were about to go off in Ulster, the communicating classes in Britain and America concentrated their attention on the 'youth revolution' in the shape of Miss Bernadette Devlin. Miss Devlin was 21. By winning the mid-Ulster by-election for the Irish Republicans she gained immediate international fame. Within 24 hours she was being hailed as 'Ireland's Joan of Arc'. The headline writers went ecstatic, especially as her arrival at Westminster coincided with an emergency debate in the Commons on the Ulster disturbances. 'Student Power comes to Westminster.' 'Bernadette's Triumph', proclaimed the caption writers.

Her speech was filled with bigotry and class war phrases. She had as much respect for the facts and accurate statistics as she did for the Unionist establishment. The then Ulster Premier, Chichester-Clark, described her address as 'pure nihilism'.

Ah, but she was a student (at Queen's University, Belfast). She was young. She was agin' the Government. She was a 'with it' girl of the tumultuous times. She had an impishly attractive appearance, modish views and Celtic patter. For television it was an invincible combination. The harsh and tragic realities of Ireland took a back place in face of personality politics: especially when the politics of the personality coincided with those of the programme-makers.

---

* Notable among them was a plural system of voting in local elections, heavily weighted in favour of property-owners and businessmen who might each have up to half-a-dozen votes. By this means local government was kept in the hands of 'responsible elements'; almost invariably Protestant.

To be a student in the sixties was bliss. To be a revolutionary student was very heaven.

Interviews and invitations to lecture poured in upon Bernadette Devlin. She was invited to write her life story. She appeared to be at one with the revolutionary students of Paris who, about the same time, were shaking the foundations of de Gaulle's Fifth Republic. And whose motto was, in the words of Daniel Cohn-Bendit, their leader: 'We are inventing a new world. Imagination in seizing power.'

What the media was doing was inventing a popular heroine, in the shape of Miss Bernadette Devlin. But it was not imagination, it was the gunmen, who were on the verge of seizing power in Ireland. The tragedy was that the media concentrated on the misdemeanours of moderate Unionists while ignoring infinitely more dangerous and sinister elements.

The presence of the British Army in the streets of Northern Ireland was the perfect target for the IRA, or the 'Provos' as they were sometimes called. It roused memories of 'The Troubles' of 1919-21. Here, again, was the brutal oppressor on Irish soil. The fact that the soldiers were protecting Irish Catholics was irrelevant. They were in Erin. Once the first British soldier was killed, the fearful narrative unfolded.

Northern Ireland became a 'media event': that is to say, television reporters and camera teams descended on the Province resolved to get a good story. Naturally they concentrated on the 'oppressed minority', the Roman Catholics. The articulate among them were those with a particularly strong sense of grievance. They sensed that the natural sympathy of the interviewer was with the under-dog and reacted accordingly. The IRA campaign was helped immeasurably by this media connection, for it enabled the Provos to operate at two levels: the terrorist one, designed to frighten 'the Brits' out of Northern Ireland and the propaganda one aimed at convincing the public on the mainland that the British connection with Northern Ireland was brutally wrong anyway. It was, as one IRA leader put it, 'The policy of the Armalite rifle and the ballot box'.

A community subject to sustained terrorism appears to go through different phases. First, disbelief that it is happening and that things will soon quieten down. Then resolve to restore order at the expense of civil liberties, followed by a desperate search for political remedy, then by a furious resolve to hit back, indiscriminately and finally resigned acceptance of violence as a feature of everyday life, with terror as simply one more element to add to mugging, rape, murder.

In the first half of the seventies, Ulster experienced each and every phase. The Special Powers Act was invoked to impose internment without trial of known subversives. As the British Army was the instrument of this policy – proposed by Stormont, endorsed by Westminster – it became the target for IRA attacks. In 1972, 103 British Army soldiers, plus 25 members of the Ulster Defence Regiment, were killed in Ulster; a further 578 were injured. Stung by the casualties the Army hit back, the forces killing thirteen IRA supporters on 'Bloody Sunday'. At which the IRA promptly hit the Paras HQ in England, inaugurating the programme of mainland bombing which reached a climax three years later in the bombing of a Birmingham pub.

Enraged by what they regarded as the supine indifference or active collaboration of the Southern Irish Government in the IRA bombing of the North, Ulster extremists launched their own bombing offensive in the South in 1974, killing 25 Eire citizens in one day. A strike of Protestant workers in Ulster also wrecked Westminster's planned power-sharing executive in Belfast, designed to remedy the Catholic minority's complaint that it was denied any share in government of the Province.

By the mid-seventies terror had a life of its own in Northern Ireland. It had no credible, or even definable political objective. A Border poll held in 1973 demonstrated an overwhelming majority for Ulster remaining part of the UK. It was estimated that at least 25 per cent of that majority was contributed by Roman Catholics. Which meant that three-quarters of the Northern Irish electorate was opposed to a United Ireland. How many in the Irish Republic favoured the forcible incorporation of Ulster in the Republic could not be established as no poll was ever conducted on these lines. But it became increasingly clear that the prospect of a million turbulent Protestants being absorbed into rural Eire filled the Dublin politicians with dreadful foreboding.

Conceivably the British Parliament might have terminated the Union unilaterally, but the prospect of an Irish civil war – certainly spreading into the South – was such as to deter any UK government from such a course.

So terror became terror for its own sake in Ireland and across the globe.

CHAPTER THIRTEEN

'Long Live Death'

Terrorism, as political action by other means, is as old as man. But in the modern world terrorism for its own sake, in the form of nihilism, dates from the Russia of the 1870s. The feeling of hopeless destructiveness which overcame the intelligentsia of Czarist Russia found expression in a campaign of murder, culminating in the assassination of Czar Alexander II. The nihilists were not concerned with innocent bystanders as they reckoned that lives were well lost to the cause of bringing down the social structure. Their own lives were forfeit and they weren't too worried about what came later as they were convinced it would have to be an improvement on the existing situation. Needless to say, they had no time for reform. Alexander II probably prompted his own death by freeing the serfs and taking the first steps towards constitutional government.

The Russian nihilists were totalitarians and the response they provoked was equally total: the imposition of a police state on the Russian nation; a model that was to be copied and refined when the Communists seized power in 1917.

Lenin used the nihilists. He didn't praise them. The difference between public reaction to the terrorists then and the reaction to them in the 1960s and 70s may be explained by what happened in World War II. In July 1941 the BBC reported, in tones normally accompanying a great Allied victory, that a senior German officer – he turned out to be a colonel – had been shot dead in the Paris underground. In retaliation, the Germans shot scores of hostages: and the British people thrilled at the brave defiance of the French. So was born the 'freedom fighter' and, shortly afterwards, the phrase: 'One man's freedom fighter is another man's terrorist.'

The shooting of the German colonel on the Paris underground was not the first such assassination in the Nazi-dominated Europe. There had been such killings in the streets of Warsaw well before that, but this murder was the first since Soviet Russia had entered the war and brought the powerful, well-organised French Communist movement into the war against Hitler. The Communists were proud of carrying the struggle against the oppressor into the streets and not at all concerned about reprisals: indeed they welcomed them as creating still greater hatred for and hostility to the Nazis.

Churchill himself had instructed the cloak-and-dagger brigade of the Special Operations Executive to 'set Europe ablaze'. So both Britain and Russia had a common aim and a joint interest in portraying the civilian killer as a hero or heroine. Those whom the Germans denounced as bandits, the Allies lauded as glorious members of the Resistance. At least the Resistance had a clear foe and an undoubted purpose: the removal of the Germans from the countries they occupied.

The Jews who gunned down British soldiers in Palestine had also a clear objective: getting rid of all who stood in the way of the creation of the State of Israel. Similar clarity prompted the EOKA terrorists (or freedom fighters) in Cyprus to take the lives of British servicemen, civilians and Turks in the sacred cause of uniting Cyprus with Greece.

Sometimes the objectives were achieved – Israel came into being – sometimes they were not. Cyprus did not join Greece and the Greeks lost one-third of their land to the Turks. Yet in all cases the romanticisation of the guerilla movements proceeded apace. For one thing there was the appeal of the underdog, struggling against military force. For another there was the attraction of the Robin Hood syndrome: swashbuckling outlaws audaciously turning the tables on the mighty.

Many journalists had a natural empathy for such movements, especially as the insurgents were naturally free with their information, for propaganda purposes, while the authorities were usually tight-lipped and much more concerned about security than public relations. So a considerable degree of media sympathy existed for guerilla fighters in the fifties and sixties and it stemmed, at bottom, from the belief that 'justice' was being denied to some group or other. Let that group become dominant – as the Jews did in Palestine for instance – and the sympathy evaporated and was promptly transferred to the new underdogs, the Arabs, who also became the terrorists.

Romanticism probably explains this attitude; a Byronic attachment to foes of authority mingled with a love for the idea of revolution. This heady mixture gave the terrorists of the latter part of the twentieth century a much more favourable press in the West than they could ever have imagined.

It was an aspect of the cultural revolution, Western style. The cultural revolution, Eastern style, was of course the model of terror for terror's sake. As a phenomenon of the Age of Change it deserves particular study.

Chairman Mao Tse-tung, 'Mad Mao' as he came to be known after his death, was bored and disillusioned. The Communist leader of close on 1,000 million Chinese had enjoyed undisputed power since his final victory over Chiang Kai Shek at the end of 1949. But by 1966 China had made disappointing progress. Communism had not changed human nature. The thoughts of Chairman Mao, diligently collected in a Red Book and distributed throughout the entire population, had not transformed the thoughts and actions of China's millions. Something really radical needed to be done. And on 20 March 1966 Mao did it. Prompted by his actress wife, the formidable and fiercely ambitious Chiang Ching, he conjured up State terrorism. Perhaps the masses could be moved or, at least the intellectuals could be stirred, through the rule of the worst.

'We need,' said Mao, 'determined people who are young, *have little education*, a firm attitude and political experience to take over the work . . . . When we started we were mere 23-year-old boys, while the rulers of that time were old and experienced. They had more learning – but we had more truth.' This was a clear invitation to the least cultured elements to wreak havoc on the community. Naturally – for in the latter half of the twentieth century, reality is described by its opposite – the process became known as the Cultural Revolution.

Victims of the Revolution were principally those who had learning and culture. They were described as 'scholar tyrants', fit subjects for punishment by millions of teenage Red Guards who were encouraged thus by Madame Ching, Mao's unworthy spouse: 'Chairman Mao often says there is no construction without destruction.' The inkwell revolution was under way. Gangs of youthful Red Guards drove professors, lecturers, teachers out of their classrooms and into the fields to do 'real work'. Neatly dressed young people were assaulted: girls with long-braided hair had it cut short; shops were ordered to stop selling cosmetics and finery. Libraries were ransacked, books burned.

School superintendents, even Communist Party leaders, who

attempted to curb these excesses were grabbed, hands tied behind their backs and paraded through the streets of Peking, Shanghai, Canton, etc with dunces' caps on their heads. Education of any kind ceased to exist. It had to, for the Red Guards were resolved to keep China 'pure' as so defined by the august resolution of the Chinese Communist Party's central committee, setting forth the aims of the Great Proletarian Cultural Revolution.

'The only method is for the masses to liberate themselves . . . let the masses *educate themselves*. Respect their initiative. Don't be afraid of disturbances.'

Meanwhile 'the masses' went a deal further than disturbances. Some 400,000 were estimated murdered during the madness. The Cultural Revolution dribbled to an end after two years. Mao, now in his dotage, appeared to have tired of it, especially as no new elemental force was released from China's huge, heaving womb. His successors estimated it had cost China ten years' development. Yet, incredibly, the Cultural Revolution found a welcoming echo in the West.

Aidan Crawley, author of the biography of General de Gaulle* reckoned that the extraordinary student uprising in Paris in 1968 stemmed directly from the example of the Chinese Cultural Revolution. However, in France '68 there was no terrorism, just vandalism: directed, as in China, against institutions and outlets redolent of the past, or of 'capitalist exploitation'.

Whether these attacks and the IRA's activities inspired the later, more deadly, outbreaks of revolutionary fervour in Germany and Italy is hard to say. The professional revolutionaries of the Baader-Meinhof Gang in West Germany and the Red Brigades in Italy may well have come into existence without examples from elsewhere. Danny Cohn-Bendit, leader of the revolting French students was an amateur compared with the hardened killers of Italian Premier Aldo Moro. Still, the ease with which millions of French workers and students could be galvanised into revolutionary activity must have been a source of inspiration to other like-minded nihilists.

In England there was a brief foray when the so-called 'Angry Brigade' terror-bombed the home of the Home Secretary, but the Angry Brigade could not compete with the IRA and it was left to extremist ideologies on the Continent to carry forward the Chinese way of death.

de Gaulle, Collins, 1969

These Western revolutionaries have been described as 'Hitler's Children'. In a sense they were: without the Second World War they would never have come into being and in their insensate love of destruction they certainly imitated the Fuehrer.

However, they could more accurately be described as the Children of Affluence. For never, surely, had a generation enjoyed the sweet things of life to anything like the degree of those who rose to adulthood in the sixties.

That it should have spawned such self-proclaimed gangsters would have seemed inconceivable to the generation reared in the depression-scarred, war-threatened thirties. It was an article of faith with progressive people in those days that, given full employment, a decent diet, good housing, education and, above all, peace any ordinary crime, never mind senseless destruction, would melt away.

After twenty years of peace, full employment, high wages and social services unparalleled in any other time in history, crime soared to epidemic proportions and some of the more articulate of the beneficiaries strove to wreck the very system which sustained them.

Clearly there must, said the progressives, be some explanation. It was sought in relativity. *Absolutely* the West European and North American populations were infinitely better off in the sixties than their parents had been in the thirties. But *relatively* there were 'obscene' differences inside western societies, between the wealthiest and the least well-off and, more particularly, between the industrially-advanced first world and the deprived, backward third world (the second comprising developing countries such as Turkey and Brazil).

So, once again, we get the equality syndrome at work. Baffled observers were apt to ask how the Third World could be helped by wrecking the First. They were apt to be answered, if answered at all, that only by shattering the old and fashioning anew could the affluent West be made aware of the inequalities and injustices it had created by colonialism, capitalism, consumerism.

To bolster this case – which was widely held by perfectly pacific folk who had no intention of procuring a revolution – a liberation theology appeared which gave philosophic, quasi-religious justification for flaying the guilty West and, at the ultimate point, for liberation-through-terror.

Faith and Liberation

No one plotted this course. But, from the early sixties onwards, there was a gathering movement that the church should become 'more relevant' to society and its problems. From the first faltering steps of Anglican modernists to full-blooded Latin American Catholic Liberation Theology represents a giant step for theology, but a small step in time. A mere thirteen years separated the appearance of the Anglican book *Honest to God* in England from the appearance of Roman Catholic priests in the Marxist revolutionary army of Sandanistas in Nicaragua.

Dr John Robinson, Bishop of Woolwich, he who had testified in favour of the publication of D. H. Lawrence's *Lady Chatterley's Lover* published *Honest to God* in 1962.* He stated his position straightaway: 'I feel it is right to rebel . . . most of my sympathies are on the humanists' side.'

He went on to say that:

Jesus is the man for others, the one in whom Love has completely taken over . . . Because Christ was utterly and completely the man for others, because he *was* love, he was one with the Father, because God is love.

That the 'others' are social outcasts of whom Jesus is the champion is given emphasis by another passage.

The test of worship is how far it makes us more sensitive to the Christ in the hungry, the naked, the homeless and the prisoner. Only if we are *more likely* to recognise him there after attending an act of worship is that worship Christian rather than a piece of religiosity in Christian dress.

Conventional prayer [went on the Doctor] on a rule book basis

* Reproduced by permission of the publishers, SCM Press.

is meaningless. Man today is no longer content to be under tutors. The fact that the old (moral) standards are disappearing is not something to be deplored. If we have the courage it is something to be welcomed as a challenge to Christian ethics to shake itself loose from the support of supra-naturalistic legalism.

The basic commitment to Christ may have been in the past buttressed by many lesser commitments – a particular myth of the Incarnation, a particular code of morals, a particular pattern of religion. We must beware of clinging to the buttress instead of to Christ. And still more must we beware of the buttress as the way to Christ.

What Dr Robinson's eloquent expression of the New Morality did was to buttress the already powerful lay arguments in favour of No Morality. That is certainly not what Dr Robinson intended, but it is what happened all the same.

Gradually over the following decade the Robinson approach to Christianity was adopted by more and more vicars, reversing the pattern of the early fifties.

In those far-off days the appeal of the Christian message was its very simplicity and spirituality, complete with 'myths' of Virgin birth, resurrection and the life everlasting. As late as 1954 the American evangelist, Dr Billy Graham, was able to pack Hampden Park, Glasgow with 100,000 congregation for fundamentalist, old-time bible-thumping religion. And he was able to repeat the success the following year at Wembley Stadium, London.

The evangelical approach persisted (and went from strength to strength in the USA) but increasingly the established Church of England allied itself with contemporary radicalism. In 1965 the Archbishop of Canterbury, Dr Michael Ramsay, endorsed the use of force to bring the whites in Rhodesia to a proper understanding of the New Morality of one man, one vote – once.

The pace-setters of the Anglican Church were resolved that the Church must not become a 'mossy fortress, defending an outworn faith with outdated intellectual weapons,' as one vicar told the *Daily Express*. The magazine *Prism*, which reflected the attitude of the radicals, commented: 'There are many men today who find traditional religion completely meaningless . . . we have reached a moment in history when these things are being said openly and there is an almost audible gasp of relief.'

There was also a noticeable decline in Church attendances. By the mid-seventies the average Sunday congregation had so shrunk that fewer than 2 million people were going to C of E churches in England: a mere 4 per cent of the population.

Those who were adamant that the Church had to be socially aware were not disturbed by this decline. Better a few zealous stalwarts than a large number of tepid waverers. Was not the early church small in numbers – persecuted and derided?

So, increasingly, Anglican leaders pointed to the beams in Western eyes – opulence, competitiveness, lack of compassion – while highlighting the nobility of the Third World (carefully avoiding the motes of the military dictatorships and one-party states of Africa and Asia). Jesus's concern for the outcast, the failures, the poor, was stressed almost to the point of disregarding His 'other world'. Christianity chimed with sociology and, at its most extreme, with outright rebellion – so long as the rebellion was directed against the West, specifically the USA. The priests who actually took part in attacking the Somoza regime in Nicaragua in the seventies unquestionably sought to right the injustices suffered by the peasants. But that they did it to clear the way for a Marxist regime is, to say the least, surprising.

Unsurprisingly, the liberal theologians, while well-publicised, remained a tiny if significant minority in the Roman Catholic church. For, unlike the Anglicans, the Church of Rome refused to move with the times if it felt the times were out of joint. Thus Pope Paul VI turned his back on progressive thought by issuing in September 1966 his encyclical on oral contraception which said, in essence:

> If the Church were to sanction artificial methods of birth control a wide and easy road would be opened to conjugal infidelity and the general lowering of morality.
>
> If the mission of generating life is not to be exposed to the arbitrary will of men, one must necessarily recognise insurmountable limits to the possibility of man's domination over his own body and its functions, a limit which no man, whether a private individual or one vested with authority may licitly surpass . . .
>
> And such limits cannot be determined otherwise than by respect due to the integrity of the human organism and its functions.

Abstention from intercourse during the wife's fertile period while allowing intercourse during the infertile period makes legitimate use of a material disposition. Artificial regulation impedes the development of natural processes . . .

No solution to overpopulation is acceptable which does violence to man's essential dignity and is based on an utterly degraded conception of man himself and his life.

Now to say that the Pope's argument was regarded by critics as specious is an understatement. First what did a celibate Pope know about sexual impulses and the over-riding need to satisfy them? Who was this obscuritanist priest to order his flock to ignore the fruits of scientific advance and cling to primitive methods of birth control? Did he believe Catholics practised birth control by restraint? Was it not positively criminal to condone anything which would add unnecessarily to the numbers inhabiting the globe and consequently to human misery? A hurricane of denunciation struck the Vatican. Not for a century had the division between Rome and the forces of libertarianism been so marked.

Pope Paul's reactionary conservatism was contrasted with the liberal relaxation of his predecessor, the jovial, avuncular, John XXIII. As Western society moved towards abortion on demand it seemed to the champions of permissiveness not merely wayward, but positively wicked, of the Pope to stand in the path of progress.

The radical element in the Catholic Church itself parted company with the Vatican hierarchy, adopting a libertarian stance not only on contraception and abortion but on celibacy. The moral divide became a political one too when revolutionary Catholicism – painting Jesus as a first-century egalitarian zealot – developed in Latin America. These people reached out to and embraced Marxist revolutionaries and did not shrink from the exercise of terror, proclaiming it as an extension of the 'just war' endorsed by theologians for centuries.

Yet Paul VI had set a lodestar for the traditional conservative authority of the Church. His Humanae Vitae encyclical, standing foursquare against sexual permissiveness, provided a rallying point which, later in the century, was to lead to a return to authority under Pope John Paul II.

Christianity retreated rapidly in Western Europe (though it strengthened in Communist-controlled Eastern Europe where it was persecuted) during the third quarter of the twentieth century. The fall in Anglican membership has been cited. The Jesuits declined from 36,000 to 27,000 during the sixties and seventies and the number of students and novices slumped from 16,000 to 3,000.

In contrast, Islam flourished and with it, the cutting edge of fundamentalism represented by the recrudescence of the assassins: the Moslem fanatics sent out to despatch Christians at the time of the Crusades.

In the Middle East, as nowhere else, was demonstrated in the period 1950–1975 the retreat of the West.

CHAPTER FOURTEEN

Faith and the Sword

Monarchy held sway over almost all of the Middle East at the start of the second half of the twentieth century. The fat, heavy-lidded Farouk reigned over Egypt. His neighbour, Libya, was ruled by the ageing King Idris of the Senussi. Morocco and Tunisia were run by France through traditional rulers, caliphs, beys, sultans (Algeria was a department of Metropolitan France). The Sudan was under the dual control of Britain and Egypt. Iraq was a kingdom. So was Jordan and both were under the decisive influence of Britain, as they had been when they were delivered to the British Empire as League of Nations mandated territories after World War I. Iran was an independent monarchy ruled by its young Shah, Reza Pahlevi. The little sheikdoms on the Persian Gulf were British protectorates. The great Saud family, with King Ibn Saud at its head, ruled Saudi Arabia. On the verges of Middle East, Emperor Haile Selassie held Ethiopia, and Afghanistan too was a kingdom. Syria and Lebanon departed from the Anglo-French monarchial pattern. They were independent republics, but recently parted from their French protector – largely at the wartime instigation of the British who were not averse to a reduction in French influence. And introducing an entirely new note was the Jewish State of Israel, self-reliant by virtue of the zeal of its million-strong Jewish population, but military and economically heavily dependent on the USA.

Within the space of twenty years the Middle East picture was to be altered out of all recognition with the withdrawal of British and French power and the hopes of the Americans that they would replace the Europeans largely frustrated.

American ambitions in the area were exposed very early in the period. A Persian fanatic, Mohammed Mossadeq, rose to power in Iran at the start of the fifties. He focussed his countrymen's discontent with their lot on the Anglo-Iranian Oil company. This was the jewel in the British oil crown. Mossadeq demanded the nationalisation of the company and the seizure of the huge refinery at

Abadan. The Shah was powerless to oppose this plan for that would have demonstrated his subservience to the British. The UK Government of Mr Attlee looked for support to the USA. They looked in vain. The prospect of displacing Britain as the premier influence in Iran – or, at the very least, sharing in the oil revenues – was far too alluring for any display of Anglo-American solidarity.

As the Attlee government was on its last legs – it was to lose office in October 1951 and the crisis had arisen in the August of that year – there was small temptation for Britain to go-it-alone. Indeed Labour propaganda harped on the folly and danger of Churchill's prescription of military intervention to preserve Abadan. The US (already enmeshed in Korea) had absolutely no intention of doing other than waiting to see how matters progressed. So Mossadeq got his way and the first stone was dislodged in the Middle East structure.

Mossadeq was unwilling to be content with one triumph. Now Prime Minister, he sought the total exclusion of the West from his country's affairs. He sought to reduce the Shah to a puppet, or even get rid of him altogether and to these two ends he drew closer and closer to the Great Bear of the North – Russia.

This was not at all to America's liking. In Washington, the Democratic Truman administration had been replaced by the Republican Eisenhower with John Foster Dulles in charge of US foreign policy. Dulles was a perfervid anti-Communist (he also had small use for the British). Iran was a perfect place in which to try out the new, dynamic American foreign policy.

The Shah's supporters – notably General Zahedi of the Army command – collaborated with the CIA to encompass the downfall of Mossadeq and succeeded in accomplishing this in 1953. The Shah, who had conveniently absented himself during the Army's *coup d'état*, returned in triumph and showed himself suitably grateful to his benefactors. The British, who had approved of the coup, did not lose out completely. They shared in the new oil company established to replace Anglo-Iranian. But it was plain that the Americans intended to extend their activities far beyond Israel, which was virtually a client state and Saudi Arabia where the US oil firm, Aramco, exercised great influence.

While the Iranian crisis was coming to the boil, Egypt had undergone a transformation. King Farouk carried everything, not just his weight, to excess. He gambled to excess. He spent money to excess. He enjoyed women to excess. For an individual, it might have been a good way to go. For a monarch in the Middle East in the middle era of the twentieth century it was a sure-fire way of ensuring he *would* go.

Farouk was toppled by a revolt of his young officers. He went quietly into exile, taking his yacht and his valuables with him. In his place there briefly reigned General Neguib, a bluff soldier cast in the Sandhurst mould. Within months he was shouldered aside by Colonel Gamal Abdul Nasser, who became dictator of Egypt, ruling until his death in 1970.

Nasser was the new-style revolutionary, ever ready to utter Marxist slogans, harangue the mob from a convenient balcony, stage popular demonstrations, launch vast schemes for the welfare of 'the people' – which diverted resources from the mundane task of feeding multitudes – and clamouring all the while for more aid: to be extorted from the West by threatening to accept it from the Russians.

Nasser had an endearing frankness. In Press interviews he explained that he was getting back for Egypt what had been taken from her by the colonialist exploiters. This in essence was his message:

> My country is poor. The rich nations – and that means principally US, Britain and France (Germany and Japan did not qualify as such in the mid-fifties) must help us. It is in their own interest to do so. For we cannot trade with them unless we have the means to do so. We cannot buy their goods unless we have dollars, pounds and francs. If we do not get aid from the West we will turn to the East. So politically, as well as economically, it will pay you in the West to do my bidding.

In so far as the three Western powers were bonded together as target for diplomatic blackmail they might be thought to have common interests which would prompt common action. In fact, there were deep differences.

France was eager to topple Nasser because he was backing the Algerian rebels who were conducting a ferocious war against the French 'colons', the settlers who, a million-strong, effectively controlled Algeria and ensured that she remained tied to Metropolitan France.

Britain, under her new Premier Anthony Eden, was unsure what she wanted. As Foreign Secretary, Eden had negotiated the British troop withdrawal from the Canal Zone. Under its terms, the Zone could be militarily reactivated in event of an emergency in the Middle East. The agreement was to run for seven years and would be implemented at Egypt's request, or at least with her agreement. This strange understanding provided Britain with a face-saver for her evacuation from Egypt after 70 years. It also personified Anthony Eden's duality and irresolution.

Eden looked the part of the perfect English gentleman. He had been a brilliant Arab scholar (which helped explain his conviction that he was, par excellence, the man to deal with the Middle East), he was associated in the public mind with resistance to the dictators in the thirties – hence his rejection of appeasement – and he was being criticised at home for not being a strong enough Prime Minister.

All three motives impelled him towards a decisive Middle East policy, but their contradictions prevented its realisation. Eden did not like the Americans. He suspected them – quite correctly – of wanting to replace Britain as the primary power in the Middle East. They had achieved as much in Iran. They were the provider, financier and champion of Israel. They exerted paramountcy in Lebanon. Eden wanted to pursue an independent foreign policy and so he invited the Soviet leaders, Khrushchev and Bulganin, to visit London to explain British policy. His invitation did not please the US Secretary of State, John Foster Dulles. Dulles did not like Eden – the feeling was mutual – and did not approve of the junior partner having conversations with the Soviets. Dulles also reckoned that Eden was too friendly by half with Moscow.

So there was no commonality of design among the three Western powers when matters came to head in the summer of '56.

Nasser contracted to buy arms from Czechoslovakia – as much to demonstrate his independence, as need for still more weapons. In retaliation the US cancelled its promised contribution towards financing Egypt's projected High Aswan Dam. In retaliation for *that* Nasser nationalised the Suez Canal.

Suez was an international waterway governed by a convention of 1888. It was an anachronism by 1956. It could not take ships of more than 50,000 tons. It was a residue of Egypt's subjection to Western dominance. Nasser was simply exercising sovereignty and he promised compensation to the shareholders. All of which was quite

true. But it did not alter the fact that Nasser's *cumulative* actions –
fomenting anti-Western agitation, continually threatening war with
Israel (and illegally blockading Israeli ships) and finally nuzzling up
to the Soviets by purchasing arms from Moscow's satellite – could
only be interpreted as destructive of Western influence.

What to do? The simplest course would have been to let Israel
decide matters. As the target for Nasser's hate she had good cause to
strike at the hand that held the dagger. But could Israel win on her
own? And if the Jews attacked Egypt would not other Arab states –
notably the pro-British monarchies of Jordan and Iraq – feel obliged
to come to Egypt's aid?

These genuine reservations led to Eden temporising. The moment
for a quick, surgical, strike passed. Finally, after much secret
comings and goings between, British, French and Israeli leaders and
their military advisers a scheme was concocted which assured the
worst of all possible worlds. Completed at Sèvres on 24 October it
provided for an Israeli offensive beginning on 29 October. This
would give Britain and France the opportunity to re-occupy the Suez
Canal Zone – and hopefully bring Nasser down. In appearance the
British and French would be acting as policemen separating two
belligerents whose fracas might endanger world peace. In reality – as
the Suez Canal was deep in Egyptian territory – the Anglo-French
action looked uncommonly like the police taking the side of the
burglar.

The final appalling blunder was to keep the entire project secret
from America and to launch it one week before the US Presidential
election. Eisenhower was furious. He ordered the US Treasury to
sell sterling. A financial crisis was added to other burdens borne by
Eden and his distracted Cabinet.

Success, of course, justifies everything. It was not forthcoming, or
anyway not in sufficient degree. The RAF 'took out' the Egyptian air
force with clinical precision. The Israelis advanced on schedule and
stopped where they had secretly agreed to stop, ten miles short of the
Canal. But the British Army was desperately slow in getting ashore
and got bogged down in Port Said. The swift occupation of the whole
Canal Zone was not achieved. In addition, the Egyptians had sunk
ships in the Canal which denied it to the world's trading nations.

To complete the picture, global attention was diverted from the
sight of Russia bludgeoning the Hungarian revolutionaries to
Britain and France bludgeoning Egypt.

Within a week of starting Operation Suez the British Cabinet buckled under international pressure – even the Russians joined in, threatening to rain rockets on London – and brought the venture to a halt.

Pierre Mendès-France, the French politician, succinctly remarked that 'the two strongest powers, Russia and America, had prevailed over the two less strong, France and the UK'. He was right. But the consequences of Suez were far wider than the assertion of the stronger over the weaker.

The second stone in the Middle East edifice had been dislodged. British influence in Egypt had ceased to exist. It had not, however, been replaced by American. Nor by Russian. But by Nasserism, a de-stabilising agent which sent spasm after spasm through the Middle East. Within eighteen months of Suez the monarchy in Iraq was swept away, the King, Faisal II, and his veteran Prime Minister, Nuri es Said, murdered. In place of this conservative administration a revolutionary movement under General Kassem was established. Kassem himself was soon overthrown – and murdered – but Iraq had become not only unstable in itself but a source of de-stabilisation to others. The third stone had been dislodged.

At this, the Americans took fright. For the first time American forces became directly involved in the Middle East when US marines landed on Beirut beach. British paratroops moved into Jordan. Now the Americans, who had been residuary beneficiaries in Iran and Egypt of the dislike visited on the British and French, became objects of hate.

America's position in the Middle East was flawed by her passionate partisanship for Israel. This could be explained by any number of reasons: the financial and political clout of the Jewish community in the USA, the largest in the world, including Israel; the natural sympathy for a small nation struggling to stay free; admiration for the democratic nature of Israel, the only democracy in the area. America was regarded by the radical Arab leaders as Israel's protector and, as such, became the focus for rising fury.

In contrast, as Britain adopted a lower profile British intervention – notably in Kuwait in 1960 to bolster Kuwaiti independence against a threat from Iraq and in Oman in 1971 when Communist rebels menaced this Persian Gulf sheikdom – proved acceptable and effective.

But even if the US had been totally free of partiality and had conducted her diplomacy with maximum tact and her military operations with impeccable competence, she could have done little to secure peace and the relaxation of tension in the Middle East. The area was splintering into feuds which had been suppressed during the long centuries of Ottoman domination and barely controlled during the brief decades of British Imperialism.

These bloody rivalries had little to do with ideology. Syria and Iraq had socialist regimes and were at each other's throats. The animosities were sometimes religious (Shia Moslems versus Sunni); more often tribal. King Hussein of the Hashemite Kingdom of Jordan was the target for frequent assassination attempts in the fifties and sixties, conceived and directed by his Arab neighbours who had long hated the Hashemite family.

And always, of course, was the problem of Palestine and the millions of Palestinian refugees demanding the return of the land which the Israelis had 'stolen'. The Arabs only came together in common rage at Israel. Like the Black African countries with South Africa, Israel was the common object of hatred and the sole unifying factor. The Arabs had tried to crush the Jewish State at infancy and failed. The Israelis had fought a successful campaign against Egypt in '56. Sooner or later the Arabs would try again, or the Israelis would pre-empt them. In the event it was the latter case.

In six days in the summer of '67 the Israelis took the Sinai peninsula from Egypt and stationed themselves on the Suez Canal, captured Jerusalem from the Jordanians and fought off the Syrians and Iraquis. Short of nuclear war, Israel was safe for generations. But within the Arab states and between them tension and bitterness mounted.

Before Nasser died, in 1970, his successor as agent of instability had appeared next door in Libya. Colonel Muammar Gadaffi led a group of young officers in the overthrow of King Idris to whom the British had given the Libyan throne after the expulsion of the Italians during World War II. Thus another stone of stabilty was wrenched from the Middle East structure. Gadaffi, to a still greater degree than Nasser, was committed to the destruction of Israel, revolution among the conservative Arab states and the advancement by terror of a fundamentalist Islamic code mingled with ascetic socialism. Antipathy to the West was an absolute requirement of Gadaffi's faith. And, four years after his accession to power, the opportunity of damaging the West was presented.

In 1973 the Egyptian Army attacked the Israeli positions on the

Suez Canal – the so-called Barlev Line – and broke through. The fourth Arab-Israeli war, known as the Yom Kippur war from the holy day of Jewish atonement on which it was launched, was under way. The war ended in stalemate, but it provided the Arab countries with an excuse to squeeze the West through first an oil embargo and then a five, later ten-fold, increase in the price of oil.

With startling rapidity Western trade and industry went into dramatic decline. Cheap oil – 2½ dollars a gallon from the Middle East – had helped fuel the extraordinary prosperity of the 30-year boom. Now that the tap had been turned off, industrial production fell. So did the Stock Market. In the UK and the US share prices between October 1973 and January 1975, slumped by two-thirds. Trade declined. The British balance of trade deficit rose to £2 billion. Unemployment rose inexorably.

The West was taught that its prosperous life-style was vulnerable (although North Sea and other alternative sources of oil supply tended to redress the balance) to the awful vagaries of the Middle East which more and more resembled the pre-1914 Balkans in its capacity to disturb the balance of power.

This terrible instability was shown at its most tragic in Cyprus and Lebanon in the last eighteen months of the period covered by this volume. These two territories had been centres of stability until 1955. In that year Greek irredentists led by Colonel Grivas (that rank appears to convey Messianic qualities) and supported by Archbishop Makarios, the island's spiritual leader, began a campaign of violence, murder and intimidation to force the British to quit and permit Enosis, the union of Greece with Cyprus.

The Greek Cypriots argued, quite legitimately, that the British role in Cyprus – to demonstrate a supportive nineteenth century presence for the Ottoman empire against the designs of Czarist Russia – had no relevance in the latter half of the twentieth century. The British replied that military bases were required to curb Soviet ambitions in the eastern Mediterranean and, more importantly, that to hand Cyprus to Greece would enrage the Turkish minority (nearly a quarter of the population) and provoke an invasion from the Turkish mainland, forty miles away.

After four years of bitter guerrilla warfare and inter-communal strife, a settlement was reached which secured Britain her sovereign air bases and gave the Greeks self-government in the bulk of the island and the Turks protection in the mainly Turkish enclaves of the

North. Enosis was ruled out. Makarios accepted the solution because he was to be the new President of Cyprus. A power-seeking prelate, attuned to the Byzantine intrigues of the Orthodox Church, he concluded that office was worth the sacrifice of principle.

Not so the Greek intransigents. Grivas had left them with the inheritance of no-surrender guerrilla warfare. The challenge was taken up by Nicco Sampson, a young firebrand. Encouraged by the Greek Colonels (there's that rank again!) who had seized power in mainland Greece, Sampson and his zealots tried to seize Makarios and proclaim Enosis. They failed. Makarios was rescued by the British and spirited out of the island. And, just as the British had prophesied, the Turks, provoked beyond endurance, moved in and occupied one-third of Cyprus, creating a de facto Turkish Cypriot Republic and another centre of disturbance in the eastern Mediterranean. Yet another stone had fallen from the Middle East edifice.

In that same year, 1974, a greater tragedy began to emerge in nearby Lebanon. This small country had been well-named the Switzerland of the Middle East. French-ruled for 28 years, it bore the hallmarks of its patron in the sophisticated life-style of its capital, Beirut, the svelte fashions, the elegant casino, the food and, above all, the French language. The Swiss element was just as important: Beirut was the banking capital of the Middle East, its most advanced tourist centre and the Lebanese had a penchant for neutrality which even the Swiss might have envied.

Although officially allied with the other Arab states in the crusade against Israel, the Lebanese Army was usually to be observed going in the opposite direction to the battlefield when fighting actually broke out. During times of tension the Lebanese maintained a bland 'business as usual' attitude which evoked the admiration of tourists and fierce resentment from partisans. The Commodore Hotel, for instance, proudly flew a large number of what one assumed were national flags. Only they bore no resemblance to known ensigns. So this author asked the manager why he flew them. 'Ah, sir,' replied the manager, 'by flying them we get the advantage of being seen as an international hotel without inviting any embarrassing consequences.' Such was Beirut before the holocaust.

Lebanon owed its distinctive flavour and near-democracy to a remarkable compromise. The Christians, known as Maronites, after their extreme devotion to the Virgin Mary, held the Presidency and the moderate Moslems held the Premiership. The Christians were in the minority but their commercial acumen and large land-owning gave them influence far exceeding their numbers and for the good of all. This was recognised by the Moslem ruling class, though not necessarily by the fundamentalist Shia Moslem minority or by the Druze mountain folk.

Still, with a population of less than 3 million and an area of only 6,000 square miles, it was recognised by every reasonable Lebanese that the country could maintain its stability and prosperity only by sustaining the compromise and practising political restraint. The Christian invitation to the Americans to come in to Lebanon in 1958 strained the dual control mechanism. But it was the Palestine refugees who brought it tumbling down.

Following the six-day war in 1967 refugees poured into Jordan and under the prompting of the Palestine Liberation Organisation tried to overthrow King Hussein and the Hashemite dynasty. Hussein hit back and scattered the Palestinian radicals who promptly fled to Lebanon in 1972. There they made contact with the anti-Western Shia Moslems and together they turned on the Christian-dominated Lebanese government. In 1975 civil war broke out with Syria lending support to the Moslem rebels in order to increase her own influence over Lebanon and possibly to absorb the small state in Greater Syria. Soon the war degenerated into a ghastly jigsaw of factional terrorism which tore the heart out of Beirut and reduced the country to a shambles. Forty thousand died in the first stage of the civil war and Lebanon, once the envy of less-favoured lands, descended into twentieth century barbarism. Another stone had been fatally dislodged.

Now Cyprus and the Middle East had one thing in common. As the Western powers withdrew their control – and exposed the area to the violent hatreds which outsiders had kept at bay – the United Nations had moved in to impose a new world order in place of the old. In Cyprus, UN forces had been interposed between Greek and Turkish areas from the 1960s and had taken up positions in the Israel-Egypt-Syria zone in the late fifties. Yet in both places they proved totally unable to prevent invasions and seizures of territory.

Perhaps few other events so illustrate the way things changed and the way dreams and hopes were blighted than the strange, lingering death of the United Nations Organisation.

CHAPTER SIXTEEN

. . . . Paved with Good Intentions

When the period covered by this volume began the United Nations seemed to many to be working extraordinarily well. A UN Army had gone into the field to aid South Korea push back invaders from Communist North Korea. Here surely was collective action to punish aggression: the prime aim of a world organisation established to implement a world order.

The appearance was an illusion. The UN in 1950–53 (the period of the Korean War) was very much under the influence of the United States. For one thing, the Americans were the paymasters, meeting more than 20 per cent of the organisation's costs: in practice, a good deal more as most of the Latin-American countries were in default of their subscriptions. For another, the UN's headquarters were in New York and the delegates were subject to the American way of life: a thoroughly exhilarating experience, for those whose countries still suffered from rationing, poverty, despair and other post-war melancholies. Above all, the United Nations Organisation at this period was overwhelmingly white, Euro-Atlanticist orientated and, excepting the Soviet bloc and neutralist India, shared similar aims and was unitedly resolved to resist Communist aggression. The UN Army in Korea was closer to NATO than to a true world force and, like NATO, it was American led and largely equipped by the USA.

The whole concept of the UN was, of course, an American design: one of President Franklin Roosevelt's most favoured projects, as its predecessor, the League of Nations, was President Woodrow Wilson's. It conformed to a deeply-held American instinct for universal, simplistic solutions.

Having opted out of the League in 1920 in favour of isolationism, the US felt a degree of guilt which could only be assuaged by instituting a new 'force for good'. As this happened to chime with the arrival of America at the summit of world power it followed that the new organisation should reflect American ideals and, if possible, serve American interests.

At its inception it was not envisaged that the UN would be in conflict with one of the major victor states of World War II, Soviet Russia. Rather the UN enshrined the woolly notion that collective security would ensure global peace. Such collective security would be more than alliances. It would be nothing less than a universal court of justice embodying the general will and prompting nations to act as one against any who offended against the law.

The notion was manifestly absurd and all history contradicted it. For why should an act of force by state 'A' against state 'B' prompt 'C' to come to the aid of 'B'. C might well rejoice at B's discomfiture. It is a sad but undeniable fact of life – not just of diplomacy – that 'my enemy's enemy is my friend'.

Indeed it could be said that the mirage of collective security in the pre-war years of the League of Nations diverted Britain and France from the real task of deterring Nazi Germany. That the concept of collective security actually promoted international insecurity.

In truth the UN could only really operate as the instrument of one nation's will. And that is precisely what happened in June 1950 when North Korea invaded the South. At that very moment the Soviet Union was boycotting the UN Security Council (the policy-making body on which any of the five permanent members, Russia, the US, UK, France and Nationalist China could exercise a veto) in protest against the then Secretary General Trygve Lie. The Russians, not being present, could not veto the American proposal that the UN should furnish such assistance to the Republic of Korea (the anti-Communist South) as might be necessary to repulse the armed attack and restore peace and security in the area. The *Daily Express* reported on the same day, 28 June, that both President Truman and his Republican opponent John Foster Dulles were at one in this resolve to resist aggression. 'To sit by,' they said, 'while South Korea is overrun by unprovoked armed attacks would probably start a disastrous chain of events leading most probably to world war.' Memories of British appeasement of Hitler and the fatal consequences were still immensely strong.

America's allies immediately fell in behind the US and sent troops to support the South. Their numbers were far smaller than those despatched by the US, 40,000 against 350,000, and the casualties suffered were in proportion of 2 to 100, but it *was* an international army. It *did* respond to a resolution of the UN Security Council. It *could* be construed as the first act of the global policeman, especially when the General Assembly (one nation, one vote) endorsed the action and so set the seal of world wide approval. Actually, the uniting-for-peace resolution by the General Assembly was an American ploy to frustrate the Soviet veto in the Security Council following the return of the Soviet delegate, Jacob Malik. It was to cause America much pain and grief in later years when the US itself was subjected to censure from that same body.

In the fifties that lay some way ahead. The UN was still, in the words of Adlai Stevenson, a US Presidential candidate, 'the world's last bright hope'.

Then, in 1956, the USA moved from a NATO-like stance to one of outright hostility to its oldest allies, Britain and France. The cause of the rupture was the Anglo-French-Israel attack on Egypt. The instrument for chastising the Europeans was the UN. Four hours before the Anglo-French ultimatum to Nasser to withdraw his forces from the Suez Canal expired, the UN Security Council, at America's prompting, voted 7 – 1 against the two powers and Israel. Arkady Soldatov, the Soviet delegate, congratulated Henry Cabot Lodge, the US representative: 'The initiative of the US is much to be applauded.'

Anyone wondering why the US should have swung round so completely as to win the wholehearted backing of the Soviet Union for opposing Britain and France got the answer from Mr Richard Nixon, American Vice-President. Speaking at an election meeting on November 2 he declared:

In the past, the nations of Asia and Africa have always felt we would, when the pressure was on, side with the policies of the British and French governments in relation to the once-Colonial areas.

For the first time in history we have shown independence of Anglo-French policies towards Asia and Africa which seemed to us to reflect the Colonial tradition. That declaration of independence has had an electrifying effect throughout the world.

To hammer home Mr Nixon's message, the US arraigned Britain, France and Israel before the General Assembly, where the Anglo-French veto did not operate. The mechanism the Americans had used against Russia was now applied against Britain and France. By a vote of 64–5 they were ordered to halt their forces. They

complied. President Eisenhower congratulated them for succumb-
ing gracefully 'to world opinion'. He did not mention that he had
reinforced world opinion by telling the US Treasury to sell sterling
and so provoking a financial crisis to add to the troubles of Anthony
Eden's divided Cabinet.

On 10 November 1956 came the final humiliation for London
and Paris. The General Assembly voted 63–5 in ordering the
Anglo-French forces to evacuate the Canal Zone and make way for a
6,000-strong UN Emergency Force. When Israel demurred at
quitting the Sinai peninsula which she had conquered, the US
threatened to move her expulsion from the UN. Israel capitulated.

Speaking a few weeks after these events Mr Nixon exulted:

A new force has come into being, the moral force of the United
Nations which pledges all nations to settle their differences
peacefully. Our stand was direct and simple. We denounced the
use of force not sanctioned by self-defence or United Nations
mandate. The United Nations has been saved and the rule of law
upheld.

Many in Britain applauded Mr Nixon's words. Hugh Gaitskell, the
leader of the Labour Party, observed: 'It is not our job . . . to decide
for ourselves, but to accept the decisions of the United Nations.' The
Liberal *News Chronicle* welcomed the UN Emergency Force as 'the
first contingent of the international police force to implement
international morality.' The police force was paid by the USA and
the morality it served was US interests. It was to sustain this role that
America adjusted her policy.

For what the Americans could see on the horizon was a host of
African countries joining the Asian ex-colonies to create a United
Nations wholly different from the one established in 1946.

In September 1956 they were informed that Britain intended
granting independence to Ghana the following March. Significantly,
John Foster Dulles, the US Secretary of State, on hearing the news
promptly abandoned the Anglo-French Suez Canal Users Association – of which he had been the founder. He and Mr Nixon and
President Eisenhower could see the shape of things to come.

And come they did. One after another newly independent African
states joined the UN until the balance was wholly altered and the
Afro-Asian group far outnumbered the old Euro-Atlanticist alliance.

On the way to that 'happy consummation' – the words were those of Kwame Nkrumah, the self-styled Messiah of Ghana (overthrown by a coup in 1967) – the UN made its supreme effort to become the flaming sword of internationalism.

The occasion was the collapse of law and order in the Congo (later Zaire) when granted independence by Belgium in July 1960. The man who master-minded UNO's effort to command the international stage was a pale, cold-eyed Swede, Dag Hammarskjold. Hammarskjold had succeeded Trygvie Lie as Secretary General of the UN as part of the continuing tradition that Scandinavians were naturally neutral. But whereas Lie was 'neutral' in the sense that he didn't mind who stopped the Russians, Hammarskjold was determined on positive neutrality, on interposing the Third World countries of Asia and Africa between Russia and America and doing it at the expense of the retreating colonial powers.

The US was still in its phase of glad-handing the black and brown newcomers when the Congo received its premature 'freedom'. As organised government there collapsed the UN Security Council – Britain and France abstaining – decreed that the Organisation should 'provide such military assistance as may be necessary until . . . the national (Congolese) security forces may be able to fulfill fully their tasks.'

This was an invitation to UNO to intervene in a civil war, in defiance of its own charter. Hammarskjold seized on the resolution as an opportunity to use the Congo as a laboratory experiment in international intervention. At Suez his role had been to discharge the decisions of the General Assembly, which he had done with exultant spleen, denouncing the Anglo-French action while pointedly ignoring the Soviet invasion of Hungary which occurred at the same time. Now, in the Congo, he had the chance to turn what he termed his 'international priesthood' of UN civil servants into the arbiters of world politics.

Dag Hammarskjold was the ideal High Priest. He was celibate; or, anyway, he was a bachelor, who had once rejected a girl because she did not understand T.S. Eliot. He was the intellectual enthroned. He read poetry in his few leisure moments. He had a 'room of stillness' at UN HQ where, along with a slab of Swedish iron ore and a Beskow abstract, he could be alone 'to feel the sky and the earth and hear the voice that speaks within us'. This Joan of Arc-like utterance did not refer to the Voice of God, but to the voice of conscience. His conscience told him that the future lay with the 2,000 million people of the Third World. This required the denuding of Western influence. Hammarskjold welcomed the prospect. He had no affinity with the West, although tactically he had to keep in with the Americans. After all,' he remarked once, 'we cannot do without them.' He never forgot who paid the piper. Yet he had effectively distanced himself from his Western origins. He described himself as a Sputnik that had taken off from Sweden but was now no closer to one country than another and he expected his staff to be equally denationalised.

Article 100 of the UN Charter stated:

> In the performance of their duties the Secretary General and the staff shall not seek or receive instructions from any Government or from authority external to the Organisation. They shall refrain from any action which might reflect on their position as international officials responsible only to the Organisation.

Further, the UN Preparatory Commission laid down that: 'Loyalty to the Organisation . . . involves a broad international outlook and a detachment from national prejudices and narrow national interests.'

As the controlling Power, the US had made one derogation from these international rules. In 1953, shortly before Hammarskjold became Secretary General, the US Government, at the prompting of Senator McCarthy, had dismissed US officials of the UN suspected of Communist sympathies. That apart, Hammarskjold, the political eunuch, had a staff of political eunuchs to carry out the new morality of UNO. This was to erase the injustice of centuries and usher in the rule of numbers – the up-coming 100 Afro-Asian states who would provide a permanent majority. The day of the underdog was about to dawn.

To force the rebellious Katangese under Moise Tshombe to accept the Congolese Central Administration, Hammarskjold himself led two companies of Swedish UN troops across the border into Katanga. Behind him were thousands more UN soldiers: Ghanaians, Moroccans, Ethiopians. On 20 July 1960 Hammarskjold proudly declared: 'The UN has embarked on its single biggest effort under UN colours, organised and directed by the UN itself.' This vainglorious boast provoked Andrei Gromyko, the Soviet Foreign Minister, to describe Hammarskjold as 'this Field Marshal'.

It was not too much of an exaggeration. By the summer of 1961 the UN Army numbered 17,000, one-quarter of them supplied by India (whose forces had just invaded Goa, without a whisper of protest from the UN).

The UN troops were deployed against Katanga; that is to say they became embroiled in a civil war and succeeded only in extending the chaos they were supposed to prevent. Not only that, they were beaten by the Katangese. The 'Field Marshal' decided to intervene personally and try to persuade Moise Tshombe, the Katangese leader, to stop fighting. Hammarskjold flew off to Ndola to meet Tshombe. His plane crashed and the Secretary General was killed. So was the UN's ambition to be the midwife of the New Order.

The Congo operation masked a decisive change in the powers' attitude to UNO.

In the year Hammarskjold died, sixteen new African states joined the Organisation. The Russians decided it was verging on the ludicrous. Indeed to make sure it paralysed itself, Nikita Khrushchev, the Soviet Premier, suggested there should be *three* Secretary-Generals – one for the West, one for the Communist World and one for the neutrals! The British, still smarting from the UN punishment of their Suez escapade, went into action. Lord Home, the Foreign Secretary, censured UNO for condoning India's aggression on Goa.

In a speech at Berwick in December 1961 he commented:

When we have reached a stage when a large part of the Organisation dedicated to peace openly condones aggression, when an Organisation founded to sustain law and order encourages politics which must endanger it . . . this can mean the beginning of the end of the United Nations.

Five weeks later Premier Harold Macmillan voiced still graver doubts:

UNO is based on the principle of national sovereignty. But one nation, one vote, does not correspond to the power position in the world. Some of the greatest powers, such as China, are not even members.

(Communist China was excluded from UNO at American insistence because Chinese 'volunteers' had fought against the UN army in Korea. 'China' was represented by the nationalist remnant in Taiwan.)*

> I am told, [Macmillan went on] that you can get a two-thirds majority from member nations who pay 5½ per cent of the budget. I do not say that votes should go in proportion to contributions, but there is a certain unreality about what is happening.
>
> At the end of 1961, 52 countries out of 104 have not paid their contributions for that year. Six have not paid for two years . . . Here indeed is power without responsibility.

He also remarked that some governments had given their representatives at UNO permanent instructions to abstain. He might have added a piquant note. The speech of a Latin American delegate was found annotated with the marginal observation: 'Weak point – shout.'!

Disillusionment and condemnation could hardly be clearer than this British reaction. The French went further. President de Gaulle referred to the UN as 'that thing' and refused to pay France's share of the Congo episode's cost. Moreover, by moulding the European Economic Community into an Association of the Fatherlands he established a significant power bloc outside the UN.

Much more significant was the Cuban crisis of 1962. It had the same significance as Sherlock Holmes's dog that didn't bark. The UN was ostentatiously ignored when the USA and the USSR clashed over the siting of nuclear missiles in Castro's Cuba. The deal whereby Russia removed the missiles in exchange for an American promise not to invade Cuba was arranged directly between President Kennedy and Mr Khrushchev. The UN Security Council was not consulted. And when the US wanted to verify that the rockets were in fact being removed, she turned to the Red Cross. Russia agreed that observers from that organisation should be used. Castro acquiesced. This particular procedure was not carried out because the US finally decided on aerial verification, but the point was that both the Soviet Union and America preferred the Red Cross to the UN.

From that moment onwards more and more the UN was ignored in international negotiations.

* Communist China was admitted in 1973, replacing Taiwan as a permanent member of the Security Council.

For the United States, nemesis at UNO was not long delayed. Having bested the Soviets at Korea, the French and British at Suez and having successfully excluded Communist China, the US herself fell victim to the new clamorous Afro-Asian majority she had helped to bring about and tried so hard to appease.

In the sixties it became increasingly obvious that the UN was a forum for blackmail. The example set by Colonel Nasser, 'if you Americans don't give me money I will go to the Russians', was followed by the newly-emergent African states. What annoyed the Americans, who appreciated that the ex-colonies were perfectly entitled to play one side off against the other, was that these states did not stay bought once they'd got the money. And as the number of nations at UNO practically trebled – from 51 to 144 – between 1945 and 1975 (with another 20 or so in the wings), the Americans swiftly saw that the scope for blackmail was boundless.

More than 100 billion dollars was disbursed in aid from the West to the underdeveloped lands between 1955 and 1975. The likelihood is that most of the money was wasted by vainglorious leaders desperate to set up airlines, build plush hotels and create industries at the expense of agriculture. The peoples of these countries did not benefit to anything like the extent they should have done from the beneficence showered on their leaders. But that was hardly America's fault.

What the citizens of the US saw was ingratitude on a massive scale. The more America gave the more she was denounced by the recipients. As the US became more and more involved in Vietnam, the chorus of denunciation at the UN reached deafening proportions. In addition, America's child in the Middle East, Israel, became the target for a crusade of hate.

The Jews, the most persecuted people on earth, were themselves accused of 'racism' at the United Nations. Humpty Dumpty, 'when I use a word it means what I want it to mean', would have been at home there. In March 1975 a committee of the UN, exactly mirroring the composition of the General Assembly, condemned Israel as 'racist' by 76 votes to 29 with 27 abstentions. When the General Assembly ratified the vote, the US ambassador to the UN spat out his country's rage: 'The United States,' he declared, 'does not acknowledge, will not abide by and will never acquiesce in this infamous act.'

In nineteen years the US had come a long way from Mr Richard

Nixon's proud declaration that 'a new force had come into being, the moral force of the United Nations'.

That General Assembly vote, itself a culmination of a decade of anti-American anti-Israel polemics at UNO, marked the Americans' final disillusionment at the instrument they had inspired and fashioned for the better ordering of the world. The monster had turned against its creator. And Americans who, in 1946, had rejoiced at the prospect of UNO being established in New York, now began petitioning their Congressmen for the organisation's removal, preferably to Tashkent or Timbuctoo. The practice of UN delegations using their diplomatic immunity to ignore anything from parking tickets to rape charges roused still more resentment as did the size of the delegations which were often ludicrously out of proportion to the importance, or wealth, of the nations sending them. In the Soviet Union's case, the delegates also included a fair number of KGB agents.

But as the USA turned away from, and against, UNO the West was forced to face the fact that the great majority of states in the world were poor, undemocratic, unstable and liable to plunge into fratricidal wars, or wars with their neighbours, or dreadful famines.

The UN, which was supposed to be the light of the world in 1950, was manifestly the light that failed by 1975. The 'have-not' nations had remained basically that, despite the aid lavished upon them. The UN, far from benefiting them, actually aggravated the tendencies which left them poor, small and vain. Money channelled into industry and weapons starved agriculture of the resources it needed. Much of this finance came from UN agencies and encouraged the governments of the new states to fund schemes that diverted manpower and cash from farming –thereby cancelling out the major scientific and technical advances in land fertility.

The UN, by providing a place for every country – marching towards the 200 mark – reduced the appeal of federation in the recently de-colonised states. The hopes of the British Colonial Office for such developments in the West Indies, Central Africa, East Africa and the Middle and Far East were thus frustrated. Of course the desire to strut the world stage at UNO was not the main reason for the failure of federations (not at all in the case of Malaya and Singapore) but it was a contributory cause, certainly in the case of the micro-states in the West Indies.

Indulging vanity was the chief 'benefit' UNO conferred on the leaders of the emerging nations and in doing so, in giving them a high profile which they would otherwise never have possessed, UNO did them – and the larger nations which they plagued – a grave disservice. In the words of Shakespeare's Coriolanus:

> Your dishonour mangles true judgment. –
> Not having the power to do the good it would
> For the ill which doth control it.

By one of the extraordinary paradoxes that so etched the period, the nations excluded from UNO – and, indeed, the very nations which the original United Nations had done their utmost to destroy – demonstrated a capacity for poise, civic virtues and economic success which earned the admiration and envy of the world. Germany and Japan demonstrated in the years from 1950 to 1975 how defeat could be turned into victory and how the prophets of doom could be confounded.

CHAPTER SEVENTEEN

Victory from Defeat

When Harold Macmillan viewed the destruction wrought in Europe by World War II he vowed that if he were a young man his only doubt would be to which other continent he would emigrate.

At the heart of Europe lay Germany: devastated, divided and despairing; her population at near-starvation level; ninety per cent of her industry destroyed or severely damaged; 70 per cent of her homes smashed. No nation in history had suffered such physical carnage as Germany. Many in Britain thought no country deserved it more. Twice in the short space of twenty years the Germans had plunged Europe into war. She should, said her foes, be castrated: industrially, financially and militarily.

This policy of insensate revenge did not survive the end of the war. The British are bad haters. But even if it had it could not have been implemented because, with the onset of the Cold War, the Western democracies needed a prosperous, contented and allied West Germany. Would they get it? In 1950 it was still anybody's guess.

Germany was split down the middle with a 1650 kilometre 'inter-zonal border' of barbed wire, stick grenades, mines, trenches and watch-towers separating the imprisoned people of East Germany from their compatriots in the West.

Could Germany recover with nearly half her pre-war territory torn from her? Would her people in the West be tempted to seek re-unification by embracing an alliance with Russia as the price demanded? Could German industry, even with the billions of dollars of American aid, be rebuilt to compete successfully in the second half of the twentieth century? And, the most haunting question of all, would the terrifying fanaticism of the Teuton break out again – would Germany start World War III?

This last loomed largest in public opinion in the UK. In the years from 1950–1955 the topic of resurgent Germany was a constant theme of letters to the *Daily Express* – usually from ex-Servicemen (and their wives) of two world wars. This response unquestionably prompted Lord Beaverbrook, the *Express* proprietor, to indulge in a furious campaign, in his newspapers, by public meetings and poster propaganda, opposing West Germany's rearmament and integration into NATO. The prospect of Germans in uniform sent a thrill of horror down the spines not only of the British but of the peoples in countries which had experienced Nazi occupation. How could the Germans be trusted? How could they change their spots?

The very triumph of West German industry lent weight to these latent fears. For the recovery of West Germany, made manifest by Coronation Year, 1953, demonstrated what a formidable people the Germans were. How long before they turned their remarkable talents and demonic energies to recovering their 'lost lands'? How could those dedicated zealots of the Hitler Youth and Nazi SS Divisions who, outnumbered, had often outfought the Allies in 1944 and '45 even as the Third Reich was collapsing around them, possibly become good democrats and trustworthy allies?

The possibility seemed absurd. For twelve years the Nazi regime had moulded every facet of German life. The young had been indoctrinated from infancy with the belief in race superiority, the total supremacy of the state over the individual, the virtues of ruthlessness and strength ('strong as Krupp steel' and 'heart of iron' were two of Adolf Hitler's favourite aphorisms) and a conception of the leadership principle which left no room for family, or any other non-State relationship.

Fanaticism was bred in the bone. How could such people be turned into democrats? Deep doubts and unease afflicted British and US politicians and commentators as late as 1952.

True, West Germany – consisting of the three Western Zones of the former Third Reich – had achieved an astonishing economic revival. Under the aged Dr Konrad Adenauer, *'Der Alte'* and his Economics Minister Dr Ludwig Erhardt, the social market system had worked brilliantly. Briefly, this gave full rein to the laws of supply and demand. Controls and regulations created by Nazi policies, wartime shortages and Allied demands were swept away. Without rationing and building and manufacturing licences there could be no black market, which flourished only when people were prevented from doing what they would do naturally. 'If there is a demand, someone will supply it,' was the Erhardt philosophy. Hand in hand with that free market doctrine went protection of the currency.

Twice in a lifetime the Germans had suffered rampant

unendurable inflation: after the First World War and immediately after the Second. Never again! So when Erhardt replaced a near valueless currency with the new Deutschmark, confidence was regained. Work was to be Germany's salvation. The work ethic replaced State worship as the motivating force in the Federal Republic. The *Wirtschaftswunder*, the economic miracle was under way.

It was helped to a considerable degree by Marshall Aid, named after the US Secretary of State which paid for the replacement of ruined factories. But without the will to work, money alone would have been useless – as the recipients of Western aid in other countries had shown.

Then West Germany also benefited from other circumstances which would not, at the time, have counted as assets. Germany's industry had been virtually destroyed. She could, and did, rebuild with the best of new machinery. There was no obsolescent tail, as with the British, to hinder economic growth.

Hitler had destroyed the German trade unions. He had replaced them with the single *Arbeitsfront*. That, in turn, had been dismantled by the Allies. So the slate was clean. A British trade union delegation, including Victor Feather who was later to preside over the Trades Union Congress, drew up a charter for union reform which was to give Germany a labour system infinitely better than that 'enjoyed' by the British. Sixteen industry-wide unions were created, so there could be no demarcation disputes between craft unions in the same industry. Binding arbitration and the outlawing of political strikes completed the scenario for industrial peace and productivity. German discipline did the rest.

Most 'disruptive elements' had either been physically liquidated by the Nazis or had long since fled: some to Moscow where they were also liquidated if they failed to conform to Stalin's version of Communism. Thus the Federal Republic was not faced with wreckers.

Most valuable of all – though heavily disguised as an asset at all – was the army of refugees from the east. Some eight million Germans fled the Soviet occupation of their country and to that total was added millions more compulsorily displaced by Czechs and Poles. These people arrived in Western Germany with nothing but the resolve to make something. They proved to be the organisers of economic victory.

For the refugees were, in the main, the fittest, the most skilled, the most ambitious and largely Prussian. They provided the Federal Republic with a formidable professional, entrepreneurial and managerial class.

The combination of a well-organised, if docile, work force and a driving resolve to build from nothing (1945 was known in Germany as Year Zero) proved irresistible. By 1955 West German output exceeded that of the whole Reich in the mid-thirties. By 1965 Germany, in terms of gold and foreign currency reserves, was, per head, the richest country in the world. By 1975 the £ and the dollar had fallen to one-third of the value against the Deutschmark they had enjoyed in 1950.

It was a dazzling accomplishment and unimaginable a quarter of a century earlier. Yet still more astounding was West Germany's conversion to democracy.

Konrad Adenauer, devout Roman Catholic, family man, political realist and sceptic, had much to do with this. The constitution which he outlined to the occupying forces laid stress on the old estates of Germany: Rineland, Westphalia, Schleswig-Holstein, and so on. By giving them their own assemblies, the Federal Republic would counter-balance power at the centre, in Bonn. The electoral system was a sound compromise between simple majority, single-member constituencies and proportional representation. Half the Federal members were elected on the first method and half on the second, with the proviso that no party obtaining less than five per cent of the total vote would be represented under the proportional system. The memory of the inter-war years of the unstable Weimar Republic with its multi-party intrigues was too vivid to risk excessive democracy.

Even so, Adenauer and his Christian Democrat Party were in power with the narrowest of margins and dependent on the support of other more extreme Right-wing parties. The Bundestag, the Parliament, seemed very fragile. Weimar too had had its constitution, a model of its time. Germany had enjoyed economic prosperity in the twenties. Then had come the world-wide depression, bitter political infighting – and Hitler. Could not the same happen again?

When unemployment grew to 1,000,000 plus in the Federal Republic pessimists prophesied doom. They were confounded. Germany stayed stable. Adenauer and his party were re-elected again and again. Gradually it was borne in upon the public of the

Western nations that Germany or, more exactly, West Germany, had undergone a sea change.

This was no temporary derogation from the heel-clicking Prussian militarism of Bismarck or the Fuehrer-worshipping adulation of the Nazis. It was a real conversion. Or a return to an older, more virtuous, Germany.

Certainly Adenauer personified the Germany of family, honour, enterprise and personal honesty. His Socialist opponents came to adopt his own philosophy and to differ with the Christian Democrats on matters of degree, not substance. So, when it came about that in 1969 the Socialist opposition won office, there was no change in Germany's basic programme of responsible free enterprise and total loyalty to the Western Alliance. The German Federal Republic had become a respected and envied pillar of the Western world; welcomed back into the comity of civilised nations. Once only during this period did the old fears surface: when, as part of European defence against Russia, German rearmament was proposed in 1954.

Straightaway Beaverbrook's *Express* warned the British of the danger of putting the Germans back in uniform. 'Don't Let the Wehrmacht March Again', sang the headlines.

Readers, and a wider public through posters, were reminded of what had happened before when the Germans had rearmed. As the *Express* campaign chimed with Soviet anxiety – real or simulated – on the same subject, a broad coalition was formed to oppose the German defence posture.

Strangely the Germans, though slipping into uniforms as to the manner born, refused to be militaristic. They did their National Service conscientiously enough. They invented ˙ some excellent weapons of war, but the armed services held no glamour or temptation for Hitler's children, those who had been born and bred in the *Hitler Jugend*, the *Arbeitsdienst*, the Party, and who had fought with such stunning courage and bloody ruthlessness, although mere teenagers, in the dying days of the war.

The Beaverbrook campaign, which would have come alight had the Germans demonstrated their Teutonic bloodlust, sputtered out. The German Miracle was as total as it was unexpected. And it was part of a European transformation in which the other two defeated Continental states, France and Italy, played decisive roles. Two of their post-war leaders, Alcide de Gasperi of Italy and Maurice Schumann of France represented, with Adenauer, the resurgence of

Christian democracy and the ideal of the European concert. All three built on the ruins of the past.

Poor, distracted France which fell in six weeks to the German invader in 1940 was, like the Weimar Republic, a victim of excessive, lunatic democracy where every little party was represented in the Chamber and each blackmailed the other for the fruits of office.

Defeat and German occupation changed that. The Third Republic of *Liberté, Egalité, Fraternité* (and stupidité) was replaced with the regime of Marshal Pétain devoted to *Famille, Patrie, Travail*. For all its brutality and corruption, the Vichy government introduced reality and reform to France and although General de Gaulle had his band of devoted followers, Vichy and Pétain were widely supported in France. The French collaborated heartily with Hitler's New Order and many able French technocrats, notably Industry Minister Bichelonne, a friend of Nazi Production Minister Speer, advanced to positions of influence. French agriculture was modernised and the system of parcelling the land into smaller and smaller proportions to accommodate the peasantry's numerous male offspring was altered to yield sensible consolidation in favour of the oldest: incidentally freeing great numbers of peasants for France's belated industrial revolution.

In that sense Vichy acted as a clearing ground for France's regeneration. The political system did not keep pace with the economic until in 1958 de Gaulle became President of the Fifth Republic which, like Adenauer's constitution, gave France stability. Before that Schumann (a perennial Foreign Minister) and Adenauer had, in 1950, concocted the European Coal and Steel Authority, predecessor of the European Economic Community, the Common Market.

In this venture they were joined by Italian Premier Alcide de Gasperi, who had fought off the Communist threat and, with the help of American money and Frank Sinatra's voice – he campaigned for the Italian Christian Democrats – won the vital election which halted the Red tide in Europe.

Neither France nor Italy, however, enjoyed the political stability conferred on West Germany by her constitution. Huge Communist parties (the French one had 6,000,000 voters, 900,000 party members and its own farming advisory service) threatened their fragile parliamentary systems.

A stronger outer wrapping, a political-economic equivalent to the

North Atlantic Treaty Organisation, was required to bind the menaced countries of Western Europe together. The Christian Democrat parties favouring such a union were in power in all three countries and so began the preparation for the European dimension to the Atlantic Alliance: the European Economic Community.

The thinking behind its erection was that instead of a grandiose union imposed from the top, the nations of Western Europe should grow together organically through mutuality of interests. The Franco-German coal and steel community provided a useful test ground.

In 1957 the treaty establishing the EEC was signed in Rome. It laid down the objective of creating a common market in trade between the Six (Holland, Belgium and Luxembourg having joined France, Germany and Italy) by the progressive abolition of tariff barriers and the erection of a common tariff against the rest of the world. Free trade in Western Europe in industrial goods was to be matched by a carefully constructed form of protection and subsidy for farming. Thus when agricultural prices fell below a certain level – to be decided regularly by the six Farming Ministers – the mechanism of intervention would be triggered and the offending surplus of grain or meat or wine would be put into store thereby stabilising prices at a higher level. This led, in time, to the creation of grain mountains and wine lakes but that was considered a fair price to pay for assuring the peasantry reasonable prosperity and winning their support.

The structure of the EEC lodged ultimate power with the Council of Ministers – usually foreign ministers or their deputies – meeting regularly in Brussels, but also, frequently, finance or agriculture or environmental ministers depending on the topics requiring agreement. They were supported by a commission of civil servants. Voting in the Council, and on the Commission, was weighted according to national populations with a heavy bias in favour of the small states.

A European Parliament initially with nominated, later with directly-elected members, to add some democratic flavour and a European Court to adjudicate on commercial disputes between companies and the Commission completed the picture.

The EEC was not a supra-national State (though a number of European Federalists, notably M. Schumann, wanted it to become one). When Charles de Gaulle became President of France – and gave France a new, fifth Republic and a constitution that ensured parliamentary stability and presidential authority – the 'Europe of the Fatherlands' definitely ousted the federalist concept. The single veto was sustained, whereby one nation could refuse to accept a Community direction if its national interest was threatened, and a halt was called to amalgamation.

The late fifties and sixties saw a fantastic increase in European prosperity. France adopted economic reforms comparable to those inaugurated by Erhardt in Germany. Inflation was ruthlessly curbed by Jacques Rueff, an economic technocrat who imposed the discipline of the free market on his country. Production leaped upwards, sometimes by nine per cent a year. On every front – exports, housing (the French housing stock rose by 40 per cent between 1950 and 1975), cars, farming output – France surged ahead until she was almost up to Germany's wealth-creation. Italy too advanced, though hindered by a political system which still echoed the anarchic liberalism of a previous era.

The Western Europe of 1975 was unrecognisable to the shattered Continent of 1950. As Britain floundered searching for the formula of economic growth, the six member states leaped ahead. In 1950 UK national wealth per head was, at $940, nearly double that of the population of the Six. Twenty-five years later the average in the Six, at nearly $3,000, was higher than that of the UK. In cars, Britain was far outstripped by France, Germany and the Low Countries. Only in television sets and telephones per household did the UK keep the lead.

It was assumed that the transformation in Western Europe's fortunes arose from the foundation of the Common Market. Actually this was not true, as all three major economies – particularly the German – had bounded ahead well before the Market was established. Nor was it true that the historic enmity between France and Germany had been buried by the two countries' new-found amity in the European comity. Peace between France and truncated Germany owed far more to fear of the Russians and the guardianship of America than to the EEC.

Nonetheless the fact of Europe's resurgence, contrasted with Britain's relative failure, induced many in the UK to believe that membership of the Common Market would produce the most beneficial effects in Britain. 'It would', said Harold Macmillan, then Prime Minister, 'act like a cold shower on the British economy.' The

Express sourly commented that people 'often caught pneumonia from taking cold showers'.

For Britain, membership of the Community represented a tremendous shift in attitudes and policy. In 1951 Winston Churchill had talked of a united Europe, but he excluded Britain from the infra-structure, stoutly maintaining that if England had to choose between the Continental land mass and the blue sea she would always choose the blue sea.

Moreover, since the economic crisis and subsequent slump of 1930, Britain had rebuilt her prosperity by following a policy of Imperial (later Commonwealth) preference; i.e. admitting Commonwealth food and raw materials free of tax to the UK and exporting British manufactures to these territories which were admitted at preferential rates of duty. In addition the Commonwealth territories, less Canada, traded in sterling. British agriculture was protected by a system of subsidies and deficiency payments so as to secure a prosperous home farming industry while continuing to supply the public with cheap food. Entry into Europe meant the complete overthrow of this system.

Events, however, were forcing the pace as the Empire vanished and trade increasingly was directed towards Europe: 10 per cent in 1950, 40 per cent in 1970. So in 1960, Britain applied to join the Common Market. Express Newspapers conducted a brilliant campaign against the move, ably assisted by President de Gaulle who disliked Anglo-American interference, feared the dilution of the European-ness of the Market if Britain came in and was able to veto the UK's proposed membership because Britain demanded special terms to accommodate Commonwealth interests. While paying lip service to the value of Britain as a partner Dr Adenauer, the German Chancellor, was delighted at the UK's exclusion. He didn't like England either (the British occupation forces had expelled him from the Mayoralty of Cologne) and he suspected the British of wanting to do a deal with Russia.

By 1971 both de Gaulle and Adenauer had departed the scene. The British, under Premier Edward Heath, had shed the Commonwealth entanglement and the French and Germans, under President Georges Pompidou and Chancellor Willy Brandt, were much more eager to embrace Britain lest it become not the Trojan Horse for America as de Gaulle had feared, but the stalking horse for the Japanese.

For the other astonishing triumph of the post-war world was the rise and rise of that other island kingdom: Nippon.

Hatred of the Japanese had been greater than that for Nazi Germany. The Germans, on the whole, treated British and American war prisoners fairly well. The Japanese regarded prisoners as failed soldiers, as cowards who had forfeited the right to be treated as a valorous foe. So they were starved, beaten, worked to death. The Red Cross had no place in the Japanese scheme of things so food parcels rarely arrived for POWs. Relatives did not know if their loved ones lived or died.

The Japanese method of waging war emphasised the difference between East and West. The Nipponese hardly ever surrendered, no matter how hopeless their position and they had a tendency to butcher small groups of enemy soldiers who attempted to parley or surrender.

Japanese fanaticism reached a peak of self-sacrifice as the war entered its final phase. Having achieved total air and sea supremacy, the Americans still had to sacrifice 12,500 dead in taking Okinawa in 1945. The Japanese losses were an incredible 180,000 dead.

Not even the Hitler Youth or the SS could rise to the heights – or fall to the depths – of Japanese fanaticism. Kamikaze, suicide pilots, dived their bomber planes on to Allied warships. There was fierce competition to man these death planes and the pilots proudly sported the white scarf signifying the divine wind which would, as it had before, save Japan from foreign invasion.

When the atomic bomb was unleashed on Japan there was much satisfaction in the West. It was widely accepted that the Japanese had richly deserved the punishment visited upon them. It seemed inconceivable that these devoted servants of the Emperor, these Oriental zealots who welcomed death could ever be readmitted to the ranks of the civilised.

Once again, as with Germany, the prophets of doom were confounded. First, Japan found a man who believed in wedding tradition and freedom – US General Douglas MacArthur. He ruled Japan as a benevolent despot between 1945 and 1950. He saw to it that Japan enjoyed a constitution bearing a striking resemblance to that adopted by Federal Germany. Then Japan too got a domestic politician, Yoshida Shigeru, to match Germany's Konrad Adenauer in conservative guile and purposefulness.

Emperor Hirohito remained as Japan's sovereign, though shorn of his 'divine' power, and the Japanese adopted Western-style democracy to suit their own brand of belief in the strength of the family and the authority of age. Thus their governing party (and it never ceased to govern since the day it was established) bore a title custom-made for the West: the Liberal Democratic Party. It was, in fact, profoundly conservative.

So with the hierarchy in place, a strong pro-consul to bring Japan into the second half of the twentieth century and a political system which ensured stability with economic opportunity, Japan entered upon a period of expansion to astonish the world.

Between 1950 and 1975 Japanese industrial production rose by 10 per cent a year. The number of cars rose one hundredfold. Japanese shipbuilders reigned supreme. Japanese transistors, radios and watches conquered markets everywhere. The same happened with motor cycles, sweeping away European competition with contemptuous ease. Calculators, computers and all things electronic followed. Herman Kahn, the American futureologist, had forecast that Japan would become the premier industrial power in the world. By the mid-1970s his prophecy was coming close to reality.

Yet Japan should have been the classic case of a nation needing help from the West. Her densely populated islands lacked raw materials. The major excuse for her imperial adventures before 1945 had been to ensure raw material supplies. Now, shorn of her empire, she ought to have experienced extreme privation. Instead she enjoyed immense expansion.

The Japanese miracle may have many explanations, but the prime one was surely the sense of discipline pervading the whole population. Family loyalty was simply and comfortably transmitted to company loyalty. Japanese workers and managements never thought of *not* producing the best at the most competitive prices. That priceless asset was built in to the character of the people. Free enterprise gave it the chance to ensure Japanese dominance on a global scale.

Most of Japanese enterprises – 95 per cent – were small concerns, but they furnished the parts for huge conglomerates which had the most sophisticated world marketing systems and enjoyed the closest business relations with the banks, furnishing long-term finance at reasonable interest rates. This mechanism helped, of course, to attain growth, but it was the combination of family loyalty, self-discipline, hard work, enterprise and pride which truly gave

Japan her enviable record.

Even the quintupling of oil prices in 1974 could not stem the Japanese advance.

Although wholly dependent on imported oil, Japan absorbed the price rise with scarcely a tremor.

By 1975 the defeated ones of World War II could look with a certain smugness at the victors. The US and UK were running slack and fitful economies and rising deficits and demonstrating political ineptitude of a quite awesome degree which had led to the resignation of both the President and Vice-President (a unique event) in the US, and the virtual abdication of government by Parliament to the trade unions in the UK. The Soviet economy was failing to produce even the necessities of life in sufficient quantity to meet public need and was forced to buy supplies of food and manufactures from abroad.

In 25 years the world had been turned upside down and the question was no longer the exultant 'Who won the war?' but the doleful 'Why did we win the war?' The British experience provided an object lesson in the failure of nerve and sinew, discipline and enterprise.

CHAPTER EIGHTEEN

A Tale of Turpitude

'Ah, gentlemen,' Winston Churchill remarked in 1952 (in the author's hearing) 'we Tories must never again be suspected of being anti-union.' The remark betrayed the Conservative Premier's desperate anxiety not to be thought anti-union or anti-working class. Churchill was neither, but three events in his life had left that impression with Labour leaders or, at any rate, had given his political opponents the opportunity to portray him as a reactionary ogre.

The first was when as Liberal Home Secretary Churchill had allegedly let loose the troops on striking miners in Tonypandy, South Wales, causing the death of a number of strikers. This was the opposite of the truth. Churchill had restrained the troops from going to the aid of the Chief Constable who had requested them to control riots. No one died in Tonypandy. Four rioters *did* die in nearby Llanelli, but they were not miners and they were victims of their own drunken folly: they set fire to a railway truck full of alcohol. But the two incidents got muddled in left-wing minds and Churchill emerged as the (mythical) scourge of labour.

When the Dardanelles campaign failed that was another black mark against Churchill, as he was the Minister (First Lord of the Admiralty) who had initiated the venture. Casualties were blamed on his cold-heartedness. Finally there was Churchill the arch-anti-Communist ('The foul baboonery of Bolshevism') who tried to suffocate Leninism at birth and who resolutely resisted the politically-inspired General Strike of 1926. On these counts he was adjudged to be anti-Socialist (which he was) and that was transmitted into anti-trade unionist (which he was not).

Churchill blamed his landslide defeat in 1945 on his reputation as a union-baiter. One of his main aims on being returned to power in 1951 was to rid himself of this slur. In so many words his industrial relations policy was: 'What the unions want, the unions get.'

Sir Walter Monckton, his Minister of Labour, saw to it that these instructions were carried out. As neither European nor Japanese competition was a factor in the Churchill years of 1951–55, no immediate damage was inflicted on British competitiveness. But as the Churchill years followed six of Mr Attlee, when a Labour Government had gone out of its way to translate every union objective into legislative reality, the unions began to regard this right to do as they pleased as an unalterable fact of life.

'Doing as they pleased' was, almost literally, true. Trades unions in the UK could not be sued for committing tort, civil wrong. A.V. Dicey, the constitutional lawyer, described it as a 'unique form of privilege'. It was without equal in any other nation. On top of this the unions were given statutory right to contribute towards a political party (the Labour Party, its political arm) and were allotted places in directorates of State-owned industries. It would have required an angelic disposition and restraint not to have abused the privileges heaped upon them.

The abuses were manifold. More pay for less work was one. Protected inefficiency was another. Fevered defence of outdated crafts was a third. The most common dispute in the fifties was caused by one union striking against another for 'poaching' its craft. This was politely described as a 'demarcation dispute'. The very considerable industrial lead Britain had built in the thirties and consolidated during World War II vanished.

Anthony Eden who briefly succeeded Winston Churchill had no taste for domestic issues and no desire to curb the unions – his first act as Prime Minister was to concede demands to prevent a rail strike – was followed in turn by Harold Macmillan who was even more resolved than Churchill not to provoke union discord. As a young MP in Stockton he had vivid memories of the effect of the depression on the workers of north-east England. He was resolved to heal the 'two nations' rift. He was, emotionally and sentimentally, on the side of the unions – and he was Premier for six years. Thus, from the best of motives, Conservative Prime Ministers had entrenched union power.

By the late sixties when another Labour government under Harold Wilson was in power and beholden to its union paymasters, the trades unions had enjoyed a generation of exceptionally privileged treatment. And during this period they had also enjoyed full (in truth, over-full) employment.

With a labour shortage, managements had been inclined to pay for sloppy workmanship. Managements themselves had become sloppy and incompetent. The fat years when, for instance, Britain built 40 per cent of the world's merchant shipping, were about to give way to the lean years as the defeated nations, France, Germany, Italy and Japan, prepared to launch their products on the market. Materially and, more importantly, psychologically, the UK was ill-equipped to meet the challenge.

The protected Empire markets which had provided the springboard for economic recovery in the thirties (the UK regained first position in the world export league in 1933) had become a feather bed and one, moreover, from which the British were about to be displaced by the arrival of aggressive German and Japanese salesmen. The soft and easy markets were about to be snatched away, were indeed already being grasped by the lean and hungry men from Bonn and Tokyo.

To exacerabate matters, the composition of the leadership of the principal British unions had changed, very much for the worse. For decades, the giant transport workers had been under firm anti-Communist control: initially that of Ernest Bevin, later with Arthur Deakin in command. However, Deakin's chosen successor died within a few months of taking over and the leadership fell vacant and finally fell to a staunch left-winger, Frank Cousins. He, in turn, was succeeded by a still more demanding radical, Jack Jones.

Heading the second biggest union, the engineers, in the late sixties, was another strong foe of capitalism, Hugh Scanlon. Other smaller unions threw up equally forceful left-wingers who were more interested in smashing 'the system' than operating it. These leaders were usually elected by a tiny proportion of the membership (4–10 per cent) as ballots were held at branch meetings attended mainly by activists.

This political leavening worked to the disadvantage of British industrial relations and British industry generally, burdening UK management with politically-inspired disruption not experienced by their American, German or Japanese competitors.

The British car industry dominated Europe in 1950. Twenty-five years later the only British-owned volume car manufacturers, BL, could command a mere 27 per cent of the British market. In that same period strikes had put Rootes out of business and driven Chrysler, the US firm, from manufacturing in the UK.

Communist shop stewards at British Leyland boasted that they could call a strike over the price of canteen tea. This motor manufacturer presented a case history of the vanquishing of the victor.

Triumph in war was a major factor in the downfall of the British motor industry. There were no competitors in Europe from 1945–50. Complacency produced mediocrity. Poor quality cars, lack of after-sale service, indifferent marketing, angered and disillusioned millions of potential customers so that when Volkswagen, Fiat, Renault appeared they swiftly swept up the market on the Continent. Even the appearance of the brilliant 'Mini' in 1960 could not change the course of events.

British Leyland (an amalgamation of Morris, Austin and the Leyland bus and lorry company) was plagued with strikes, often losing up to 40,000 cars a year. With seventeen different unions (against Volkswagen's one) there were endless disputes and the company was never able to generate the cashflow necessary to raise production levels and quality control. With 200,000 employees during the period profits remained derisory (about £6 million a year) and the company was finally nationalised in 1975.

This was, indeed, a deadly pattern which afflicted aircraft manufacturers, shipbuilding, steel production, cables, bus operators. Inefficiency and union troubles forced firms to seek State aid, culminating in State ownership and the provision of public funds with no accountability.

Strikes and low productivity became known as 'the British disease'. Working days lost due to labour disruption rose from 3 million in 1961 to 23 million in 1972. UK productivity in many industries was one-third of American, one-fourth of German and one-sixth of Japanese.

Both political parties in England recognised the swiftly deteriorating industrial situation. In 1968 a Royal Commission reported on what should be done to restore discipline, harmony and sense to industrial relations. In January 1969 the Labour Government produced its policy based on these proposals, entitled 'In Place of Strife'. Premier Harold Wilson told his party:

This plan is essential to our economic recovery. Essential to the balance of payments. Essential to full employment . . . That is why I have to tell you that its passage into law is essential to Labour's continuance in office. There can be no going back on that.

'Going back' is precisely what Mr Wilson had to do. The powerful union leaders baulked at the modest provisions designed to bring the unions within the law, at least so far as binding contracts were concerned, as well as providing individual workers with protection against the abuse of the closed shop (where individuals were obliged to belong to one union on pain of dismissal) and the right of employees to redress where they had been unfairly dismissed by their employer.

Harold Wilson, stung by the union barons' opposition to his scheme, exclaimed, 'Take your tanks off my lawn, Hugh' (Hugh Scanlon, President of the Engineering Union). To no avail. Hugh's tanks remained. Wilson, it was, who surrendered.

This marked the last time when both great parties might have agreed on a bi-partisan approach to industrial relations. Instead, when the Conservatives, after winning the 1970 election, introduced an Industrial Relations Bill similar to 'In Place of Strife', Labour and the unions conducted a vitriolic campaign against it. 'Kill the Bill' was the slogan and killed it was when Labour won the 1974 election. Instead a measure was introduced *increasing* the legal immunity enjoyed by unions taking strike action over disputes originating overseas (i.e. in British plants of multi-national companies) and giving greater legal protection to unions inducing breach of contract. The Conservatives proclaimed their total opposition to this legislation and so any prospect of consensus was removed.

Nineteen sixty-nine was also the last chance for British industry to reform itself before the full weight of Japanese competition was felt and before the oil crisis of 1973 was to thrust the Western world into its first full-blown recession since World War II.

As a result of union obduracy and Labour timidity (and of earlier Tory connivance with both) the UK was the most vulnerable of all economies when the blow fell. Unemployment doubled from 500,000 to 1,000,000 between 1973 and '75. Inflation trebled from 8 per cent to 25 per cent. Only the successive discoveries of oil in the British sector of the North Sea prevented a collapse of the £ in foreign exchanges.

The year 1975 saw a fundamental change in the Conservative approach to industrial relations represented by the election of Margaret Thatcher. Her predecessor, Edward Heath, came from the same mould: children of lower middle class parents who rose by their own talents to dominant positions in the Tory Party. Both represented a break with the patricians. Both proclaimed their faith in free enterprise and competition. Both advanced themselves as conviction politicians.

Heath however had been scarred by his experience of twice fighting – and losing – to the National Union of Mineworkers. He had been dismayed by the violence of picketing in the first coal strike, of 1972, and was deeply afraid that were he to permit market economics to prevail – leading to the closure of pits, shipyards and factories – he would provoke riots in the industrial towns and pit villages of the north. Glasgow was one place where he was warned that closure of a subsidised shipbuilding yard would create mayhem. In these circumstances Heath backed away from confrontation and increasingly hankered after the more bland recipes of Whitehall civil servants. Which, being a former civil servant himself, he found fairly congenial.

The Tory Parliamentary party rebelled against this passivity and, more to the point, against Heath's record of one election victory to three defeats (1966, 1974 twice) and replaced him with 50-year-old Margaret Thatcher. In doing so they were creating a precedent. In choosing a woman the British Conservatives were the first major party in the Western world to go for petticoat government. They had been the first to select a Jew, Benjamin Disraeli.

Of greater consequence was the fact that they had chosen a woman resolved to reverse the collectivism of two generations.

From the 1920s collectivism, amalgamation, nationalisation had been the pattern. Margaret Thatcher sought to reverse the trend, helped by public repugnance at trade union dictatorship, anger at nationalised industrial incompetence and the clear failure of the non-enterprise society.

The intellectual ground for the return to market economics had been laid over a period by the consistent work of the Institute of Economic Affairs under the direction of Ralph Harris (later Lord Harris of High Cross). Mobilising academics and articulate free enterprise businessmen the Institute had, from 1958 onwards, argued the case for letting the market do the job of allocating resources, satisfying demand, unleashing new products which the State could manifestly not achieve. In its way the Institute of Economic Affairs did for free enterprise in the third quarter what the Fabians and the Left Book Club did for Socialism in the first half of the twentieth century.

Initially these arguments made little progress. The 'mixed economy' appeared to be delivering the goods. Between 1951 – when the absurdities of rationing and detailed controls started to be abolished – and 1964 the standard of living of the British people doubled. The target for this achievement had been set by R.A. Butler, a leading Tory politician, at twenty years. It had been accomplished in just over half the time. The public expected the rate of advancing prosperity to improve.

It was largely because Mr Harold Wilson, with his talk of refashioning Britain 'in the white heat of the technological revolution', seemed more likely to achieve this than the Conservatives' Sir Alec Douglas-Home (formerly the 14th Earl of Home) that Labour narrowly won the election of '64, ending thirteen years of Tory rule.

The standard of living continued to rise for the following nine years but, intermittently, and with increasingly frequent balance of payment crises and higher inflation. The era of effortless prosperity had ended and, with the quintupling of oil prices in 1973–4, the British economy started to go backwards, with falling living standards, declining gross national product and swiftly burgeoning unemployment.

Britain's relative decline – masked as it was by *absolute* improvements – now came starkly to the fore. And, for the first time in 50 years, intellectuals began to question the validity of the collectivist argument.

Was it sensible to have the commanding heights of the economy – coal, steel, rail transport, gas, electricity, much road and air transport – controlled by the State and subject to constant political interference? Was it sensible to encourage, with subsidies and grants, private manufacturers to site factories in places of higher-than-average unemployment even though the labour force in those areas was neither trained for nor sympathetic to the type of work on offer – as happened with the Chrysler car plant near Glasgow? In short, should natural market forces be frustrated by Government decree for 'social ends' when they could result in losses to the private firms (Chrysler quit the UK) and consequently greater damage to the social framework?

Such questioning would have been inconceivable ten or twenty years earlier. Then 'indicative planning' was the method accepted by both parties. That had helped pull Britain out of the great depression of 1930–33, had been the administrative 'starter' for rearmament, an essential tool of the wartime economy and post-war reconstruction. It was built into the thinking patterns of senior civil servants. It had been the conventional wisdom for a long time, buttressed by the persuasive writings of the West's most formidable economic thinker of the thirties, John Maynard Keynes.

But, one after another, the free market economists who had been muted in the glory days of indicative planning and collectivism began to give voice through the IEA. The intellectual mood was changing. Margaret Thatcher daughter of a self-made businessman (a Grantham grocer), believer in thrift, self-reliance, hard work, discipline and the Victorian values in general, articulated the growing public doubts in the political field, while academics challenged the conventional wisdom on the theoretical plane.

National failure was the spur to challenging the sacred cows of the planned economy, even that chief sacred cow – perpetual full employment.

It was a painful process. Almost as painful to the British as contemplating the defeated in battle enjoying economic triumph at the expense of the victors 30 years after the war's end.

CHAPTER NINETEEN

America's Nightmare

At this same junction, 1975, the Americans were almost as downcast. The central pillar of the American political system, the Presidency, had just fallen victim to scandal and misuse of power unequalled in American history. Never before had a Vice-President been obliged to resign for taking bribes and his President forced to quit lest he be impeached by Congress. Andrew Johnson had come within an ace of being impeached in 1867, but he was the victim of the malignancy of post-Civil War zealots eager to extirpate anyone who had the smallest sympathy with the defeated South.

President Richard M. Nixon had been accused of subverting the Constitution and his deputy, Spiro Agnew, had been exposed as corrupt. These were charges graver by far than any which had been levelled at previous occupants of the White House. And thinking Americans were uneasily aware that what became known to history as the Watergate Affair had more sinister implications than the misbehaviour of the State's two principal citizens.

It was conceivable for a misguided electorate to choose two clever miscreants. But if the American system had any soundness at all it was surely inconceivable that one of them, the senior, the President himself, should have been successively senator, Vice-President for eight years, President for four and re-elected with a landslide majority while all the time being a criminal.

Thinking Americans wondered . . . and anguished.

The story of Watergate is important to this narrative as a classic illustration of how, in a crude phrase, democracy can 'get its knickers in a twist'. Of how, from trivial origins, a crisis may evolve – or be created – which can bring down a Government and precipitate a paralysis of the will. It also illustrates the degree of change in the relative powers of the US Executive and the media.

Oscar Wilde did once observe that while the President ruled for four years, journalism ruled forever. But under the impact of the Depression, War and the Cold War, American presidents from

Roosevelt to Lyndon Johnson had gathered to themselves authority and prestige that made them seemingly impregnable. Then along came Richard Milhouse Nixon.

What made Nixon different was that he had earned the loathing of journalists and TV commentators by appealing (in the eyes of media operators) to the lowest instincts and most crass prejudices of the populace. What irked his critics more than anything else was the success which had attended Nixon's methods. The man had collaborated with the anti-Communist witch hunter Joe McCarthy; had, indeed, defeated a Liberal Californian, Helen Gaghahan, to reach the Senate and then gone on to become Dwight D. Eisenhower's running mate for the Presidential race in 1952. On being attacked for accepting dubious funds he had gone on nation-wide TV to deny the charges and make – again successfully – an appeal to the voters' sentiments by bringing in the Nixon family dog.

Partly it was his right-wing politics, partly it was his intense, almost paranoic ambition, partly it was his heavy-jowled five o'clock shadow appearance: 'Would you buy a second-hand car from this man?' was an effective poster from his Democratic opponents. Some, or all, of these factors explained Nixon's dislike-rating with media. Within his Republican Party, however, he advanced remorselessly: aye ready to come to the aid of a troubled Congressional candidate, to raise funds for the Party machine, to speak where anyone would listen. His devotion to the Party paid off and he was selected as Republican candidate for the 1960 election against the glamorous, articulate, self-deprecating darling of the media, Jack Kennedy.

Nixon lost but by a whisker (and possibly because the result could have been slightly doctored in Illinois). The anti-Nixon Press exulted and when he failed to win election for the governorship of California two years later it seemed as though his career was over. 'You won't have Nixon to kick around,' he sourly commented to newsmen on conceding defeat.

Yet six years later he narrowly defeated Hubert Humphrey for the Presidency. The man who had been rejected by the media became the occupier of The White House. Mutual suspicion between the President and the White House corps of reporters marked his reign. Nixon could not forget how unsympathetic most journalists had been (though not the owners of newspapers or radio/TV stations). The newsmen suspected him of moulding the news to suit himself and his administration: a method as old as the US itself.

None of this may have mattered had not America been entering a dark night of the soul: racial riots, setbacks and bloodshed in Vietnam, a stumbling currency, the loss of the old certainties.

Richard Nixon appealed to the traditional in American society, to the 'silent majority', to the patriotic, hard-working, basically conservative American. Whether the appeal was cynical and solely self-serving – as his opponents alleged – is beside the point. It was overwhelmingly successful. Nixon won a colossal majority against his very liberal opponent, George McGovern, who was the beau-ideal of many journalists.

Yet in November 1972, as he stepped before the exulting crowds of his supporters under the blazing lights of the television cameras, Richard Nixon was doomed to go down to history as the only American president to be driven out of the White House.

Five months previously a task force of naive Nixon supporters – paid administrative assistants – had broken into the Democratic Party headquarters in the Watergate building, Washington. The operation was as silly as it was illegal. The author has been told by the then chairman of the Democratic Party machine that any information about the Democrats' election strategy would have been known to their opponents 'within hours', so leaky was the system.

Political spying and theft of political material was, anyway, part of the American tradition. Only a year before, administration papers had been stolen and passed to the *New York Times*, a sworn foe of Nixon. Previous presidential candidates had made it their business to find out what their opponents were up to by hook or by crook.

The break-in at Watergate had profound significance only because the 'élitist, unelected Press' – Nixon's words – chose to play it up for all it was worth. Not in their wildest imaginings however did the Press, principally the *Washington Post* and the *New York Times*, foresee the effects.

The Watergate burglars were arrested in June 1972. The event itself roused little attention until blazoned across the front page of the *Washington Post* in October, just before the election. It failed to halt Nixon's victory march but it did lead to legal proceedings which opened a whole can of worms.

One after another the President's confidential agents admitted to illegal methods: phone tapping, use of the Revenue to discover incriminating material on political opponents, break-ins. Gordon

Liddy, one of the Watergate burglars, was initially sentenced to twenty years in jail for refusing to testify against his chief. (That sentence was swiftly reduced on appeal.) Other Nixon aides, notably Robert Haldeman, whose German name gave rise to a reverse racial slur that Nixon was surrounded by a Berlin Wall, were arraigned.

On Friday, 13th July 1973, it was revealed that the President kept tapes of conversations held in The White House. There was nothing sensational or unique in that. Roosevelt, Truman, Eisenhower, Kennedy, Johnson had followed this procedure lest recollections of conversations should differ.

What gave Nixon's enemies their opportunity to blacken the President was (1) his initial refusal to publish the tapes of confidential staff and strategy meetings, and (2) the fact that when he was obliged to permit their publication they demonstrated the banality, crude vulgarity and sheer bloody-mindedness of those taking part. 'Expletives deleted' spattered the pages of the printed tapes. In the moral battle with the media, Nixon had lost his Waterloo.

The tapes were published in May 1974. Nixon resigned in August, having first received an executive pardon from his successor, the Republican Congressional leader, Gerald Ford.

The departure within a twelve-month of the President and his Vice-President was a shattering blow to American morale coming, as it did, at the same time as final defeat in Vietnam. For the Nixon-Agnew resignations revealed structural weaknesses in the American system. If a President was a real rogue it was desperately difficult to get rid of him.

In a Parliamentary system, the ruling Party could swiftly replace the rascal with someone else. Richard Nixon 'toughened it out' for almost two years – and could have forced an impeachment process for another two – to the grave injury of American government, indeed to its near paralysis.

During the period of Watergate the US slithered to humiliation in Vietnam and permitted Marxist governments to seize power in the former Portuguese colonies of Angola and Mozambique, while the US economy was denied the attention which its weakening state demanded. Previous spasms of moral righteousness – as in the anti-drink, anti-immigrant twenties – had not had such far-reaching effects because the US played a small part on the international scene. In the seventies a wholly different situation obtained; the US was the paramount power in the West and waywardness and folly had fearful repercussions.

Suppose, however, that the President was not a rogue at all but a much maligned man, not the perpetrator of a conspiracy, but its victim. That was the Nixon line. He claimed that the media, the metropolitan press and the three major TV networks, had undermined the presidency by enticing public servants to disclose confidential information to the public prints. The revelations of the exceptionally well-informed 'Deep Throat' contact to the *Washington Post* was a case in point. The media had misused the information, filleted and distorted it to destroy confidence in the Administration.

To defend himself against their campaign of lies and half-truths, Nixon had been obliged to resort to underhand methods himself. The corruption was not that of the President, but of the media exercising power without responsibility.

So, in 1975, the American people faced this dilemma. US democracy gave the Press (including radio and TV) a constitutional position comparable with Congress, President and Supreme Court. It was truly the Fourth Estate. If it were denied information openly it would seek to get it covertly. In turn the Administration, *any* Administration, would seek to frustrate that aim, else private decision-making would become impossible. Further, the Administration could actually provide disinformation, designed to discredit the media in the eyes of the public.

Such a 'war' could break out at any time and was inherent in the American democratic system. Most times such tension was constructive: keeping the organs of government on their toes. But as the two-year Watergate saga had shown, it could be appallingly destructive: of trust, confidence and the very capacity of the country to defend its own and its allies' interests.

Once the Senate had cribb'd cabin'd and confined the President – as when it frustrated Woodrow Wilson's plan for America to join the League of Nations in 1920. Now, it was Press and TV which had reduced Lyndon Johnson to bid the nation a tearful farewell (his prestige wrecked by the media's description of the Vietnam war) and had forced Nixon to quit. The force which patriotic Americans had long looked upon as a guarantor of liberty had assumed an influence at which patriotic Americans looked askance.

It was all so different from the scene at the start of the second half of the twentieth century, 'The American Century'. Then the

Americans occupied a position of almost total command. Militarily they had a monopoly in the West of the atomic bomb. They had the leadership, and indeed control of, the United Nations forces in Korea. They dominated NATO.

Their influence in every sphere of life was all pervasive. They bade fair, in the words of the American economic writer of the twenties, Ludwell Denny, to encompass the Americanisation of the world. By the early sixties, for example, US investment in the UK was *fifteen times* its level before World War II. The *Daily Express* published a list of routine domestic products from soap powders to refrigerators, from cars to food, which were American-owned. It was estimated that a British housewife could go through the day without ever touching any consumer good that was not American: from the Westclox alarm that awakened her to the Monogram electric blanket which sent her back to sleep.

In computers, aviation, electronics, business machines, the US was pre-eminent; to American companies, the world was their oyster. The cream of European technical schools and universities considered a period in the US essential to the advancement of their careers. Many postgraduate engineering and science students remained in America, finding the opportunities for pay and promotion and responsibility far finer than in their own countries. What came to be called the 'brain drain' seemed set to ensure the US of a constant flow of the brightest and the best from Europe and Japan to the Americas, thereby strengthening the Home base and weakening the competition.

American capitalism in the fifties and early sixties was in its most expansionist phase for forty years. With Europe and Japan prostrate, at least in the early phase, and Britain discarding her Empire as quickly as constitutions could be written for the successor states, America was in the driving seat.

The dollar was the international medium of exchange against which every other currency measured itself and in which the value of many products, notably oil, was denominated. Gold had been virtually demonetised, retained for decorative purposes, but excluded from international commercial transactions and kept at its 1934 level of 35 dollars to the ounce by US orders. Dollar domination symbolised US power and might, encapsulated by the Camelot of the Kennedy presidency.

Then it all started to unravel.

Possibly, the change in American mood was sensed by the tall, magisterial figure of Professor Kenneth Galbraith. In 1958 he published a book called *The Affluent Society* which, among other things, deplored 'public squalor amid private affluence'.

This marked the start of a radical change in US attitudes, which received enthusiastic White House support as soon as Eisenhower had left the Presidency. The regular budget deficit was introduced by President Kennedy as a means of countering poverty. After his assassination, his successor Lyndon Johnson took up the cause with fervour. Whereas Kennedy had come from a rich family, Johnson had known poverty in his Texan upbringing and he also knew there were votes in welfareism. An old American political joke had it that 'no one shoots Santa Claus'.

As the *Daily Express* reported in August 1964, he welcomed the launch of what he called 'The Great Society' with the words: 'For the first time in the history of the human race, a great nation is able to make and is willing to make a commitment to eradicate poverty among its people.' Between 1950 and 1975 American welfare spending rose twenty-fold until it was absorbing 12 per cent of gross national product. The budget deficit rose too: to billions of dollars, then tens, then scores of billions.

A trade deficit followed. European and Japanese import penetration turned US trading returns from black to deepest red. In consequence the dollar weakened. So-called 'Euro-dollars' began to circulate outside the control of Washington. In 1971 the US Administration admitted that the dollar was no longer as good as gold and ended the American guarantee to purchase ingots at a fixed pre-war price. Within a twelve-month the dollar price of an ounce had doubled. Within four years it had risen 20-fold. The American dollar was still first in currencies on the basis of its acceptability in commodity trading. It trailed a poor third to the Deutschmark and the Yen in strength and prestige.

Welfareism as an ideal for alleviating poverty, but unearned by economic growth, had proved for the US as expensive an experiment as the Welfare State for the UK.

America, like Britain, prospered absolutely in the quarter-century from 1950 to 1975. But, relatively, America shrank as great slices of her economy – one-third of the automobile industry, one-half of electronic information technology and an increasing part of aviation – was supplied by outsiders. Even oil, in which the US was 90 per cent self-sufficient, fell by the wayside. Imports accounted for 40 per cent of consumption in 1975.

While America writhed in the toils of Vietnam, Germany and Japan and, to a lesser extent France and Italy, penetrated markets in Latin America and in the Pacific, previously regarded as an American preserve. Then the victorious 'defeated' nations began to lend money to the US and Washington moved remorselessly from being the No 1 creditor nation towards being a major debtor state.

As the quarter-century drew to its close, Americans could count much more lost than garnered. World power had proved not only expensive but largely illusory. The nuclear balance with the USSR (Russia exploded her first atomic bomb in 1949, to be followed in subsequent years by Britain, France and China) effectively fettered freedom of action, for nothing could be done that would risk a third, nuclear, war.

In 1959 Cuba, which had been effectively an American dependency, with US right of intervention accepted in theory if discontinued in the Cuban constitution, and with an American base on the island, fell to Fidel Castro and Communism. Castro began exporting his Marxist doctrine to neighbouring countries. While America had once punished 'naughty republics' (as an Express headline in 1909 described anti-Yanqui Central American states) it was powerless to overthrow Castro because he was linked to the nuclear-armed Soviet Union.

An American attempt to destroy Castro by using dissidents ended in humiliating defeat in 1961. A year later President Kennedy succeeded in forcing Nikita Khrushchev to withdraw nuclear-tipped missiles from Cuba, but only on agreeing not to invade the island or attempt again to topple its Communist leader. There could have been no clearer demonstration of the inhibitions made manifest by the nuclear equation.

Similar factors restricted US freedom of action in the Middle East. The US supported Israel, armed her, financed her. But America did not control her. Whenever Israel felt herself mortally threatened – as in 1956 and again immediately before the Six Day War of '67 – she acted wholly in self-interest and without thought of what effect her actions might have on US Middle East policy.

Therein lay the fatal flaw in the so-called Pax Americana. World power had come to Washington at the very moment that it could not – because of the nuclear balance of terror – be effectively deployed.

In the Western hemisphere, in the Middle East and, most of all, in the deadly paddy-fields of Vietnam, the US in the two-and-a-half decades covered by this work, discovered that the 'American Century' was far removed from the American dream.

To rule an Empire one accepted unpopularity. To bear the burden of responsibility for keeping the peace without power to enforce one's will, invited unpopularity and contempt. Mao-tse-Tung's jeer that America was a 'paper tiger' echoed and re-echoed throughout the world, especially after defeat in Vietnam.

'What the hell did we fight the war for?' expostulated an American prosecutor after minor Nazi war criminals were released in 1951 ten years before their term was up to ensure West German support in the Cold War. His plaintive lament might have been the peace-cry of the victorious democracy of World War II.

Britain, in the words of US Secretary of State Dean Acheson, 'had lost an Empire and had not found a new role'. America had not found an empire but had had to adopt the costly role of defender of the West. Both nations had moved far from the teachings of Adam Smith and the self-regulating disciplines of the marketplace and had embraced welfareism, with its top-heavy government, over-intrusive bureaucracy and diminishing will to work.

The spoils of victory were poisoned.

In contrast the losers had, at the victors' insistence, become model democrats. They had expanded political freedom into the economic sphere and, having had an appalling lesson in the inherent wickedness of the all-powerful State, eagerly embraced the free market doctrines of the good Scottish eighteenth century moral philosopher Adam Smith. So West Germany and Japan flourished mightily becoming, in tandem, the strongest economic power on the globe and among the most stable nations in the West.

It was a triumph for peaceful reconstruction few would have conceived possible in 1950. To the peoples who made it possible – principally the Americans – it was not an unmixed blessing.

CHAPTER TWENTY

The Happy Story

Was anything an unmixed blessing in the new world of the final half of the twentieth century? One would be tempted to answer: 'Yes' in the revolution of health, material standards and the quality of life for the masses.

Most dramatic and most beneficial of human advances in the quarter-century has been in the field of medicine. It is significant that the greatest changes for good have come about as a result of unplanned human endeavour.

Sir Derrick Dunlop, chairman of the British Medicines Commission observed in *The Times* on 9 November 1970 that: 'Since the October Revolution, the Soviet State-owned industry has not produced a single new drug of therapeutic importance.' In contrast, private companies in Europe and America, prompted by the rough and tumble of the free market, produced a string of life-saving or life-enhancing drugs. Between 1950 and 1975 life expectancy in the West rose from an average of 64 for men (68 for women) to 70 and 76. And their quality of life was transformed by the sulphonamide and penicillin drugs, the Salk vaccine and others which practically eliminated scourges such as tuberculosis, polio, pneumonia of previous generations. The marvels of heart surgery saved tens of thousands who would have been condemned to death in earlier days. Asthma, rheumatoid arthritis, even the lowly – yet painful – haemorrhoids have succumbed to the medical revolution.

It is no exaggeration to say that the advance in medical science in the 25 years from 1950 to 1975 was váster than in the previous 250 years. Once, comparatively young men and women who had contracted tuberculosis simply waited patiently for death. In the 25 years such threatened lives were saved: swiftly and completely.

Synthetic insecticides and anti-malarial drugs, notably Paludrine and Daraprin virtually eliminated malaria in parts of the world infested with the disease.

The story of penicillin properly belongs to an earlier period, but the rapidity and extent of the derivatives from Sir Alexander Fleming's discovery are firmly fixed in the 1950–75 era.

Take the development and progression of one series of drugs produced by Beecham, the British food and pharmaceutical firm.* On the advice of Sir Ernest Chain (joint developer of penicillin in reasonably stable form) Beecham embarked on research to create penicillins with a broader spectrum of anti-bacterial activity to counter the germs successfully resisting the earlier penicillin. Beecham isolated the penicillin nucleus in 1957, allowing the company to add side chains, thereby providing new compounds for countering a new range of bacteria. After clinical tests a powerful oral penicillin, Brexil, was marketed two years later. In 1961 came the vital remedy for penicillin-resistant staphylococcus. This drug, Celbennin, was described by the medical journal, *The Lancet*, as a 'major event in chemotherapy'. More and more powerful drugs followed: Renbritin, Orbenin, Floxapen. In 1972 an antibiotic drug Amoxil appeared to reduce the toll of chronic bronchitis. The Royal Society awarded its Mullard medal to four of the men principally responsible, Drs Ralph Batchelor, Peter Doyle, John Naylor and George Rolinson. Their achievement, declared the Royal Society, marked 'one of the most significant advances in the chemotherapy of bacterial disease in the last decade'.

As a number of UK, US and Continental drug firms advanced against bacteria on the penicillin front, an 'accidental' discovery – not unlike the happy accident of the penicillin spore which landed on Fleming's culture – enabled Fison, a drug and agricultural chemical company, to come up with Intal for dealing with asthma.

A weed growing wild in the Middle East, called khellin, was known to have medical properties beneficial to asthma sufferers. Fison's chemists analysed khellin seeds, isolating a number of compounds from which they synthesised new chemicals – although it belongs to a different group from the anti-asthma constituent in khellin and acts in a different way.

Dr Roy Altounyan, a chronic asthmatic, used himself as a human guinea-pig, giving himself artificially-induced asthma spasms and testing hundreds of synthesised compounds in identical circumstances, week after week, month after month. In 1965 the synthesised

---

* I am indebted to my co-author Peter Grosvenor for much of the material here – see *The British Genius* (Dent) by Grosvenor and McMillan.

compound which came to be called Intal emerged. Safe and simple to use – inhaled as a powder – Intal symbolised the medicines which came to be taken as a matter of course during the sixties and seventies but which, not long before, would have been hailed as miracles.

Equally miraculous was the advance of 'spare part surgery'. In 1960 Sir Peter Medawar won the Nobel Prize for medicine along with Sir Macfarlane Burnet, for his work on tissue transplant. Living spleen cells from a mouse of one strain were injected into the veins of a new-born mouse of another strain. Six weeks later skin from the first mouse was grafted onto the other mouse and the graft survived. Had it not been for the injection, antibodies would have formed and destroyed the graft within ten days of transplantation. Sir Peter had proved the existence of immunological tolerance induced by injections.

From thereon an incredible series of transplant operations took place, culminating in the heart transplants performed by the South African, Christiaan Barnard.

At the start of the period Russell Brock (later Lord Brock) conducted the first 'blue baby' operation to remove an obstruction in a heart valve. Later came 'hole-in-the-heart' operations to deal with an abnormal hole between the chambers of the heart. Valves came to be replaced as regularly in the human heart as once they had been in radios. Kidneys from dead donors gave new life to people crippled with kidney failure. Severed arms were sewn back on. Diseased hips were removed to be replaced by artificial ones, freeing patients from pain and disablement.

Parallelling these extraordinary accomplishments were those of the scientists, Robert Edwards and Patrick Steptoe, who developed test tube fertilisation of the human egg and Francis Crick and James Watson who unravelled the shape and substance of the molecule DNA (deoxyribonucleic acid) present in every human cell. Sir Laurence Bragg of the Cavendish Laboratory described the latter – in *The Times* on 16 May 1968 – as 'the most important single scientific discovery of the twentieth century . . . leading to a veritable explosion of research work in the biochemical field which has transformed our knowledge of life processes.'

In tandem, these two discoveries were hailed as the beginning of a genetic evolution.

The first had the immediate effect of permitting some infertile women to conceive. In the magazine *Nature* of May 1971, Dr Edwards commented:

> The desire to have children must be among the most basic of human instincts. Denying it can lead to considerable psychological and social difficulties. There could be a demand for thousands of babies by this means [the laboratory fertilisation of a woman's ova by the husband's sperm, replacing the embryo in the wife].

So startling had been the thrust of medical science that the conviction grew during these years that everything must give way before resolute research financed on a large enough scale.

Indeed the whole attitude to health changed in the period.

In 1950 dieting was imposed by rationing and the dream of the vast majority of the British public was to return to eggs and bacon, fish and chips, milky tea, roast beef, roasted potatoes and thick slices of white bread loaded with butter. By 1975, when all these were available, the aim had totally changed, at least among the young. Health foods were the fashion, vegetarian dishes flourished; slimming magazines multiplied on the bookstalls, and the calorie count became a daily ritual.

In probably no other period in history did views on health change so rapidly and care of health become such a pre-occupation. By 1975 cigarette smoking was regarded as a severe medical risk and a social stigma. The US had taken the lead in pointing to its dangers. In the late sixties the UK government insisted that health warnings be printed on every cigarette packet and informed the public that smoking was the greatest preventable cause of illness and death, accounting for no fewer than 100,000 deaths a year and costing more than £100 million a year for the treatment of diseases attributable to smoking: heart arrests, lung cancer and bronchitis.

As a result of this publicity campaign cigarette smoking began to decline in the early seventies, for the first time since the cigarette was introduced to the West.

The Tommies of World War I had laughingly described cigarettes as 'coffin nails' (although assured by the song 'Pack Up Your Troubles' that 'a lucifer to light your fag' was the best antidote to worry). Now, fifty years later, their descendants were being taught to regard them literally as 'coffin nails'.

Elton John set a new standard in outlandish dress, outdoing the young Noel Coward.

Punks—anything to gain attention.

As a social phenomenon the assault on smoking ranked with the anti-alcohol drive earlier in the century. With this important difference. No attempt was made to impose Prohibition on smoking as the US Government had done for alcohol in 1921. Memories of that 'Noble (disastrous) Experiment' held the hand of government. There was also the matter of the billions of revenue collected from the tobacco tax. And, most important of all, was the permissiveness which had become part of the fabric of life by the seventies. Prohibition and proscription, so far as the pleasures of the people were concerned, were not a popular option among the political parties.

True, many of those who fervently opposed smoking would have enthusiastically supported a discriminatory ban on cigarettes, but it would have been too difficult a case to argue when libertarianism was so much in tune with the times.

Libertarianism also marched with leisure and unprecedented growth in material possessions.

The jet engine, developed by Sir Frank Whittle during World War II transformed people's journeys abroad. The package holiday became as much part of the people's way of life between 1960 and 1975 as the pub, or the music hall had been to prior generations.

In 1951 fewer than 1,000,000 left the UK for holidays overseas. This was mainly due to severe foreign currency restrictions. In 1975 some 12 million people took their holidays abroad. And while the 1951 tourists had to spend three months earning their trips, the 1975 travellers spent only three weeks' earnings. Regular sunshine trips to Spain and later to Italy, Greece and points further afield became routine for masses of folk. Whether travel broadened the mind is another matter. There was no notable increase in language courses (the foreigners had to learn English) and in the most tourist-affected areas, such as Benidorm in Spain, a Blackpool-in-the-sun was created complete with English-style pubs, fish and chips and discos. Enjoyment however was unconfined.

The travellers returned to a home radically different to that of their parents. The number of houses owned or being bought by the occupier soared from 6 million to 12 million. Outside these houses – and another six million rented homes – stood a motor car. Car ownership climbed from 2.5 million in 1951 to 16.2 million. Telephones in homes quadrupled to 18 million. The same expansion occurred with consumer durables: refrigerators, washing machines, vacuum cleaners and central heating.

In its impact on women the kitchen revolution was, perhaps, the most fundamental of all. It freed them from the drudgery of the mangle, the grate, daily shopping, carpet beating. It freed them from work inside the home – to employment outside. Between 1951 and 1975 the number of women employees rose fourfold: to eight million. The proportion of *married* women at work grew to 60 per cent of those aged 16 to 60; many, of course, part-time. A wife's earnings came to be regarded as essential to the family budget as 'keeping up with the Joneses' became a national preoccupation.

This American phrase was adopted throughout the Western world to describe the urge to match neighbours' opulence. If Mr Jones had a new motor mower, Mr Smith must have one too. If Mrs Jones had the latest tumble drier, so must Mrs Smith. As a means of keeping the wheels of industry turning, the envy factor had much to recommend it. It also helped change the pattern of family life. For to sustain the labour-saving devices in the home, the wife had to labour often in other people's homes, as a 'daily'.

Another vital element in altering the role of women was the development of the birth pill which virtually removed the danger of unwanted pregnancy. Planned parenthood entered the family budget and where there was a slip-up outside marriage 35 per cent of pregnancies were terminated by abortions. Not surprisingly, the birth-rate slumped from its high in 1964 to a figure (1.82 children per household) barely allowing for the replacement of the population (2.1).

Again beginning in America – the seeding ground of twentieth century change – women's movements sprang up demanding legislative changes to match women's improved status. These feminist organisations generally bracketed women with 'oppressed minorities'. An odd description, considering that women formed the majority in every country in the Western world.

These movements received legislative acknowledgement in the UK – though, strangely, *not* in the US where the Equal Rights Amendment to the Constitution failed to receive the support of two-thirds of the States. In 1970 an Equal Pay Act provided that women should receive the same wage as men for doing broadly similar work or work of equal value. Five years later, the Sex Discrimination Act made discrimination between men and women unlawful in employment, education, training and the provision of housing, goods, facilities and services: an Equal Opportunities Commission was established to monitor the application of the Acts, administered by county and sheriff courts and industrial tribunals.

Parliament's effect on women's role was minimal compared with events over which the politicians had no control. Just as the kitchen, medical and holiday revolutions advanced without Parliamentary approval so did the revolution which overtook shopping, though here Parliament *did* have a say in ratifying a transformation-in-being.

Six years after the end of World War II shopping in Britain was still a time-consuming chore as rationing and queuing were as widespread as during hostilities. In most other combatant states, outside the Communist bloc, rationing had long since disappeared as abundance replaced shortages. Still, there were compensations. Shopping was a social activity as well as a burden. People chatted to each other in queues and to the shopkeeper and assistants who served the purchasers. Personal service was the hallmark of the individual retailer and the vast majority of shops of every description were individually owned.

However, yet again America was setting the pace: this time with the development of supermarkets, where the customers served themselves from shelves stocked at lower prices by virtue of bulk buying from manufacturers or food suppliers. Labour costs were reduced, selling space enhanced, rental costs cut – because shopping for most commodities took place under one roof and not in separate buildings.

British retailers eyed events in the US and calculated that, sooner rather than later, the pattern would be repeated in the UK. One such shrewd observer was Jack Cohen whose philosophy of 'pile 'em high and sell 'em cheap' would launch the first major supermarket chain and claim undoubted success under the Tesco banner.

But two large obstacles stood in the way of Cohen and those who thought like him, notably the up-market Sainsbury family: rationing and re-sale price maintenance.

There could be no revolution in food retailing until food (and furnishings and clothes) came off the ration and competition was restored. As late as 1952 butchers were still being paid for *not* selling meat. That is to say, the income from meat sales was so small that it did not cover the fixed costs of light, heating, wages, rent and rates.

And even when rationing was finally swept away in 1955 there remained re-sale price maintenance.

This was a system which had grown up in the 1930s to ensure fair trade for retailers and manufacturers alike. In that era of heavy unemployment, restraint on competition was considered essential to national wellbeing. Re-sale price maintenance (RPM) was such a restraint, but with positive advantages to the distribution system.

Briefly, it imposed a fixed, national, re-sale price on branded merchandise. A Mars Bar sold for two pennies in a village store in Wick or in a Woolworths in London. The retailer was obliged to sell at the manufacturer's price regardless of his ability to accept a much slimmer margin because of economies of scale.

The argument for RPM was that it enabled many retailers to stay in business who might otherwise have been forced out by cut-price competition. The benefit to the customer was that she knew the price of the product and knew it would be the same wherever she shopped. The manufacturer was assured of an abundance of retail outlets for his goods. If by ruthless price cutting retail chains were to drive the corner shop, the small man, out of business, everyone would ultimately lose: the customer, who would be at the mercy of a semi-monopolist who had driven out his rivals; the retailer who would be either living on the edge of poverty or unemployed, and the manufacturer who could find that a few huge groups of retailers could dictate prices and policy to him or even take over the manufacturing process themselves and produce 'own-name' goods.

To defend themselves against this threat, real or imagined, manufacturers agreed to impose a collective boycott on any store, or groups of stores, which dared to break the fixed price. The store would then face closure because it would be unable to stock up.

The practice of RPM was clearly in restraint of trade – that was the whole aim and object of the exercise in the slump-ridden thirties – and would have fallen victim to anti-cartel legislation in the fullness of time. However, those who were clamouring for an end to restrictions imposed by war, austerity and socialism, were in no mood to tolerate a cosy arrangement to secure supplies of goods at the expense of buyers.

Ralph Harris and his Institute of Economic Affairs loudly applauded and supported by the supermarketeers-in-waiting, started a propaganda campaign against RPM.

Their case was that if a shopkeeper wanted to sell any product at a price of his choosing, he should be free to do so. The manufacturer received payment at the price he stipulated and the customer purchased what he, or more usually she, wanted at a lower price. Everyone benefited – except the complacent or incompetent who should not be in business anyway. Fears for future exploitation by a few super-groups were groundless as thrusting new entrepreneurs would swiftly undermine commercial dinosaurs.

Lord Beaverbrook and his *Express* newspapers set themselves up as champions of RPM (not least because national newspapers, with their heavy dependence on a network of small dedicated newsagents, were intent on supporting their distributors) and a lively debate ensued in the early sixties.

The issue, however, was never really in doubt. Edward Heath, the Tory Trade Minister and about-to-be party leader, was intent on appearing the abrasive advocate of pugnacious, efficient free enterprise in order to counter Labour's Harold Wilson who had appropriated 'white-hot technology' as his gospel. Resale Price Maintenance was consigned to the scrapheap.

In June 1964 – a day or so before Beaverbrook's death – the collective boycott to sustain RPM was outlawed. The only restriction remaining on the retailers' freedom was that he should not make certain products 'loss leaders'; that is, sell a particular commodity, sugar for instance, at a give-away price in order to tempt customers to his store. That restriction was quietly ignored.

Within twelve months of the end of RPM the first super-store (26,900 sq ft) opened in Britain. The retailing revolution had begun. Within the next ten years some 200 such stores were in operation and more than 50 per cent of the country's retail trade was in the hands of large multiples. In the grocery trade the proportion exceeded 60 per cent with Sainsbury, Tesco, Fine Fare, Allied and Co-operatives in dominant positions.

Two factors saved the independents from complete liquidation: the arrival of extraordinarily hard-working Asians ready to remain open all hours and saving on wages by employing family, and the growth of voluntary chains, Spar, Wavy Line, V.G., etc, which enabled small retailers to get the cost advantage of bulk purchase by banding together and cheap credit to convert counter stores into self-service ones.

In just over a decade the face of High Streets and Main Streets was altered beyond recognition. Gone were the old individual grocers shops with their bags and jars and weighing machines and tills and counter service and chit-chat. In came trolleys and check-out points and the American fashion of bringing the car as close as possible to the loading bay.

As stores got larger and larger and more and more dependent on private cars for out-of-town shopping, they clashed with the concept of the green belts. These rural rings had been designated after World War II as vital to prevent urban sprawl. But they could hardly co-exist with mega-style hypermarkets which to be economically worthwhile needed to be situated close to large towns and cities. So began a conflict between developers and conservationists which was very typical of the era.

Quality of life against quantity was a particularly strong argument in the period. Clean air legislation had created smokeless zones and virtually eliminated smog, a dread killer-combination of smoke and fog which, in the winter of 1952, caused the death directly or indirectly of 4,000 Londoners. Clean rivers had replaced sludge caused by factory effluence. Unsightly smoke stacks and slag heaps were disappearing from the countryside, giving rise to the hope that England would regain her lost green and pleasant aspect. The same aspiration applied to the industrial districts of Scotland and Wales.

But these hopes were in complete conflict with the demands of competitive industry. Should oil, discovered amid the beautiful scenery of Dorset, be exploited, scarring the landscape, ruining the tourist trade? In previous generations there would have been no doubt about the answer: country pursuits and dreaming spires would have given way to the clamorous demands of commerce.

The sixties, however, had seen the emergence of powerful preservationalist lobbies, the middle-aged, middle class equivalents of the Flower People. They had powerful instruments in the shape of the National Trust, the Council for the Preservation of Rural England, the National Conservancy. They were staunch supporters of the quality of life and their voting potential – especially to Conservative MPs (who might otherwise have supported commerce and industry) – was far too great to be ignored.

During this period, for example, they frustrated all plans to build a third London airport, first at Maplin Sands (to preserve wildlife) and then at Stansted (to save farming land).

Farmers too however came in for fierce pressures over their destruction of hedgerows to produce cost-effective, prairie-type farming. It was no longer enough for farmers to claim that, by 1975, they had made the country 80–100 per cent self-supporting in meat, eggs, milk products, wheat and potatoes. Production as an end in itself was no longer acceptable. The opportunity cost of intensive farming – the loss of wild flowers, food and shelter for birds and animals – was considered not worth the extra output. Just as pollution of the atmosphere could not excuse industry's desire to cut its costs.

So here was another revolution, the upsurge of the 'greens': green belts, green countryside, green farming at the expense of out-of-town shopping and housing and development generally.

The period saw the reversal of the centuries-old drift to the cities. In 1951 Glasgow hit its maximum population, just short of 1.2 million. By 1975 the population had declined to 800,000 as 'overspill' were accommodated in new towns such as East Kilbride and Cumbernauld. Liverpool, Manchester, Birmingham shrank by slightly smaller percentages, but London's decline was dramatic – a 40 per cent fall from 11½ million to 6.9 million.

Nor did people move only to satellite towns (of which 32 were built in the period) or suburbs. The areas which recorded the greatest increases were East Anglia, the West Country and eastern Scotland.

The apparently irreversible concentration of population in the metropolitan conglomerates was reversed: unplanned and, initially unrecorded. This 'return to the land' was accompanied by an unprecedented increase in house purchase, as has been said, doubling from 6 million to 12 million over the 25 years. And as people moved out of town and city flats, so the ratio of houses to apartments rose to four houses to one apartment. The percentage of municipally rented property fell to 30 per cent against double that for private ownership (the balance being privately-let accommodation).

There were, however, big disparities in this distribution of home ownership. In Scotland about two-thirds of houses were municipal, often let at extremely low rents – in 1950, for example, a three-bedroom modern terrace house could be had for 40 pence a week. Twenty-five years later they still lagged behind the rest of the United Kingdom. Reflecting, said some, Scotland's relative poverty; causing, said others, the very distortions and refusal to face reality which, more than anything else, held back Scotland and made her one of the poorest areas in Europe.

CHAPTER TWENTY ONE

Lion Rampant

The period 1950–1975 saw the rise and rise of Scottish nationalism fuelled initially by a feeling of neglect and latterly by 'Scotland's oil' and throughout by the belief – which grew as the era advanced – that small was beautiful.

In the period 1950–1975 nationalism flourished as never before: the number of states at the United Nations trebled, to 143. And the unity of the United Kingdom of Great Britain and Northern Ireland was shaken to its foundations by the rise and rise of Scottish nationalism.

A feeling of separateness had always existed in the Northern Kingdom: understandably so as it had joined itself to England in 1603 to enable James VI of Scotland to succeed the childless Elizabeth of England and so constitute the United Kingdom. Scotland's Parliament had disappeared in 1707 to make way for a UK Parliament in Westminster and Scotland had been compensated by receiving a disproportionately large number of MPs in the House of Commons.

Compensation, larger by far than any representation, lay in the opportunities opened to, and seized by, Scottish merchants in the burgeoning British Empire. Scottish industry, shipbuilding, commerce, banking, prospered mightily so that, in 1882, *Marshall's Dictionary of Statistics* reported:

> Scotland possesses more wealth for her population than any other country in the world. Her fortune has quintupled since 1840 . . . we may search Europe's annals and we shall find nothing to equal the rise of Scotland in the above period. . . Such is the prosperity of the bulk of the people that Scotland has now an average of £272 per head of the population, as against England's £262.

By 1950 Scotland's average income per head was one-sixth lower than England's. There were many reasons for this, not least

Scotland's failure to develop new industries to replace the declining basic ones of coalmining, shipbuilding and steel, but the decline rankled. A Scottish National Party was founded in 1928 and a Scottish National MP was actually elected in a by-election in the closing days of World War II. He was heavily defeated at the succeeding General Election.

An appeal for greater administrative powers for Scotland (to enhance those of the Secretary of State for Scotland) received two million signatures in 1950 and an added spice of romantic folklore when students from Glasgow University 'reprieved' the ancient Stone of Scone – traditional coronation Stone of the ancient Scottish kings – from its resting place in Westminster Abbey, where it had lain since being seized by Edward I six and a half centuries before. As previously recounted (see page 21) they were obliged to return it the following year when the Attorney General threatened to prosecute. King George VI was truly upset at the disappearance of the Stone, fearing the loss of its mystical significance could weaken the monarchy. Maybe it did. Certainly the accession of his daughter caused a furious outcry north of the Border. Not because of the person of the Monarch – Elizabeth and her Scottish mother were immensely popular – but because of the title Elizabeth *II*.

Politically, however, the Scottish Nationalists made no headway whatsoever. The country was split evenly between the Conservatives (35 seats) and Labour (35) with one lone Liberal. Scotland had her own legal system, her own educational structure, her own mini-civil service and five Government ministers.

Yet the two major London-based parties had serious weaknesses. The Conservatives were badly served; the quality of their MPs was extravagantly low. In 1957, for instance, Scotland's Tory MPs boasted as fine a crop of knighthoods and baronetcies as had ever been gathered together. No fewer than one-third of Scottish Tory MPs were 'Sir'. But this blaze of chivalry was dulled by one cold fact. There was not a single Scottish MP in the Cabinet – outside of the Scottish Secretaryship which was reserved for Scots. The knighthoods and baronetcies were consolation prizes.

Furthermore, the Scottish Tory MPs were not particularly Scottish. Most of them were educated in England: no fewer than eight at Eton. This mixture of the remote and the ineffective produced a strong reaction from the electorate. In the following nine years the Tories lost twelve seats.

Labour's ascendancy induced complacency. The party boasted that, in Scotland, its successful candidates weighed their votes and didn't just count them. That was true in some cases: most of all in the heavily industrialised central Scotland division of Hamilton, where Tom Fraser enjoyed a majority of over 16,000.

Then it happened. At a by-election in 1967 Mrs Winifred Ewing, law graduate, housewife and mother of three won the seat for the Scottish Nationalists. The next year they swept the polls at local elections. The party's membership soared to 150,000 – fifteen times larger than their total *vote* two decades previously.

Labour itself had once been the party of Scottish Home Rule and its propensity to centralise decisions in Whitehall and so betray its earlier promises partially explained defections to Scottish National- ism. But only partially.

At heart, the sudden explosion of Scottish Nationalism was a sixties-style revolt against the established order. It was part of the belief that if you changed the structure you would somehow produce instant Utopia. The mood might well have passed – it was ill-suited anyway to the dour practicality of the Lowland Scot (and the Lowlands embraced four-fifths of Scotland's population) when oil was discovered in massive quantities under the North Sea off the east coast of Scotland.

Immediately the Scottish Nationalists changed tack. Previously they had stressed Scotland's poverty and neglect – although Scot- land received, proportionately, much more than England from State funds – as reasons for cutting the bond with England. Now they trumpeted: 'It's Scotland's oil!' and launched their election campaign of October 1974 on a platform of immediate independ- ence. Their vote soared to 30 per cent and they gained eleven seats.

All at once it seemed that 370 years of union would vanish: sunk in a sea of oil. Plans were hastily drawn up by both Conservative and Labour parties – Labour having narrowly won the election – to pre-empt full independence by offering 'devolution', a system of Home Rule, with a Scottish Assembly legislating for Scottish affairs.

Again it appeared that purely party calculations were to impose fundamental political changes on the nation, that fear and appeasement were to be the principal counsellors. The *Express* commented that 'producing more politicians and bureaucrats for Scotland, is like trying to cure diphtheria by injecting the patient with typhoid'.

It is a significant commentary on the sixties and early seventies that momentary spasms were confused with main movements. Change, change of any kind, for whatever purpose, was endemic to the scene.

The Scottish Nationalists had not produced a single figure of any significance: no Charles Stewart Parnell, let alone a William Wallace, yet Scotland seemed destined to disrupt the union of centuries in a matter of months.

Thus was demonstrated the excessive volatility of the age. And nothing mirrored that volatility – more, helped to create it – than the magic moving picture box in the corner of the livingroom. Television.

CHAPTER TWENTY TWO

The Goggle Box

It was on a February evening in 1950 that public and politicians became aware of the impact radio could have on the electorate. The familiar gravelly tones of the Radio Doctor came across the air waves urging the voters to dismiss the blunt, homely advice of author J.B. Priestley to support Labour and to endorse the Conservatives instead. It was a party political broadcast by Dr Charles Hill and it indubitably swayed great numbers of people to switch their votes.

Priestley had been an inspired choice for Labour. So persuasive had been his wartime postscript talks that Churchill himself became apprehensive that the wartime truce was being broken and Labour was stealing a march on the Tories. When Priestley was wheeled out in the 1950 General Election as Labour's Secret Weapon, the Tories felt they had to counter with someone who had equal broadcasting charisma. The choice fell on Charles Hill, their candidate for Luton, whose voice was familiar to the radio audience, talking daily about the advisability of regular bowel movements, but reassuringly about not getting too worried if there were occasional lapses.

Familiarity, reassurance, medical prestige: the mixture worked. And if it worked for 'steam' radio how much more effectively would well-known personalities sway opinions in the television age?

The nine-inch box in the corner of one million livingrooms was about to become the single most formative feature of people's homes in history. Within the next 25 years virtually every house in the land would have a set, 20 per cent would have two.

A television service in the UK had operated before the war, but it was confined to London and the South. From 1951 onwards the TV aerials spread like a rash across the whole nation. The Queen's decision that the Coronation should be televised gave the new medium tremendous promotion. TV parties were organised where the proud owners exhibited The Box and chairs were arranged around the set as in the cinema. These 'television parties' became a regular feature until everyone got their own set.

Control of television, as with radio, was vested solely in the British Broadcasting Corporation, chartered by Parliament, financed by licence fee, administered by a board of governors (sound Establishment figures) and run by professionals who worked to a strict remit which excluded vulgarity in any guise.

A radio comedian who also figured prominently in the early days of television, Arthur Askey (who was pretty 'blue' on the music-hall stage) wrote these words for his signature tune: 'Clean – if I'm not very clever – but only 'cos I've got to be'. They neatly summed up the BBC's philosophy, as handed down by the Corporation's first Director-General, the great John Reith. Reith imposed the strictest codes on his broadcasters and in the naturally deferential twenties, thirties and forties no one thought of breaking them.

If the 'brute force of monopoly to do good' – Reith's words – had continued, would the codes? Was television the engine of change, or merely its mirror? Who can tell. Even as late as 1954 the *Sunday Express* recorded, with surprise and shock, that Gilbert Harding had removed his dinner jacket to reveal red braces in the programme *What's My Line?*

What changed this attitude and broke the BBC mould was the introduction of commerical television. British advertisers before WWII had been obliged to use Radio Luxembourg to tout their wares over the wave-lengths. They were resolved that, so far as the infinitely more popular selling medium of television was concerned, they would not be frozen out. Commercial companies and advertising agencies formed the Popular Television Campaign and set out to persuade Parliament and public that choice was right, proper and inevitable.

Propaganda concentrated on persuading Press owners that they would become the operators of the commercial TV stations and journalists that there would be far more openings for their talents. In the Commons, attention was focussed on the governing Tory Party to convince doubters that they should prove their devotion to free enterprise by striking off the shackles of broadcasting monopoly.

The campaign's success was by no means assured. The bulk of the Press was in mortal fear of TV's competition for advertising. Initially Beaverbrook favoured commerical TV (he thought he would have total control of one programme and the *Mirror* would control the other!) but he later turned against the commercial lobby and gave his support to the antis. The Labour Party was solidly against 'sordid commercialism'. Many Tories of the patrician kind, notably Lord Hailsham, distrusted the lobby and disliked the trivialisation of television which commercialism seemed to bring, as evidenced in America.

Much indignation had been caused in Britain at an advertising shot featuring a chimpanzee, J. Fred Muggs, which had appeared in the US transmission of Queen Elizabeth's Coronation.

'Is this,' asked the *Manchester Guardian*, 'what British viewers will have to endure if the Commercial lobby has its way?'

In general, the artistic world was opposed to commercial television, believing it would sacrifice quality and minority interests to the lowest common denominator.

However, there were important elements in the Conservative second tier of Ministers, especially Lord Woolton and Selwyn Lloyd, who were wholly in favour of breaking the BBC monopoly and giving advertisers their opportunity. Churchill, Eden and Butler, the Party's three chiefs in 1954, were not particularly interested in the issue, but they did require safeguards. And so a compromise was hammered out.

Television companies in the UK would not be owned outright by any one individual or company. Groups would get together to seek a franchise from the Independent Television (later Broadcasting) Authority. Their 'cultural qualifications' would be examined. No company would be permitted to sponsor programmes – as in the USA. Advertisers would buy 'slots' which, according to price, would appear at peak viewing times or non-peak times. The country would be split into regions so that, effectively, each region would provide a monopoly for the chosen contractor. This, it was reckoned, would provide a temptation to entrepreneurs to risk investing in this new and hazardous venture. So tempting was it that Roy Thomson, the Canadian press-owner who won the Scottish TV contract, described it as 'a licence to print money'. Network committees would determine distribution of programmes.

This was a typical British approach, a blend of gentility and competition, glazed with semi-monopoly: all in the name of taste and high standards.

In September 1955 commercial television – or independent television as it preferred to be known as – went on the air without a hitch. Archibald Graham, secretary to the advertising committee of the Authority and effectively its advertising controller, was pleasantly surprised at the technical slickness of the first evening's operation.*

The advertisements were not obtrusive. They were limited to a maximum of six minutes per hour, spaced as evenly as possible, taking account of natural breaks and were networked to split-second timing.

Fears that advertisers would delude the public by making false claims were swiftly dissipated. True, the advertising committee received complaints, but they were mainly of a trivial or silly nature, such as that one dairy firm was using a block of wood to demonstrate the silky softness of their butter. When it was pointed out that real butter would have melted under the intense heat of the old-style TV lights, the complaint was withdrawn.

Good taste was, generally speaking, sustained in the content of the advertisements. Occasionally Graham had to take advertisers to task, as with the one who wanted to show his client's product – a medicinal drink – as an aid to a heaving, sweating woman in labour. Graham swiftly convinced the eager promoters that this was not acceptable.

Indeed, the responsibility of the commercial companies and their agents exceeded the hopes of their supporters.

Advertisers did not, could not, control the content of any programme, but they exerted some, indirect, influence. For if a programme on a regular schedule proved consistently to have little appeal, advertising slots at that period would have few takers. So, in a sense, the discipline of the box office did exert influence in independent television.

'Ratings' entered the language. How high a programme stood in the ratings, i.e. how many viewers watched it (the figure being determined by a representative sample of households whose TV sets had been specially adjusted to measure choice and by random tests of public opinion) decided its fate.

Within months of ITV appearing, the commercial system had captured 70 per cent of the viewers, leaving the BBC with less than one-third where once it had held 100 per cent.

The BBC was worried. The newspapers were even more worried.

* In conversations with the author.

The impact of television advertising was electrifying. Initial doubts swiftly disappeared. Viewers rushed in their thousands to have their sets converted to receive the new channel and, of course, all new sets were so constructed. Shops reported an enormously increased demand for a product on the morning after it had been advertised on TV; 'as seen on TV' posters began to appear at the point of sale.

In the past salesmen had told chemists to stock up with a particular brand because 'The *Express* will be running a full page ad'. Now 'telly' alone stole the show. Advertising jingles entered the popular repertoire at the very moment that conventional pop music became un-whistleable.

Press advertising plummeted. No longer did Beaverbrook Newspapers return some cash to advertisers when profits exceeded £1,000,000 a year. No longer could newspapers afford to subsidise their cover price from advertising revenue. Vulnerable or poorly managed newspapers vanished from the scene. In 1960 alone the famous Liberal newspaper the *News Chronicle* and its sister paper, the *Star*, ceased publication. So did five national Sunday newspapers and a number of considerable provincial papers including the *Bulletin* in Scotland and the *Dispatch* in Birmingham, plus a clutch of evening papers.

Naturally, those engaged in television swelled with proprietorial pride. They were the inheritors. To them belonged the kingdom of communication. 'If it doesn't happen on television, it doesn't happen.' The slogan summed up the mood, and the mood was one of supremacy and arrogance.

The Press was on its knees. Radio was all but forgotten. The struggle was clearly between the BBC and the commercial companies and now the BBC decided to fight back: to challenge ITV on the populist battlefield and wait until an appropriate date for the launching of a second public service channel (BBC 2) to cater for minority interests.

With the appointment of Hugh Carleton Greene, brother of Graham Greene the author, and a man of broad tolerance, liberal outlook and trendy notions, the BBC began to chase the ratings.

Old-style impartiality fell by the wayside. So did the gentler types of comedy and drama. Programmes became provocative, hard-hitting. Comedy was spliced with satire and malice. Realism permeated drama. Sex raised its seductive head. The showing of *Stamboul Train* broke new ground in permissiveness. 'Auntie' BBC

Television . . . the great moulder, or moving wallpaper?

Jack Nicklaus, multi-millionaire of golf.

The face of satire: David Frost and Ned Sherrin.

threw away her stuffy image, donned a mini skirt and cavorted with the best, or the worst, of them.

Did the Corporation produce the Swinging Sixties or merely project them? Both, of course.

The circumstances were in place. Premier Harold Macmillan (whose choice was Carleton Greene) did not exactly say '*Enrichissez-vous*', but such were the mores of his reign. The country, in common with the Western World, was experiencing a spectacular increase in material prosperity; living standards were set to double every fifteen years. The 'goodies' were on view, not least in ITV's shop window and the public were encouraged to 'get it now'. 'Buy now, pay later' was the constant theme.

Television was unquestionably the medium of the masses. The working class had come into its own at last: not through revolution, but through the cathode ray tube.

Recognising where the buying public lay and how to appeal to it, independent television – Granada the contractor – presented *Coronation Street*, the first British TV soap opera (derived from melodramatic serials produced in the USA and frequently sponsored by soap companies).

Coronation Street embodied the true conservatism of the British working class. It was northern (Manchester), chummy (terrace houses), warm and recognisable. The pub was central to the story; the characters were real, vivid and true, in the sense that viewers could identify with them.

Coronation Street soared into the ratings stratosphere. Clearly gutsy working class drama paid. The BBC responded with a realistic police series – this time set in Liverpool – called *Z Cars*. But it also stepped into satire with *That Was The Week That Was* in which Youth (with a capital Y) was encouraged to bait and discredit their elders. This was considered by TV critics to be very funny and refreshingly different. It symbolised a departure from BBC traditions of respect and respectability so severe as to represent a cause of permissiveness. The Corporation was now in the business of creating opinion and not simply reporting it.

Carleton Greene maintained that that was the Corporation's job. He and his governors and staff were being true to the BBC's reputation for independence: an oft-cited example of which was John Reith's rejection of Winston Churchill's demand, during the General Strike of 1926, that the Corporation should broadcast only

Government announcements.

In the sense that the BBC was maintaining its independence from the governing party of the day – and from the opposition for that matter – the arguments mounted by Greene and his supporters were valid. During his 10-year tenure at the BBC – from 1959–69 – each party held office for five years. The complaint from both parties was not of party bias but of a sneer-and-jeer philosophy.

The *Daily Express* in an editorial went so far as to say: 'The BBC should be re-named The Anti-British Broadcasting Corporation.'

Harold Wilson who entered his Premiership in 1964, became so exercised about the Corporation's wilder moments that he appointed Lord Hill (the same Dr Charles Hill who had served the Conservatives so well) to be chairman in order to bring the Corporation to a proper regard for its responsibilities. That was in 1967. It was to be the first – but not the last – occasion for mounting tension between the Corporation and its nominal pay-master, the government of the day.

While the Corporation remained a monopoly it showed respect for the country's institutions of which it was a major ornament itself. But once it was obliged to compete, as it had to do when commercial television arrived on the scene in the late fifties, it felt it had no more obligation to adopt a deferential pose.

In a sense, the Corporation enjoyed the best of both worlds. It was not subject to the box office constraint of commercial television (receiving its revenue from a State-enforced licence fee) and it could proudly wave the flag of independence should any Government dare to criticise it. It enjoyed, in fact, power without responsibility: the very vice Stanley Baldwin had accused the Press barons of exercising in 1930.

A strong, resolute, puritan-type Director-General might have reined in his staff. But a strong, journalistically-inclined libertarian DG would spur them on. And, once freed of restraint, it was the journalist's natural tendency to go out looking for stories and to 'create' them if none made themselves easily accessible. Naturally, these were not inventions, but they were often grossly exaggerated accounts of individual grievances which were made to appear widespread abuses. 'Good' current affairs television was argument, dissent, exposure, denunciation. When BBC radio faced competition in the seventies from local commercial broadcasting, it too followed the path set by TV. Reporters went on the grievance trail, sure that if they could find one they could make a story out of it.

It is always easier and more profitable to write or film or speak about failings than about successes; to criticise rather than praise.

'Good news is no news' and papers which concentrated on the better side of human nature (including one named *Good News*) went out of business. That's human nature.

So events and personality combined to drive the BBC in a certain direction in the sixties and, in terms of regaining viewership, it worked to some extent: ratings *did* improve, though not to level-pegging with ITV.

On the broader front of 'educating the masses', television proved a massive disappointment. Excellent programmes from A to Z – from architecture, astronomy, archaeology, antiques to zoology – drew millions of viewers but they were largely people who would have read about these subjects anyway. BBC2 promoted the Open University study course: again, hopes of a huge new student audience of workers were disappointed. Where the vicar had taken his degree at Oxford, the vicar's wife took hers at the Open University.

Indeed television reduced the inductive process required by reading and in that way contributed to a diminution of mental activity. By 1975 children under sixteen were watching TV 21 hours a week. Their comics and boys' and girls' papers reflected the change from print to pictorial. Papers such as D.C. Thomson's *Hotspur, Rover* and *Wizard* which, in 1950, had been almost entirely written stories were transformed into picture-stories with balloon captions. The *Boys' Own Paper*, a worthy journal which stretched thought and encouraged participation in hobbies, went out of business altogether.

During the same period the reading quantity of the popular press declined with the disappearance of solid-type papers such as the *Daily Herald* and *News Chronicle* and their replacement by picture papers such as the *Sun*. In turn, these papers and others, devoted more and more space to the fictional characters in television serials so that they became more 'real' than many flesh and blood characters who peopled the news.

This change in the perception of what concerned the public was entirely the work of television.

In previous decades, cinema actors and music hall performers had engaged tremendous public interest. Movie company publicists worked overtime to create a demand for their 'products' and then to satisfy that demand with 'signed' photographs, fan magazines and clubs. International actors and actresses were larger than life. Hollywood was the dream factory of the world.

But no one mistook the dream for reality, the shadow for the substance. Fictional characters were recognised for what they were. And, anyway, actors took different parts in different films so that they were not permanently associated with one role. Thus Clark Gable was not forever Rhett Butler, in *Gone with the Wind*, or Bette Davis a scheming bitch in a never-ending serial.

Television, a far more intimate medium than the cinema, communicated directly with the family in their home and the fate and fortunes of the fictional serial family on the box was a palpable factor in real family life: often the sole topic of conversation uniting the members.

So TV, instead of making life more real made it more fictional: fact and fantasy got so confused that when a serial character 'died' the newspapers reported it as a tragic event. Even radio had shown the power of fantasy when, in 1955, Grace Archer of the Archers serial was 'killed' in a fire – and hundreds of people sent condolences to the fictional Archer family in the series of that name.

Television vastly extended the scope for that identification between listener-viewers and the serial characters. Sociologists espied escapism in this involvement with fiction, a subconscious desire to opt out of an increasingly violent and confrontational society.

Whether that was so or not television did nothing to disguise conflict outside the home – quite the contrary, it revelled in it.

Television scanned the world to bring riot, war, death, starvation, into the livingroom. As freedom for cameramen and reporters to roam was a Western phenomenon (the Communist East being closed) an impression of excessive violence in the West was transmitted. The distorting lens of the camera gave the impression that Los Angeles was aflame when race riots hit that city in 1968. In fact, more people died as a result of road accidents in the US that day than were killed (26) in the Los Angeles disturbances. The constant showing of war films from Vietnam, night after night, probably weakened American resolve to continue the war. In that respect, television changed the course of events. And led to Governments excluding television teams from future military interventions.

In the UK television coverage of violent incidents in the coalminers' strikes of 1972 and 1974 aggravated the conflict and may have intensified the polarisation of political attitudes.

What TV manifestly did *not* do was increase political awareness and participation in politics.

In 1950, when TV was a minor element in national life, 83.9 per cent of the electorate voted in the British General Election. Near the close of our period, in October 1974, when TV was installed in 92 per cent of homes in Britain, the percentage fell to 72.8 per cent.

Fears that a political super telly-star would emerge proved unfounded. Some performers were, admittedly, better than others. In the US, John F. Kennedy, in 1960, was adjudged to be more tele-visual than Richard M. Nixon. Nixon's five o'clock shadow and shifty look were reckoned to be political death on the little screen. Yet Nixon, in 1972, won the Presidential Election with a record majority.

From the fifties onwards of course, politicians dared not ignore television (long gone were the days when US Presidential candidate Adlai Stevenson thought the TV adviser was someone to repair his set while on the campaign trail). They were briefed on their appearance, their accent, their mode of dress and every party occasion was adjusted for TV. But where cameras and microphones were admitted to legislative assemblies, as in Canada or (microphones only) in the UK, there was no noticeable increase in public interest in political debate.

With television, show business came first. It remained, in essence, a medium for entertainment. And it revolutionised the prospects of all who could entertain, in whatever capacity.

Nowhere was this more true than in sport.

In 1950 professional footballers in the UK were governed by fixed maximum wages and contracts tying them to their clubs for as long as the clubs chose to keep them. Ten years later, footballers were 'in the driving seat', free to re-negotiate contracts, to work abroad, to earn as much as they could, regardless of what their team-mates were paid.

The Players Union was the instrument of change, but the conditions for change were created by television. BBC and ITV would televise successful teams – and pay handsomely for doing so. With the financial rewards of victory so enormously increased, managements could not wait to train up young local hopefuls. They had to buy talent in the transfer market. They could not do that while the maximum wage and the (near) lifetime contract existed. So both were swept away. Without television that would not have happened, or at least would not have happened so swiftly and completely as it did.

How different, how very different from the BBC's complaint, in 1930, that the Football Association was demanding *payment* (!) for the Corporation's goodwill gesture in broadcasting the Cup Final.

As with football, so with golf. Television turned professional golfers into household names. Where once winning the British Open championship was a matter of honour (and £100), so victory in that tournament or in one of the three major American competitions which, together, made up the Grand Slam, made the victor a millionaire overnight. For not only were prizes raised a thousand-fold but endorsements and future TV appearance fees increased income to seven figures.

The same golden TV rule applied to tennis. Wimbledon wisely bowed to the inevitable and scrapped the 'amateurs only' rule at the close of the sixties. By making the Wimbledon Tennis Fortnight (and its equivalent in the US) an international event, capturing the attention of hundreds of millions of viewers across the globe, TV ensured fortune for the winners and those close to them.

By the mid-seventies snooker, a game commonly associated with dingy halls, skill at which provided evidence of an ill-spent youth, was claiming the attention of TV. No sport, no pursuit – not chess, not bridge, not darts – but could be raised to a multi-million venture through the exposure of the TV camera.

The academic who yearned to appear on TV and who, on being asked what he considered a fair fee, replied: 'If I send you a cheque for £50 will that be all right?' was not so far wide of the mark. For many, not even remotely concerned with the medium, television opened the golden gates. For others, naturalists, historians, botanists, art connoisseurs, it brought national and international recognition and a very considerable income.

Those who went on television to explain the mysteries of antiquity, the magic of the rose, the complexities of art, were not necessarily the most gifted, but each possessed a talent for communication and an identifiable personality. They too had cause to bless the medium.

Writers, producers, directors, actors and actresses, found new opportunities on TV which was just as well. For the most badly crippled of television's victims was the cinema industry.

In 1950 there were more than 6,000 picture houses in the UK. They were visited regularly once a week by 40 per cent of the population, and by 10 per cent twice a week. By 1975 the number of cinema screens (for a number of cinemas had two or three mini-theatres) had fallen to 1,700, and admissions had slumped to less than 20 per cent of the 1950 figure.

Radio emerged in a less battered state than the film industry because the growth in motor-car ownership (quintupling in the 25-year period) provided a new market for car radios and the lengthening traffic tail-backs ensured that motorists, and their passengers, listened more and more to the radio.

The theatre shrank – especially in the provinces – but survived and, in the West End (less so on Broadway), showed many signs of vigour. Soccer endured a steady decline in attendance from 1950 to 1975, but this was due not so much to television as to the availability of competing attractions for expenditure as rationing gave way to abundance and Saturday afternoons to joint family shopping sprees.

The impact of television on the community was pervasive, but less fundamental than had been hoped – or feared.

It did not appear to have altered voting patterns. In our 25-year term the Conservatives were in office for 17 years, Labour for 8: not dramatically different to the Conservative/Radical ratio of previous generations (much the same voting pattern was evident in the USA between Republicans and Democrats). No spell-binder anywhere emerged to ensnare the public.

On a more prosaic level, British television produced some outstanding programmes and series and a fair amount of mediocre 'moving wallpaper'. The US, with a far greater output, produced a still higher proportion of trivia. Much of that found its way into British TV – and that of other nations.

In 1968 the *Daily Express* recorded on occasion four out of five hours of peak viewing time given over to American imports.

America's huge output – designed to satisfy up to a dozen channels – and a common language, made the UK a natural market for US products (though, in turn, Britain did well in selling programmes to the American public service TV system). The American programmes were, by and large, well-made, undemanding movies, but often they had a background of crime and, in the race for bigger audiences, they tended to become more and more violent.

These programmes and an increasing reliance on explicit sexual scenes in domestically produced programmes, provoked Mrs Mary Whitehouse, an Essex housewife and former teacher, to form a Viewers and Listeners Association to oppose the 'cult of violence and lewdness'.

Permissiveness and its impact on the cultural scene have been discussed elsewhere in this work. Television was brought on to centre stage because its influence was so pervasive and its effect on children so much greater than any other medium.

Needless to say, the debate on television's responsibility for the upsurge in crime and moral looseness (the factor of five was a constant in the period: five times more crime; five times more divorces; five times more illegitimate children) was inconclusive.

One criticism thrust at TV and not effectively rebutted was that it bred copy-cat behaviour. Let one group of hooligans be televised invading a football pitch or looting shops in pursuit of racial or political protest, and others would follow suit, reckoning the publicity was worth the small risk of arrest. Judging the frequency with which one outburst followed another (violent demos in the sixties, football and racial outbreaks in the seventies) there seemed to be something in that argument.

On the other hand, champions of television claimed that the sight of mobs attacking the police swung public opinion in favour of the maintenance of law and order.

Over the 25 years during which television covered the whole country there was a notable decline in behaviour, totally reversing the experience of the previous 60 years. The cinema and the radio, equally universal, had not produced that effect. So was there something particularly powerful and malignant about the television screen, and callous about those in control of it?

No conclusive answer could be given. Callousness undoubtedly existed among some executives where the urge to get high ratings or create a sensation over-rode other considerations. The desire to appeal to one's 'peer group', i.e. fellow producers, directors or writers with whom one was in daily touch, unquestionably influenced attitudes and eroded responsibility.

But there was no indication that people involved in television were less sensitive than those in banking, tourism, retailing or any other service trade.

The countervailing elements – press and politicians, advertisers and pressure groups such as Mrs Whitehouse's association – laid constraints on television and the fickleness of public taste meant that even the most successful and arrogant executive could be brought down to earth with a bump.

TV. A force for good? A force for evil? A bit of both – or neither one nor the other?

Efforts have been made to answer these questions, but they cannot be decisive. Television is a mere mechanism. It cannot be separated from the other forces that have moulded our 20th century.

It is time to attempt to draw up a balance sheet: to try to determine how we have changed, and perhaps why we have changed, in the 75 years from 1900 to 1975.

CHAPTER TWENTY THREE

The Balance Sheet

I began this book by contrasting the change in attitudes between 1950 and 1975 and observing how much greater they were than the change in material circumstances over the same period. Looking back over the 75 years of the twentieth century, the changes in attitude *and* material circumstances almost beggar description.

In practically every compartment of life an unimaginable transformation took place.

Longevity rose some 75 per cent so that the Biblical score of three-score years and ten was comfortably overtaken by the majority of men and, more especially, women. People's health improved dramatically so that they not only lived longer, they were lively longer. In 1900 grandmothers of 40 retired into the shadows, well suited to their black bombazine (though they may well have conducted a shadow government in the home) whereas by 1975 women of 60 or 70 were brightly dressed, attractive and taking a full part in community and social life. So full indeed that in 1975 the Conservatives for the first time in British political history elected a woman leader.

Three-quarters of a century earlier such an event would have been considered utterly inconceivable. Not only were there no women in Parliament; women did not have the vote. Legally they were, in many respects, chattels with rights severely circumscribed at law. They were 'gentle creatures' – so gentle that they were barred from listening to Dr Arthur Marshall address an audience at the Exeter Hall, London on purity. The reason for their exclusion was that the refined would be horrified by disclosures of impurity while the lower type were kept out because they were the cause of impurity.

Chivalry, often of an excessive kind, still commanded respect. A wretched labourer, Thomas Barrett of Woodbridge, Suffolk, was jailed for 21 days for 'profaning and insulting' Miss Bessie Alexander. He had kissed her against her will. It was automatic for men to open doors for ladies, to help them in and out of cabs, to raise their hats on passing one of their acquaintance or on being introduced. It was axiomatic that gentlemen rose when ladies entered a room, that they should offer ladies their seats on a crowded tramcar or omnibus. Men accompanying their wives, or any other female for that matter, walked on the outside of the pavement so as to shield the lady from mud thrown up by passing vehicles or worse, in the case of horses.

Pregnant women were treated as pieces of precious porcelain. Their 'condition' was not, of course, referred to in polite society but their slightest whim evoked an immediate response from solicitous menfolk.

Duels were frequently fought on the Continent where a woman's honour was at issue. In Spain, in October 1904, the Marquis Pickman was shot dead after horse-whipping a captain of the Civil Guard who had cast lustful eyes on the marquis's beautiful wife. A court of honour, presided over by a General, decided that a duel with pistols under the severest conditions, only fifteen paces separating the combatants, should be fought. The captain was the better shot.

A precise monetary value could be – and was – placed on a woman's honour and her blighted hopes when betrayed by perfidious suitors. Breach of promise suits in the courts provided women with redress at a time when she was woefully short of other rights. If a man made a maid pregnant or blighted her prospects by remaining engaged for years only to abandon her at the end, or enticed her by promises of marriage to spend money on her 'bottom drawer', she had legal redress. She could sue him in the courts and extract damages from him to compensate for her lost virginity or dreams of marriage.

Some women took precautions against their loved ones denying that they had ever intended marriage. The *Daily Express* recorded this signed declaration produced in evidence at a breach of promise case at Preston Court on 15 December 1905.

Vouch of honour – I, Richard Ernest Lang, hereby promise to marry Mary Ann Gordon on whatever date shall be selected by either party. Signed April 1904.

Lang later got engaged to another girl. The jury assessed damages against Lang at £75. (Say, £850 at 1975 values: always remembering

that £75 probably represented one-third of Lang's annual earnings
as an upholsterer.)

On the same day, a watchmaker of Nottingham, one Harry
Wilson, foolishly admitted to his swain, Mary Tunnicliffe, that he
had £40 in the Savings Bank. He was relieved of that sum when the
jury found that he had broken his promise to wed Mary, who
received the cash.

The Marquis of Northampton agreed to pay the former Daisy
Markham, an actress, £50,000 (£600,000 at 1975 values) for not
marrying her. By the time the case came to court, in July 1913, Daisy
had become married to a Mr Moss. Nonetheless, the Marquis
clearly consenting, she won her record-breaking sum. The
marquis's father (the son was the then Earl Compton) had
forbidden the marriage.

Of such material was the dramatic part of a woman's life formed,
though there were many in the lower strata of society who counted
themselves lucky to get away without a belting on a Saturday night,
and even respectability on the outside, in middle class marriages,
sometimes concealed behaviour that veered far from the codes of
chivalry and courtesy.

Nonetheless, the codes were there. In return women were
expected to be ideal wives and mothers, while the unmarried ones of
good background would get jobs as 'superior domestics' or 'ladies'
maids' at £25 per annum and keep – against an average of £15–£18.

Much advice was expended on how wives and mothers should
comport themselves.

An item headed 'Things a Woman Wants To Know' in the second
issue of the *Daily Express* in 1900 declared: 'The higher education of
woman is in itself an admirable thing, but the highest education of
woman will be to show her how to become a good mother and how
best she may work for the perfection of the race.'

In the seventies such a view might have brought the writer into
conflict with – if not invited prosecution from – the Race Relations
Commission and the Equal Opportunities Commission. Then it was
considered wholly in keeping with the image of Britain as the
twentieth century Rome complete with dedicated Romano-British
matrons.

Newspapers and magazines were filled with advice on how to
become buxom, how to dress infants so that they were decently clad
in the winter and not suffocated ('by two thick rollers of flannel

bound tightly round the abdomen') in summer. Women in adverts were constantly adjured to improve the condition of their hair so as not to let down their husbands.

Husbands were urged to treat their wives at all times with courtesy and consideration. But the word in the marriage service which applied to women only was 'obey'. Along with the children they were supposed to do just that. Father was indisputably head of the family. As well expect the children to vote as expect women to do so. Mr H.H. Asquith, the Liberal Prime Minister, said quite bluntly in answer to the growing suffragette campaign for the vote, 'Your sex is not fitted, by nature, for the function'.

The increasingly passionate and violent campaign for the female franchise led to an explosion of anger from those, men *and women*, opposed to women voting. Letters in the Press deplored the extremities of the feminists: notably an assault on MPs in the Central Lobby of the Commons in 1906 and the mass breaking of plate glass windows in London's Oxford Street, and reached heights of stridency rivalling the most militant suffragette.

'These neurotic women clamour for a vote. What they need is a fire hose.'

'Hard labour and salt and senna' . . . 'the birch' . . . 'strait jackets' . . . 'half-a-dozen mice'.

Some women took to wearing anti-suffrage badges 'so that we can retain the respect of men'.

The respect of a good man – and his hand in marriage – was the right and proper ambition for a woman. Indeed many thought that it was frustration at not getting what every woman (biologically) needed which drove females into the suffrage movement.

Mayor Gaynor of New York succinctly summed up this attitude in a newspaper interview.

About 1,500,000 women in your country have no man and they are desperate. If they are allowed the vote, that will not get them husbands, and husbands quiet women wonderfully . . . (Wives) like their husbands and children so much that they do not want to be bothered by other matters. They would say, 'Let father attend to this matter. It puzzles our little heads too much'.

The vote, which women won after their sterling service in World War I, did not lead to a huge increase in women members of

Parliament, despite the fact that women made up 52 per cent of the electorate. In 1975 the percentage of women members – 3 per cent – had hardly changed in 30 years.

The change in the role of women came about for entirely different reasons than the vote. And this change was largely packed into the generation between 1950 and 1975.

Safe anti-pregnancy measures, which could cope even with the momentary loss of self-control, reduced almost to zero the chance of an unwanted pregnancy. Those sperm which did slip through the net were caught by the abortion legislation which, in all but a handful of cases, eliminated the burdensome embryo. The Abortion Act of 1969 allowed the termination of a pregnancy by a registered medical practitioner where two such practitioners decided that its continuance would involve a greater risk to the life of the pregnant woman or of injury to her mental health or disturbance to existing children in the family. Under this wide-ranging justification (plus the possibility that the unborn child might be mentally or physically handicapped) abortion-on-demand was virtually legalised. The number of abortions swiftly rose to exceed 130,000 a year, representing 35 per cent of pregnancies outside of marriage and nearly 10 per cent within marriage: in total, about 15 per cent of the birth rate of 800,000 a year was aborted.

What had been in 1900 – and still was in 1950 – a crime, the removal of an unborn child, was by 1975 quite acceptable.

That was perhaps the most dramatic change, not only in the position of women, but in the moral climate.

Those who favoured abortion-on-demand – though the qualifications were frequently spelled out, the reality was very close to that description – argued that a woman's body was her own and she should be free to do with 'foreign elements' as she chose.

The principle of abortion under certain circumstances – grave risk to the life of the mother – had been sanctioned by religious and legal authorities in the past. Abortion legislation simply took this process further along the road of individual rights. It gave a liberal interpretation to the sanctity of life: tipping the balance of argument in favour of the wishes of the living woman instead of the not-yet-living child.

An article in the *Express* in the mid-sixties pointed out the curious irony that Parliament was abolishing the death penalty for the most vicious and brutal murderers in the high cause of the civilised society, while at the same time sanctioning the destruction of unborn life, also in the name of the civilised society.

But however the morality argument might go, medical and legal advances had transformed the outlook for women.

Marriage property legislation strengthened the rights of women, removing unjust disabilities though, at the same time, men too shed liabilities.

Mutually supportive (or restrictive) covenants were being broken down because the cause of individual freedom (or licence) was with the grain of the period.

Divorce, again in the sixties, was made so easy as to become, almost, divorce-on-demand. The irrevocable breakdown of a marriage became the principal reason for parting. In 1950 fewer than two divorce decrees were granted per 1,000 married couples in England and Wales (considerably fewer in Scotland and Northern Ireland). By the mid-seventies the figure had increased five-fold and Britain was moving towards the American pattern of one divorce for every two marriages.

How many marriages of the pre-sixties vintage were mere shells, hurtful associations that poisoned the lives of parents and children? Surely it was better, argued the proponents of divorce reform, that these pretences should be ended. Moreover once separated from uncongenial partners, divorced persons could seek new ones and indeed by 1975, 10 per cent of all marriages were by people who had been divorced.

Those who opposed the weakening of the marriage bond – some sections of the established churches and a minority of MPs – claimed that easy divorce would lead to irresponsible coupling with little thought being given to the marriage vow and less to the children of the union. They were, however, spitting against the wind.

A swift reply to the charge of irresponsibility was that 'trial' marriages would increasingly become the custom. As they did. By the mid-seventies the proportion of women living with men whom they later married was rising towards 20 per cent. Cohabitation occurred more frequently for divorced and separated women than for single ones and often it did not end in marriage, but in a 'stable relationship'.

Thus in the mid-seventies the number of illegitimate births – many jointly registered by the parents – was, at 15 per cent of live births, 300 per cent the level of illegitimacy in 1951. Clearly marriage was no longer necessary, as George Bernard Shaw once observed, to create 'the maximum temptation with the maximum opportunity'.

Men, in the last quarter of the twentieth century, could have sexual enjoyment without the contractual obligation. Women could have the same because of their opportunities for work and for putting children into creches were now so much greater than they had been earlier in the century.

Four times as many women were employed in 1975 as a generation earlier. At 8,000,000 and rising women's skills were more attuned to the changing society than those of men. Heavy industry, in Britain and the West as a whole, declined dramatically in the 25 years as Far Eastern competition and automation cut employment in shipbuilding, coal, engineering, iron and steel.

While manufacturing declined the service industries grew: distribution, leisure industries, information, tourism – many ideally suited to part-time employment for married women with children. Even domestic service – a mainstay of female employment in the early part of the century – made a come-back, with many women taken on to look after the houses, and the children, of their fellow females who had gone out to paid work!

The young woman of 1900 transported to 1975 would have been bedazzled, and probably shocked and bewildered beyond measure at the freedom enjoyed by her sisters. Every convention, every church admonishment, every legal bar to her liberty had been removed. In addition, she was protected against discrimination and sexual harassment at work.

The 'man's world' of her own existence, summed up in the suffragettes' song 'Men treat as merest playthings the mothers of their race. . . we have no voice or say; no voice in making cruel laws we may not disobey', had vanished completely.

Where it would have been a sin, punishable by expulsion from the family home, to bear an illegitimate child, it had become commonplace to do so. Where 'living in sin' with a man would have meant being cut off without a shilling, so now parents introduced their daughters and the men with whom they lived without so much as a blush, or a word of explanation.

A social revolution so profound that it altered the entire basis of society, had been accomplished with hardly an angry word, let alone loss of blood. Economic, legal and medical change had ushered in the female Utopia. Or had it?

Happiness is not quantifiable. In drawing up a balance sheet for women the material benefits, the acquisition of rights, the abolition of constraints are recognisable and countable. The debits are far less obvious. The disappearance of many little courtesies paid by men to women may be counted as one. So may the loss of permanence in marriage and in family relationships.

Loneliness among women became a major factor of ill-health in the period from 1950 to 1975 as the quintupling in the sale of tranquillisers and the vast increase in appeals to such organisations as the Samaritans (founded in 1953) testified. The extended family where everyone knew their place, from grandma (aged 50 perhaps) sitting in a place of warmth and honour, to the breadwinning father and the domestically-minded mother, to the youngest child, could be restrictive, frustrating and cloying: it could also be vastly reassuring. The lost children of the sixties, who entered the drug culture, were often the products of 'liberated', well-off – and broken – homes.

The weakening of family life has to be set against the gains for women's rights and freedom in the balance sheet. All part of the total transformation of the ordered structure of society, known to supporters and detractors alike as the English class system.

Cecily Frances Alexander's line from the hymn 'All Things Bright and Beautiful':

> The rich man in his castle
> The poor man at his gate
> God made them high or lowly,
> And order'd their estate.

were as accepted by the vast majority of Britons 60 years after she wrote these words in 1848. They were sung regularly in classrooms no less than in churches. By 1975 that verse had completely vanished from desks and pews and the title 'All Things Bright and Beautiful' was associated with a book by the veterinary surgeon, James Herriot, about the farms of Yorkshire.

In 1900 this exchange was recorded in the columns of the *Daily Express*:

Coroner: 'As a chemist, you know you should not take anything for granted.'
Chemist: 'Well, I was looking at it as a gentleman.'
Coroner: 'But chemists are not supposed to be gentlemen.'

If such an exchange had occurred in 1975 the coroner would have been removed from office on the grounds of insanity.

In the England of 1900 the (unpaid) House of Commons was composed, almost entirely, of landowners, wealthy businessmen and wealthy lawyers. The two Labour MPs were dependent on trade union subscriptions as was John Burns, a Socialist who backed the Liberals. The House of Lords, co-equal to the Commons, was wholly the preserve of inherited privilege in the form of the aristocracy. Many, in both Houses, were related to one another. In some respects, Tories and Liberals were more like family parties than political parties. Hilaire Belloc's jibe that the real difference between the parties was that one lived by women, champagne and bridge, while the other rested upon bridge, women and champagne, had more than a touch of truth in it.

In the villages, the squire ruled unopposed, as secure in his traditional duties as in the affection of the villagers. That was his view. And, judging from the tranquillity of the countryside in 1900, it must have been largely true. Sustaining the squire and the established order was the vicar, belonging to the Anglican Community which was described as 'the Tory Party at prayer'.

The Welfare State did not exist in even the most rudimentary form. When minimal retirement pensions (40p a week for over-seventies, subject to means test) were introduced – 30 years behind Germany – many aged recipients assumed that it must be *Lord* George, not Lloyd George, who was responsible for this outstanding bounty.

A gigantic chasm separated the rich from the poor. Sir Edward Wills of the tobacco family died leaving £2,531,207 (about £27 million by 1975 values). A mere £37,000 was exacted in death duties. The American spouses of 10 leading sprigs of the aristocracy were reckoned to have brought £33 million to their husbands in dowries alone.

At the same time about 1,000 out of 6,000 children born in greater London died before they were one year old, according to a report from Sir Edwin Chadwick of the Home Office. Many of them perished from malnutrition.

Yet there was a complete absence of revolutionary fervour in Britain. At the 1900 election, with universal male suffrage, the Conservatives were returned for a second successive term with a very large majority.

Envy of the wealthy and the aristocratic was confined to the small Socialist Party. People in employment regarded those out of work for any length of time as being bone idle. Imprudence and folly were blamed for poverty which, anyway, was alleviated by charity.

The moral climate, the social mores of the time, were not conducive to radical change. When it came, from the Liberals in 1906, it was partly to seize the initiative from the office-holding Tories and partly to fend off the challenge of Socialism on the Left. The power of the House of Lords was clipped and it was made subsidiary to the Commons, but the established order of things, the class structure and social framework, was left intact.

And so it appeared to be in the 1950s. For it was then that the term 'Establishment' came into general, and pejorative, use. It was first mentioned by journalist Henry Fairlie* to distinguish the comparatively small group of politicians, senior civil servants, judges, businessmen, industrial and military chiefs, university vice-chancellors, who ran the country and came almost exclusively from the same public schools (i.e. fee-paying), the same universities – Oxford and Cambridge – the same regiments and were members of the same clubs. In short, that the Old School Tie still waved over England's battlements. Shortly afterwards, another journalist, Anthony Sampson, brought out his *Anatomy of Britain* which repeated the charge and went much further in defining Britain's relative industrial decline in terms of the influence wielded and the stultifying effect produced by this out-of-date circle who, despite apparent differences, shared similar attitudes, fostered each other's interests and blocked the path of advancement to real talent.

As this was the period when the English Theatre was afire with revolt – John Osborne's *Look Back in Anger* and *The Entertainer*, Allan Sillitoe's *Saturday Night and Sunday Morning*, Shelagh Delaney with *A Taste of Honey* – the economic and social dismemberment of the Establishment took on an emotional element too.

There seemed considerable justification for the claim that the ruling classes came from a narrow and privileged caste. The leader of the Labour Party and Premier in 1950, Clement Attlee, and his successor Hugh Gaitskell, were products of the public school system: Attlee of Haileybury, Gaitskell of Winchester. Attlee, as his letters

* Though the distinguished BBC political broadcaster, Edward Thompson, states that he heard Hugh Kingsmill and Malcolm Muggeridge using the term in the 1930s.

showed, was often more interested in the doings of old boys than in the proceedings of his Party Conference. The Tory leaders of the fifties and early sixties, Winston Churchill (Harrow), Anthony Eden (Eton), Harold Macmillan (Eton) and Alec Douglas-Home (Eton) seemed to fit the same mould. The principal reformer in the Tory Party, Richard Austen Butler, differed from them only in that he had not gone to Eton or Harrow. He was educated at the equally privileged establishment, Marlborough.

The *Economist* journal coined the phrase 'Butskellism' to describe the consensus between the parties based upon a shared vaguely 'progressive' view of society. This establishment was buttressed by some 6,000 individuals, the so-called 'great and good' who staffed royal commissions and other quasi-official bodies, usually giving their time and abilities free, but with a definite Lady Bountiful attitude all the same. Most of the Great and Good had also been to public schools.

Here, so averred the critics, was proof that the ruling class had not really changed, despite three periods of Socialist government and the advance of the trade unions, since the start of the century.

The groundswell of revolt against 'The System' and its alleged failings manifested itself in 1963. Middle class – and ambitious – Tories of the stamp of Iain MacLeod and Enoch Powell were enraged at the manner in which the Old Etonian Alec Douglas-Home was foisted on them as Party Leader, and Premier, in succession to the Old Etonian Harold Macmillan. MacLeod denounced the magic circle which chose Tory leaders and, backed by his fellow MPs, the process was put in hand for electing the Conservative leader by the whole Parliamentary party. Within 18 months that system produced the grammar schoolboy Edward Heath as the Tory leader and the grammar schoolgirl, Margaret Thatcher, as his successor.

In that same year, 1963, Harold Wilson, the grammar schoolboy (whose claim to have been a barefoot youngster was ridiculed by Macmillan who said that if he was ever barefoot it was because he was too big for his boots) succeeded the public schoolboy, Hugh Gaitskell as leader of the Labour Party and was, in turn, succeeded by Jim Callaghan, another politician with an impeccable record of state schooling.

The virtual take-over of the communications industry by talented non-public school products in the same period brought an end to the

Establishment's alleged power to control, direct and manipulate national affairs. The criticism died away too – as did the charge that the Establishment was to blame for Britain's poor economic performance.

How far was the criticism justified? While Britain *did* double her standard of living between 1950 and 1970, other countries did better still. Britain's share of international trade fell and productivity remained depressingly low compared with German, American and Japanese.

Was that the fault of a classically-educated elite whose snobbish inversion of values put a class emphasis on the arts at the expense of science, engineering and technology?

Or was a far more important cause of British failure the progressive consensus which opted for the quiet life of giving the unions what they wanted without requiring much in return?

Maybe a mixture of both plus a genuine public desire to put leisure and welfare ahead of production and prosperity.

Or was there another cause, not so much the dominance of class privilege, or the progressive consensus, or even public opinion, but the bureaucratisation of Britain?

One overwhelming change in Britain during the first three-quarters of the century was the rise and rise of the Civil Service. War, depression and austerity combined to enlarge the Service sevenfold. By 1975 the Civil Service numbered over 700,000 and, for 25–30 years had been responsible for a host of industries: coal, gas, electricity, railways, steel, shipbuilding, motor manufacture and road transport. In 1900 these industries were in the hands of private enterprise. Many of the directors of the firms may indeed have been 'Establishment' figures who got on the boards because of whom they knew, not what they knew, and whose names looked good on the company notepaper. But no one was prevented from starting a business, be it a coalmine or a shipyard. No planning process or Act of Parliament blocked his way.

From 1950 to 1975 it was the Civil Service and its appointees who commanded the dominating heights of the economy. Safety first was the watchword. Avoidance of 'destructive competition' was the prime motive of management.

So while one Establishment was dismantled in the sixties and seventies, another one (which, curiously enough, used the term to describe its own permanent membership) moved in to take its place.

The Civil Service, which had been an instrument of policy in 1900, had become, in fact if not in name, the policy-maker during the third quarter of the 20th century.

Although its leadership, the so-called mandarins, the permanent secretaries, deputy secretaries, under and assistant secretaries, were admitted to the administrative corps only after having taken an honours degree at university (a small number of exceptionally able individuals were admitted from outside the university system) and having passed the civil service examination, most of these people continued to come from the public school and Oxbridge sector.

So 'the Establishment' had much the same character as before. What had changed was its function. In 1900, industry was far more open to entrepreneurship than was the case in 1975. Meritocracy – as measured by examination results – was in command, but the commercially-minded and enterprising were much less in evidence.

The change, apparently so fundamental, may have helped to stultify the economy it was meant to restore.

Anyway, the old Establishment would have disappeared with the demise of empire and the opportunity of service-beyond-self which it represented.

That class structure vanished because of another vast change: the transformation of the British from 'effortless superiority' and belief in themselves and in the destiny of the white races, to a much more humble and apologetic posture.

In the balance sheet, one change is consequential upon another. The change from 'dominion over palm and pine', to 1950 Commonwealth, to 1975 member of the European Community, is a measure of how much things changed.

*

It would be difficult to over-emphasise the jaunty assurance of the British – and of westerners generally – in the early years of the twentieth century. The unfortunate Chinese were being punished for daring to permit armed gangsters (Boxers) to attack the concessions enjoyed by Europeans. Chastising the 'yellow pagans' was the last united act of Old Europe (plus Japan and the USA). It exhibited the whites in supreme arrogance and confidence. And nowhere was that confidence more surely felt than in Britain.

Over one quarter of the population of the globe the Union Jack fluttered. The Royal Navy patrolled the shipping lanes of the world, untrammelled and unchallengeable – and such had been the case for 100 years. Every second merchant ship at sea flew the Red Ensign and these ships could sail round the world and only put in to ports under British control. Not since the days of Rome had one state held such authority.

Rudyard Kipling, poet of Empire, warned the people against becoming 'drunk with power' and held the awful example of Nineveh and Tyre before them. His words were lost in the roar of exultation at the parade of forces from the 'Empire on which the Sun never Sets' (an Irish writer observed that the sun didn't set on the British Empire because God couldn't trust the Brits in the dark).

Splendid isolation was British foreign policy – until fear of the new Germany with her massive naval armament, sent Britain, in short order, into partnership with Japan, France and Russia.

Outside of Europe, Britain ruled complacently and without a cheep of protest from the ruled. The Empire was the 'Great Civiliser' bringing peace, the rule of law, transport, irrigation, minimum interference with the customs, habits and religion of the peoples (though the missionaries were intent on winning souls for the Christian faith and frequently clashed with British settlers and traders who were more interested in getting value from native labour or local resources). Foes of the Empire said the British were running it for what they could get out of it. By 1900 that was a lot less true than it had been in previous centuries. The Empire drew young men to administer it – frequently in lonely, dangerous and plague-infested spots for a modest remuneration. The Empire offered a fine arena for service-beyond-self.

Outside the bounds of Empire, Britain made her presence felt whenever she had a mind to do so. The ubiquitous presence of the Royal Navy ensured prompt payment of debts to British citizens from Haiti to Tahiti. Haiti was one of only a handful of black-ruled nations and it was said that a white foreigner there had no need to fear local justice if his country had a navy.

Second to the UK in carrying a big stick was the United States. A five-line paragraph in the *Express* in the first decade of the 20th century observed that 'US forces were ready to move in to Nicaragua where two Americans had been murdered.' The news item was headed 'Armed Force to Punish a Naughty Republic'. President Wilson declared a police action or 'peaceful war' against Mexico for 'insulting the American flag'.

It was accepted as an article of faith that the white races (the word 'race' appeared frequently in the Press and on the lips of orators) were vastly superior to the black, brown or yellow. And it was another article of faith that the coloureds accepted their inferiority and wished only to become as near white as God and genetics and cosmetics could make them.

The American anthropologist, William Archer, was quoted in *The Morning Post*:

> Whoever may doubt the superiority of the white, it is not he (the negro); and it is a racial, not merely a social or economic, superiority to which he does instinctive homage. It does not enter his head to champion his own racial ideal, or to set up an African Venus in rivalry to the Hellenic. . .
>
> If wishing could change the Ethiopian's skin, there would never be a Negro in America. The black race, out of its poverty, spends thousands of dollars annually on anti-kink lotions, vainly supposed to straighten the African wool. The brown belle tones her complexion with pearl powder . . .

Mr Archer dedicated the book in which these views appeared to the English author, H.G. Wells.

Whether Mr Wells subscribed to these views or not, they were part of the accepted culture of the times. The black man was a 'Nigger'; Latin Americans were 'Dagoes'; Indians were 'Wogs'. The Latin peoples of southern Europe were 'Wops'; the yellow races (Chinese or Japanese) were 'Chinks'. True, the Anglo-Saxons were no more polite about each other: the Americans referring to the British as 'Limeys' and the British returning the compliment by denoting all Americans as 'Yankees'.

But when it came to asserting rights, the Anglo-Saxons first and the northern Europeans second imposed themselves on the rest of the world. They dealt out the chastisement and the others accepted it.

Such hubris invited nemesis. It came in the form of the European Civil War of 1914–1918 and in the appalling Nazi doctrines (see page 82) leading to World War II and the collapse of the Western will to rule.

In a mere eighteen years the British Empire dissolved; its unity replaced by more than two score of independent, mutually feuding states, the majority one-party or military dictatorships. Two of them, India and Pakistan, fought one another no fewer than three times between 1947 and 1972. Yet this strange amalgam of states had an identity: the Commonwealth. Originally it was the British Commonwealth, but early in 1950 the *Express* reported that Sir Stafford Cripps, Labour's Chancellor of the Exchequer, addressing an audience of Canadian businessmen, had insisted on dropping the word 'British'. Once begun, the term remained. Thus was born an association in which idealism triumphed over experience.

And now began too the process of reversing the West's effortless superiority and glowing self-confidence. Between 1950 and 1975 the whole idea that the West had more to offer the East than vice versa was abandoned. America's defeat in Vietnam and her repulse in Cuba set the seal on the Western withdrawal.

It was accompanied by a zealous elimination of all signs of racial superiority.

Beginning in 1954, the black peoples of the southern states of the USA were constitutionally granted the right to enjoy the same facilities in public services – not the 'separate but equal' proviso which had endured hitherto. In the following decade the civil rights campaign headed by Martin Luther King gained equal voting rights for blacks in the South and they emerged as councillors, mayors and congressmen.

Racial discrimination was banned, reverse discrimination (or 'affirmative action') was put in its place whereby public authorities were obliged to discriminate in favour of black people for jobs or university places. The Orwellian doctrine that 'some people are more equal than others' was thus embodied in Anglo-Saxon law.

For Britain, the retreat from global responsibilities took the additional form of joining the European Economic Community, membership of which was confirmed by a national referendum in 1975.

America began repining about her treatment of the Red Indians and Australia about her treatment of the aborigines.

The white man's burden was now not one of responsibility for bringing the coloured folks to the light, but one of guilt for past sins: a guilt which could only be redeemed by making white over black racialism a crime and black over white racialism a virtue.

In drawing up this balance sheet the past misdemeanours of white masters has to be set against the genocide practised by blacks against blacks in Uganda, Nigeria, Ethiopia and Sudan; the genocide in Vietnam and Cambodia, and the wars which have claimed 10 million victims fought between former colonial territories.

For our returning Mr Rip Van Winkle it would be one more example of a world turned upside down: to be laid beside the total transformation in morality, crime and punishment.

*

When elegant Terence Rattigan, the playwright, wrote a programme note in the early fifties that those of his profession who did not write for the demure Aunt Edna of Knightsbridge would not score with theatre-goers, he was echoing the ethos of a life that was about to vanish.

In that theatrical past, there was actually an official, the Lord Chamberlain, to ensure that Aunt Edna's susceptibilities were not abused. Nor her dress sense either. London theatre, in the early part of the century, obliged gentlemen to wear full evening dress when seated in the stalls.

This propriety was matched by the Lord Chamberlain's eagle eye for anything considered salacious – and woe betide the management that took a risk.

Mr Alfred Butt arranged to mount Max Rheinhardt's mime, *A Venetian Night*, set to the music of Friedrich Bermann. An official of the Lord Chamberlain's office attended the dress rehearsal and on the eve of the first performance a letter arrived on Mr Butt's desk, letter-headed from St James's Palace to the effect that the Lord Chamberlain was 'unable to license the performance'. Even George Bernard Shaw, not noted for a repressive attitude, wrote to the Press that his play *Mrs Warren's Profession* was refused a licence because it was too moral! He added (whether with tongue in cheek or no): 'It would be a good thing for English dramatic art if a return were made to the policy of producing plays in every way fit for a girl of 15 to see.'

Libraries banned from their shelves books and plays by Compton Mackenzie and Hall Caine because of their treatment of sex (three-quarters of a century later certain local councils banned books because they showed girls as potential housewives and mothers!).

The *Daily Express* and other newspapers gave a kind of moral licence to films which they reviewed – these were, of course, silent movies. Such pictures as *The Road to Ruin* – a cautionary tale about an Oxford undergraduate who reforms and quits liquor and dalliances – was given a high rating. Those liable to upset the most fastidious were simply not mentioned.

This atmosphere in which Terence Rattigan would have felt at home, gave way in the early sixties to an outpouring of unbridled sexuality. As woman's hems rose (the mini skirt was shortened by an inch each year during the decade) so did male temperatures. In 1970 the *Express* counted 32 sex films in the capital.

In the theatre, sexuality advanced to centre stage. Mr Joe Orton gave homosexuality a fine run – until murdered by his friend, who then committed suicide. The first nude musical came from America. The year after Orton's death in 1967, *Hair* was produced on Broadway. This cast discretion, along with clothes, to the wind and bravely displayed male and female private parts. Not to be outdone, another US company the following year put on *Che* (called after one of the folk heroes of the sixties, Che Guevara, a Cuban revolutionary who was killed while trying to promote a peasants' revolt in Bolivia). This not only had the cast appearing nude, but simulated the sex act as well.

When the New York police intervened and arrested the cast, Equity, the actors' union, insisted that performers must be told, before signing a contract, whether or not they were required to disrobe in public. This proviso had nothing to do with morality. Mr Angus Duncan, the union's executive secretary, was adamant – according to press statements – that he was guided solely by the resolve to indemnify his members against arrest and fining.

For Britain, Mr Kenneth Tynan mounted – an apt term – a show called *Oh! Calcutta!* Mr Tynan was the sixties writ large: the daring innovator, the apostle of free expression. He liberated the language by uttering the four-letter obscenity on television (Caliban would have appreciated that) and went on to boast of his show in terms of the number of people who took off their clothes; 'it out-nudes *Hair* . . . it is an evening of elegant erotica'.

There was talk of making stage plays of books whose main theme was masturbation. A novel of the period – *Portnoy's Complaint* (Philip Roth, Random House, 1969) was universally praised for its funny frankness and superb writing. Four-letter words crowded into paragraphs and the flavour of the book may be caught in one classic phrase. 'I was wholly incapable of keeping my paws from my dong once it started climbing up my belly.' The book headed the bestseller lists on both sides of the Atlantic for months on end.

Thus was morality, Victorian-style, mocked and derided. The fates were not quite so easily mocked. By the mid-seventies rape and sexual offences generally had risen five-fold from their 1950 level to 36 per 100,000 of the population in the UK (from some 300 rape cases to some 1,500 and rising swiftly).

On the question of morality in crime and punishment, standards were virtually reversed between the first half and the third quarter of the twentieth century.

Politicians, sociologists and probably a great majority of ordinary people would have been horrified at the bloodthirsty clamour for the cat (the cat o'nine tails) in a Parliamentary debate in 1912 when there had been an increase in sexual crimes against women and children.

All party support was forthcoming for severe physical chastisement for men who violated women or who procured them for immoral purposes.

Mr F.G. Mildmay, Conservative, Totnes declared: 'Flogging is a deterrent for men whose instincts are animal.'

Mr McKenna, the Liberal Home Secretary: 'I am informed that in London there are a number of young men, almost entirely of foreign origin (!) who live on young women to the extent of £15 or £20 a week. These men accumulate fortunes in the trade.

'The police say that after the first conviction, if there is power to flog . . . these men will be intimidated.'

Colonel Lockwood, Conservative, Epping: 'I would like to see flogging introduced for all offences against women and children.'

Mr Lief Jones, Liberal: 'How many members would take the "cat" in their hands and administer the flogging?'

Mr Will Crocks, Labour, Woolwich: 'There is a lot of maudlin sentiment. I am glad these scoundrels have a skin that can be tanned. If anybody is wanted to do the flogging they can call on me.'

The Hon Edward Wood, Conservative, Ripon: 'When I was at school I was whipped three times before breakfast on one occasion, and I'm none the worse for it. It had an extremely deterrent effect on me.'

Mr Austin Chamberlain, Conservative: 'The infliction of physical pain on a few men would be as nothing to the infinite misery that would be prevented.'

The anti-flogging amendment was rejected by 297 to 44, a majority of 253 for flogging.

The House of Lords ratified the Lower House's vote.

The Lord Chancellor: 'It would be an advantage if the power was given of inflicting corporal punishment for a first offence.'

The Lord Chief Justice: 'I do not think anyone can doubt the influence of flogging as a deterrent.'

The Archbishop of Canterbury: 'I am willing to risk one innocent man being flogged in a generation.'

Lord Lansdowne: 'A punishment which may not unfairly be described as "brutalising" is a proper punishment when we are dealing with men who are brutes.'

The second reading of the Bill in the Lords was passed without a division.

That the Archbishop of Canterbury should have given voice to such a vengeful comment that he would be prepared to see an innocent man flogged would have struck the late twentieth century observer as barbaric and would certainly have been indignantly repudiated by later Archbishops and their entire Bench of Bishops (who, in 1912, approved the flogging bill).

Corporal punishment for crime involving violence was sustained until after World War II and MPs (and Tory Conferences) still urged its use in the fifties. But the tide of opinion was overwhelmingly against such judicial brutality. The cat along with the gallows was banished to the Chamber of Horrors to be gazed upon by a later generation as objects of horror.

But as violence against the perpetrators of crime was banished from the statute book, violence to victims grew at an appalling rate.

A random selection of newspaper items from the last quarter of the twentieth century included such examples:

'500 muggings a week in London.' 'Woman of 85 beaten, raped.' 'Woman of 92 assaulted and left for dead.' 'Old Age Pensioner robbed and murdered.' Scarcely a day passed without such crimes – and worse – being recorded.

The ghost of law enforcement past might have asked what society was doing to counter this crime-wave. A cursory glance at the Press would not have furnished a very reassuring reply.

A man who kicked his stepson to death for blocking the view of the TV set. Three years in jail.

A man who stabbed another to death in a pub brawl. Two years.

Suspended sentence. These sentences were recorded in one year, in the county of Bedfordshire.

A husband who strangled his wife after a row. Three years in jail.

A taxi driver shot his son-in-law nine times in a quarrel about his son-in-law's marital problems. Four years in jail.

A barman was given a suspended 18-month sentence for a 'vicious rape'. A motorist who raped a hitch-hiker was fined £2,000.

The Criminal Injuries Compensation Board reflected that it was 'impossible not to be startled by the leniency shown by the Courts'.

Lord Shawcross, a former Labour Attorney-General – and the chief British prosecutor at the Nuremberg Trials of the principal Nazi war criminals – observed: 'Criminals see the chance of being caught as 6-4 against, the chance of being acquitted considerable, and if convicted, the chances are that he will be bound over or given a suspended sentence.'

The ghost of laws past might have wryly commented that society had banned cruelty to the convicted only to replace it with disdain for the victims, and that a society which put concern for the guilty before protection of the innocent was richly deserving its nemesis.

The crime rate in the UK fell by 50 per cent between 1870 and 1910 – and rose 1,400 per cent in the succeeding 65 years, almost all in the final third.

The gulf in morality between the first decade of the twentieth century and the last quarter leads us to a final examination of the greatest contrast between the two periods, the end of innocence.

CHAPTER TWENTY FOUR

The End of Innocence

At the opening of the twentieth century one assumption was common to men and women of goodwill. Civilisation was moving upwards and onwards. There might be differences of opinion about how perpetual progress could best be achieved, but the end – peace, prosperity and a higher culture – was not in question.

Socialism appeared to offer the finest prospect. Gross inequalities, avoidable poverty and the wretched uncertainty of employment would yield to a better ordering of affairs by the State.

The Socialist Party was already well established in Germany, the best educated country on earth, with a soundly established welfare system. This community of efficient souls imbued with the work ethic would show the rest of the world how to achieve harmony and contentment.

In Britain much remained to be done. Sweated labour was widespread. A 'finisher' in contract millinery received less than one penny an hour. Fewer than 20 per cent of the labour force was organised in trade unions – and lost three out of four disputes. An agricultural labourer could be dismissed at a moment's notice and obliged to quit his tied cottage. Strikers could expect short shrift. When families in pit villages owned by the mine-master failed to pay their rents because of a dispute, they were straightway evicted. Safety at work was wantonly neglected by employees and employers alike. In 1904, 1,000 people died in workshops; more than 1,200 lost their lives in coalmines and more than 400 railway servants were killed in the line of duty. (Seventy years on, four railway men lost their lives.)

The poor – deserving or undeserving, differentiation was commonplace – had a very hard time of it. Thousands occupied rat-infested slum basements in the major cities and only the hazard of disease moved the authorities to act. Death from starvation was not unknown.

Champions of capitalism argued that prosperity would broaden down from class to class as free enterprise and competition sought new markets at lower prices. Marxists and Socialists took exactly the opposing view: claiming that big capitalists would absorb lesser ones until monopoly extinguished competition and the poverty-stricken masses – swollen by a deprived middle class – rose in revolt against exploitation.

Socialists had by far the best tunes: rousing revolutionary airs and an absolute belief in the moral righteousness of the Cause. By the middle of the first decade of the century the British Labour Party and its kindred socialist groups were holding up to 3,000 meetings a week, including socialist Sunday schools where the infants were taught a different kind of catechism.

'What rights do we have?' 'The right to be fed, clothed and housed by the state.'

'How is this ideal to be achieved?' 'By dividing among everybody the property which now belongs to the rich.'

Nationalisation of the means of production, distribution and exchange was the means by which the rich would be forced to disgorge their ill-gotten gains.

Idealism, expressed by the childish voices singing, to the strains of Auld Lang Syne, 'We love the bold and boundless mind, The heart of purpose strong, Which feels the woes of human kind, And wars to vanquish wrong', gave socialism a moral dimension; a shining vision of the future, predicated on the conviction of the inherent goodness of human nature.

Those who disliked handing out other people's property – especially if they possessed property themselves – gave vent to a more prosaic and sceptical definition of socialism: 'What's yours is mine. What's mine's my own.'

Yet socialism (if not of the extreme variety which advocated the abolition of the monarchy and the establishment of state pawnshops!) undoubtedly was one of the two main idealistic and visionary movements of what was still – in the light of what came thereafter – the age of innocence.

The other driving force was the idea of Cecil Rhodes that the British Empire in alliance with its natural partner, the English-speaking United States of America and the Briton's racial cousin, the dynamic German nation, could bring peace, order, progress and prosperity to an otherwise benighted globe. So convinced was Rhodes of this ideal that he founded Rhodes Scholarships for young men of Empire, USA and Germany at Oxford University. Not only did he found a country (Rhodesia), he articulated an ideal.

Economic clothing for this political vision was provided by Joseph Chamberlain, once-radical mayor of Birmingham, now, in 1903, Colonial Secretary and High Priest of tariff reform by which the Empire would be united through the erection of a tariff wall against foreigners (some considerable adjustment would have been required to accommodate Germany and the US against whom the tariffs were directed, but doubtless an eventual compromise could have been reached).

The point about socialism and Empire trade and the vision of the Anglo-Saxon-Germanic peoples to rule the world was they were founded on the belief shared by almost everybody that universal progress and peace and innate rationality were unchallengeable. Even if such an obscene event as a European war were to supervene it was confidently believed it would last a few weeks only as the interdependence of capitalist systems, the common resolve of the working classes not to kill one another and the family links of the monarchies would all combine to bring hostilities to a speedy end.

By 1950 none of these illusions remained. The British Empire was in the process of dissolution, largely as a result of two appalling wars fought against Germany, the racial partner of Rhodes's dreams. The white races were everywhere in retreat and the 'world order', in so far as there was any, relied upon the balance of terror established by the two new giants, the USA and the USSR.

Almost no one would have foreseen such a march of events, so much destruction, death and decay.

As for Socialism (or Communism) it had 'triumphed' in the sense that more than one-third of the world professed to be following the doctrines of Karl Marx. Yet the hopes that it could be combined with political freedom to produce a Utopia on earth had been wholly blighted.

Aneurin Bevan, Labour's most brilliant public orator, told an audience at this time that if the British, 'the most mature and tolerant people on earth', could not make socialism with freedom work then the consequences would be bleak for freedom.

After ten years of war socialism and peace socialism *with political freedom*, the Labour Party, in 1951, was dismissed from office. On almost every count by which the welfare of people could be measured and compared, total state control of the economy had not redeemed the pledges of the zealots. By 1951 the public was more severely rationed than during war – while the free enterprise Germans enjoyed abundance. Housing had fallen far behind pre-World War II levels – while the free-enterprise Germans built twice as many homes as the UK. Not a mile of motorway was constructed – while the Germans remorselessly improved their roads and the cars to drive on them. Even the concept of a completely 'free' National Health Service had, by 1951, been breached and charges had been imposed.

The Welfare State was in being, but Winston Churchill's sombre words that 'if you do not create new wealth there will not be common wealth, but common poverty' could ring the death-knell of a welfare-ism not sustained by wealth-creation. And it appeared that the *creation* of wealth required a personal incentive which socialist collectivity could not furnish. Profit, competition, ownership, capital formation, started to come back into their own. Utopia was postponed.

Abroad, the actions of the USSR, the 'socialist sixth of the world' began to bear a striking resemblance to those of Czarist Russia; especially when, in 1956, Soviet troops shot down Hungarian students and workers in an agonising replay of Czarist Russia's destruction of Kossuth's Hungarian rising a century before. When the Russians repeated the annihilation of 'Communism with a human face' in Czechoslovakia, all but the most obtuse, or corrupted, had to recognise the utter failure of social engineering.

Thus, by 1975, the calm assumptions of the age of innocence had succumbed to reality. Worse, they had produced ghastly mirror images of themselves.

Cecil Rhodes's honest conviction that 'the best' should rule and that 'equal rights should be accorded to all *civilised* men' had been turned into a fearful parody by the Nazis who denied life to the 'racially inferior'.

The triumph of the working class, the 'dictatorship of the proletariat' promised by Marxism and Socialism had in the Soviet Union been turned into the dictatorship *over* the proletariat. One privileged class – the Communist Party – had succeeded another, the Czarist autocracy, while the workers remained without real rights to pursue life and liberty.

Sadness would have been the principal emotion of the Ghost of

Times Past viewing the melancholy distortion of idealism that so mocked the aspirations of the age of innocence.

Visions perish, others take their place.

Between 1950 and 1975 as these pages have tried to testify, Rudyard Kipling's old Gods of the Copybook Headings have been steadfastly ignored.

> At varying times we were promised abundance for all,
> By robbing selected Peter to pay for collective Paul;
> But though we had plenty of money, there was nothing our money could buy,
> And the Gods of the Copybook Headings said: *'If you don't work You die.'*

So it was in the mid-seventies as inflation in the UK soared ahead to 30 per cent per annum.

However, perhaps the most relevant verse of Kipling's poem referred to the sexual revolution which, along with social awareness, replaced in the sixties the vision of Utopia through economic change.

> On the first Feminia Sandstones we were promised the Fuller Life
> (Which started by loving our neighbour and ended by loving his wife)
> Till our women had no more children and the men lost reason and faith,
> And the Gods of the Copybook Headings said: *'The Wages of Sin is Death'*.

By the mid-seventies the birth rate was below the level required for the replacement of the population.

In the Swinging Sixties such an old fuddy-duddy as Kipling (who wrote those words in 1919) could be cheerfully dismissed and his warnings ignored as a 'good lay' was followed by a 'drugs high'. By the mid-seventies there were signs that the bill might be presented in a peculiarly frightening form.

So Rip Van Winkle, with whom we began this work, and the Ghost of Times Past, might wryly observe with Mr Kipling:

As it will be in the future, it was at the birth of Man –
There are only four things certain since Social Progress began:-
That the Dog returns to his Vomit and the Sow returns to her
Mire
And the Burnt Fool's bandaged finger goes wobbling back to the
Fire.

Index

I